C-2239   CAREER EXAMINATION SERIES

This is your
PASSBOOK for...

Interpreter (Spanish)

Test Preparation Study Guide
Questions & Answers

NATIONAL LEARNING CORPORATION®

COPYRIGHT NOTICE

This book is SOLELY intended for, is sold ONLY to, and its use is RESTRICTED to individual, bona fide applicants or candidates who qualify by virtue of having seriously filed applications for appropriate license, certificate, professional and/or promotional advancement, higher school matriculation, scholarship, or other legitimate requirements of education and/or governmental authorities.

This book is NOT intended for use, class instruction, tutoring, training, duplication, copying, reprinting, excerption, or adaptation, etc., by:

1) Other publishers
2) Proprietors and/or Instructors of "Coaching" and/or Preparatory Courses
3) Personnel and/or Training Divisions of commercial, industrial, and governmental organizations
4) Schools, colleges, or universities and/or their departments and staffs, including teachers and other personnel
5) Testing Agencies or Bureaus
6) Study groups which seek by the purchase of a single volume to copy and/or duplicate and/or adapt this material for use by the group as a whole without having purchased individual volumes for each of the members of the group
7) Et al.

Such persons would be in violation of appropriate Federal and State statutes.

PROVISION OF LICENSING AGREEMENTS – Recognized educational, commercial, industrial, and governmental institutions and organizations, and others legitimately engaged in educational pursuits, including training, testing, and measurement activities, may address request for a licensing agreement to the copyright owners, who will determine whether, and under what conditions, including fees and charges, the materials in this book may be used them. In other words, a licensing facility exists for the legitimate use of the material in this book on other than an individual basis. However, it is asseverated and affirmed here that the material in this book CANNOT be used without the receipt of the express permission of such a licensing agreement from the Publishers. Inquiries re licensing should be addressed to the company, attention rights and permissions department.

All rights reserved, including the right of reproduction in whole or in part, in any form or by any means, electronic or mechanical, including photocopying, recording, or by any information storage and retrieval system, without permission in writing from the Publisher.

Copyright © 2024 by
National Learning Corporation

212 Michael Drive, Syosset, NY 11791
(516) 921-8888 • www.passbooks.com
E-mail: info@passbooks.com

PASSBOOK® SERIES

THE *PASSBOOK® SERIES* has been created to prepare applicants and candidates for the ultimate academic battlefield – the examination room.

At some time in our lives, each and every one of us may be required to take an examination – for validation, matriculation, admission, qualification, registration, certification, or licensure.

Based on the assumption that every applicant or candidate has met the basic formal educational standards, has taken the required number of courses, and read the necessary texts, the *PASSBOOK® SERIES* furnishes the one special preparation which may assure passing with confidence, instead of failing with insecurity. Examination questions – together with answers – are furnished as the basic vehicle for study so that the mysteries of the examination and its compounding difficulties may be eliminated or diminished by a sure method.

This book is meant to help you pass your examination provided that you qualify and are serious in your objective.

The entire field is reviewed through the huge store of content information which is succinctly presented through a provocative and challenging approach – the question-and-answer method.

A climate of success is established by furnishing the correct answers at the end of each test.

You soon learn to recognize types of questions, forms of questions, and patterns of questioning. You may even begin to anticipate expected outcomes.

You perceive that many questions are repeated or adapted so that you can gain acute insights, which may enable you to score many sure points.

You learn how to confront new questions, or types of questions, and to attack them confidently and work out the correct answers.

You note objectives and emphases, and recognize pitfalls and dangers, so that you may make positive educational adjustments.

Moreover, you are kept fully informed in relation to new concepts, methods, practices, and directions in the field.

You discover that you are actually taking the examination all the time: you are preparing for the examination by "taking" an examination, not by reading extraneous and/or supererogatory textbooks.

In short, this PASSBOOK®, used directedly, should be an important factor in helping you to pass your test.

INTERPRETER (SPANISH)

DUTIES:
Under direct supervision, interprets Spanish into English, and vice versa. Interpreters are primarily responsible for interpreting between English and Spanish in the courtroom and other settings. They may perform simultaneous and consecutive interpretation, as well as translation of documents and other written material. Interpreters may also oversee voucher paid interpreting services and perform clerical tasks such as filing or answering inquiries, and other related duties.

WHAT THE JOB INVOLVES:
Interpreters (Spanish) clearly and accurately interpret spoken language and translate written materials from Spanish into English and vice versa while maintaining full message content, context and style at various governmental proceedings and activities for city agencies; perform clerical work associated with interpreting and translating responsibilities; maintain records of completed interpretations, translations and other assignments as needed; ensure confidential information is protected; may be required to travel to field locations to perform interpretations and/or translations; may be required to be on call for emergency interpreting and/or translating as needed; proofread, edit and revise translated materials. All Interpreters (Spanish) perform related work.

SCOPE OF THE EXAMINATION
The test will be designed to measure ability to translate conversational Spanish into English, and vice versa, and to carry out some or all of the typical tasks listed above. The written test will include:
1. Translating written material;
2. English/Spanish grammar and usage;
3. Vocabulary; and
4. Reading, understanding and interpreting written material.

HOW TO TAKE A TEST

I. YOU MUST PASS AN EXAMINATION

A. *WHAT EVERY CANDIDATE SHOULD KNOW*

Examination applicants often ask us for help in preparing for the written test. What can I study in advance? What kinds of questions will be asked? How will the test be given? How will the papers be graded?

As an applicant for a civil service examination, you may be wondering about some of these things. Our purpose here is to suggest effective methods of advance study and to describe civil service examinations.

Your chances for success on this examination can be increased if you know how to prepare. Those "pre-examination jitters" can be reduced if you know what to expect. You can even experience an adventure in good citizenship if you know why civil service exams are given.

B. *WHY ARE CIVIL SERVICE EXAMINATIONS GIVEN?*

Civil service examinations are important to you in two ways. As a citizen, you want public jobs filled by employees who know how to do their work. As a job seeker, you want a fair chance to compete for that job on an equal footing with other candidates. The best-known means of accomplishing this two-fold goal is the competitive examination.

Exams are widely publicized throughout the nation. They may be administered for jobs in federal, state, city, municipal, town or village governments or agencies.

Any citizen may apply, with some limitations, such as the age or residence of applicants. Your experience and education may be reviewed to see whether you meet the requirements for the particular examination. When these requirements exist, they are reasonable and applied consistently to all applicants. Thus, a competitive examination may cause you some uneasiness now, but it is your privilege and safeguard.

C. *HOW ARE CIVIL SERVICE EXAMS DEVELOPED?*

Examinations are carefully written by trained technicians who are specialists in the field known as "psychological measurement," in consultation with recognized authorities in the field of work that the test will cover. These experts recommend the subject matter areas or skills to be tested; only those knowledges or skills important to your success on the job are included. The most reliable books and source materials available are used as references. Together, the experts and technicians judge the difficulty level of the questions.

Test technicians know how to phrase questions so that the problem is clearly stated. Their ethics do not permit "trick" or "catch" questions. Questions may have been tried out on sample groups, or subjected to statistical analysis, to determine their usefulness.

Written tests are often used in combination with performance tests, ratings of training and experience, and oral interviews. All of these measures combine to form the best-known means of finding the right person for the right job.

II. HOW TO PASS THE WRITTEN TEST

A. NATURE OF THE EXAMINATION

To prepare intelligently for civil service examinations, you should know how they differ from school examinations you have taken. In school you were assigned certain definite pages to read or subjects to cover. The examination questions were quite detailed and usually emphasized memory. Civil service exams, on the other hand, try to discover your present ability to perform the duties of a position, plus your potentiality to learn these duties. In other words, a civil service exam attempts to predict how successful you will be. Questions cover such a broad area that they cannot be as minute and detailed as school exam questions.

In the public service similar kinds of work, or positions, are grouped together in one "class." This process is known as *position-classification*. All the positions in a class are paid according to the salary range for that class. One class title covers all of these positions, and they are all tested by the same examination.

B. FOUR BASIC STEPS

1) Study the announcement

How, then, can you know what subjects to study? Our best answer is: "Learn as much as possible about the class of positions for which you've applied." The exam will test the knowledge, skills and abilities needed to do the work.

Your most valuable source of information about the position you want is the official exam announcement. This announcement lists the training and experience qualifications. Check these standards and apply only if you come reasonably close to meeting them.

The brief description of the position in the examination announcement offers some clues to the subjects which will be tested. Think about the job itself. Review the duties in your mind. Can you perform them, or are there some in which you are rusty? Fill in the blank spots in your preparation.

Many jurisdictions preview the written test in the exam announcement by including a section called "Knowledge and Abilities Required," "Scope of the Examination," or some similar heading. Here you will find out specifically what fields will be tested.

2) Review your own background

Once you learn in general what the position is all about, and what you need to know to do the work, ask yourself which subjects you already know fairly well and which need improvement. You may wonder whether to concentrate on improving your strong areas or on building some background in your fields of weakness. When the announcement has specified "some knowledge" or "considerable knowledge," or has used adjectives like "beginning principles of..." or "advanced ... methods," you can get a clue as to the number and difficulty of questions to be asked in any given field. More questions, and hence broader coverage, would be included for those subjects which are more important in the work. Now weigh your strengths and weaknesses against the job requirements and prepare accordingly.

3) Determine the level of the position

Another way to tell how intensively you should prepare is to understand the level of the job for which you are applying. Is it the entering level? In other words, is this the position in which beginners in a field of work are hired? Or is it an intermediate or advanced level? Sometimes this is indicated by such words as "Junior" or "Senior" in the class title. Other jurisdictions use Roman numerals to designate the level – Clerk I, Clerk II, for example. The word "Supervisor" sometimes appears in the title. If the level is not indicated by the title, check the description of duties. Will you be working under very close supervision, or will you have responsibility for independent decisions in this work?

4) Choose appropriate study materials

Now that you know the subjects to be examined and the relative amount of each subject to be covered, you can choose suitable study materials. For beginning level jobs, or even advanced ones, if you have a pronounced weakness in some aspect of your training, read a modern, standard textbook in that field. Be sure it is up to date and has general coverage. Such books are normally available at your library, and the librarian will be glad to help you locate one. For entry-level positions, questions of appropriate difficulty are chosen – neither highly advanced questions, nor those too simple. Such questions require careful thought but not advanced training.

If the position for which you are applying is technical or advanced, you will read more advanced, specialized material. If you are already familiar with the basic principles of your field, elementary textbooks would waste your time. Concentrate on advanced textbooks and technical periodicals. Think through the concepts and review difficult problems in your field.

These are all general sources. You can get more ideas on your own initiative, following these leads. For example, training manuals and publications of the government agency which employs workers in your field can be useful, particularly for technical and professional positions. A letter or visit to the government department involved may result in more specific study suggestions, and certainly will provide you with a more definite idea of the exact nature of the position you are seeking.

III. KINDS OF TESTS

Tests are used for purposes other than measuring knowledge and ability to perform specified duties. For some positions, it is equally important to test ability to make adjustments to new situations or to profit from training. In others, basic mental abilities not dependent on information are essential. Questions which test these things may not appear as pertinent to the duties of the position as those which test for knowledge and information. Yet they are often highly important parts of a fair examination. For very general questions, it is almost impossible to help you direct your study efforts. What we can do is to point out some of the more common of these general abilities needed in public service positions and describe some typical questions.

1) General information

Broad, general information has been found useful for predicting job success in some kinds of work. This is tested in a variety of ways, from vocabulary lists to questions about current events. Basic background in some field of work, such as sociology or economics, may be sampled in a group of questions. Often these are principles which have become familiar to most persons through exposure rather than through formal training. It is difficult to advise you how to study for these questions; being alert to the world around you is our best suggestion.

2) Verbal ability

An example of an ability needed in many positions is verbal or language ability. Verbal ability is, in brief, the ability to use and understand words. Vocabulary and grammar tests are typical measures of this ability. Reading comprehension or paragraph interpretation questions are common in many kinds of civil service tests. You are given a paragraph of written material and asked to find its central meaning.

3) Numerical ability

Number skills can be tested by the familiar arithmetic problem, by checking paired lists of numbers to see which are alike and which are different, or by interpreting charts and graphs. In the latter test, a graph may be printed in the test booklet which you are asked to use as the basis for answering questions.

4) Observation

A popular test for law-enforcement positions is the observation test. A picture is shown to you for several minutes, then taken away. Questions about the picture test your ability to observe both details and larger elements.

5) Following directions

In many positions in the public service, the employee must be able to carry out written instructions dependably and accurately. You may be given a chart with several columns, each column listing a variety of information. The questions require you to carry out directions involving the information given in the chart.

6) Skills and aptitudes

Performance tests effectively measure some manual skills and aptitudes. When the skill is one in which you are trained, such as typing or shorthand, you can practice. These tests are often very much like those given in business school or high school courses. For many of the other skills and aptitudes, however, no short-time preparation can be made. Skills and abilities natural to you or that you have developed throughout your lifetime are being tested.

Many of the general questions just described provide all the data needed to answer the questions and ask you to use your reasoning ability to find the answers. Your best preparation for these tests, as well as for tests of facts and ideas, is to be at your physical and mental best. You, no doubt, have your own methods of getting into an exam-taking mood and keeping "in shape." The next section lists some ideas on this subject.

IV. KINDS OF QUESTIONS

Only rarely is the "essay" question, which you answer in narrative form, used in civil service tests. Civil service tests are usually of the short-answer type. Full instructions for answering these questions will be given to you at the examination. But in case this is your first experience with short-answer questions and separate answer sheets, here is what you need to know:

1) Multiple-choice Questions

Most popular of the short-answer questions is the "multiple choice" or "best answer" question. It can be used, for example, to test for factual knowledge, ability to solve problems or judgment in meeting situations found at work.

A multiple-choice question is normally one of three types—
- It can begin with an incomplete statement followed by several possible endings. You are to find the one ending which *best* completes the statement, although some of the others may not be entirely wrong.
- It can also be a complete statement in the form of a question which is answered by choosing one of the statements listed.

- It can be in the form of a problem – again you select the best answer.

Here is an example of a multiple-choice question with a discussion which should give you some clues as to the method for choosing the right answer:

When an employee has a complaint about his assignment, the action which will *best* help him overcome his difficulty is to
  A. discuss his difficulty with his coworkers
  B. take the problem to the head of the organization
  C. take the problem to the person who gave him the assignment
  D. say nothing to anyone about his complaint

In answering this question, you should study each of the choices to find which is best. Consider choice "A" – Certainly an employee may discuss his complaint with fellow employees, but no change or improvement can result, and the complaint remains unresolved. Choice "B" is a poor choice since the head of the organization probably does not know what assignment you have been given, and taking your problem to him is known as "going over the head" of the supervisor. The supervisor, or person who made the assignment, is the person who can clarify it or correct any injustice. Choice "C" is, therefore, correct. To say nothing, as in choice "D," is unwise. Supervisors have and interest in knowing the problems employees are facing, and the employee is seeking a solution to his problem.

2) True/False Questions

The "true/false" or "right/wrong" form of question is sometimes used. Here a complete statement is given. Your job is to decide whether the statement is right or wrong.

SAMPLE: A roaming cell-phone call to a nearby city costs less than a non-roaming call to a distant city.

This statement is wrong, or false, since roaming calls are more expensive.
This is not a complete list of all possible question forms, although most of the others are variations of these common types. You will always get complete directions for answering questions. Be sure you understand *how* to mark your answers – ask questions until you do.

V. RECORDING YOUR ANSWERS

Computer terminals are used more and more today for many different kinds of exams.
For an examination with very few applicants, you may be told to record your answers in the test booklet itself. Separate answer sheets are much more common. If this separate answer sheet is to be scored by machine – and this is often the case – it is highly important that you mark your answers correctly in order to get credit.
An electronic scoring machine is often used in civil service offices because of the speed with which papers can be scored. Machine-scored answer sheets must be marked with a pencil, which will be given to you. This pencil has a high graphite content which responds to the electronic scoring machine. As a matter of fact, stray dots may register as answers, so do not let your pencil rest on the answer sheet while you are pondering the correct answer. Also, if your pencil lead breaks or is otherwise defective, ask for another.

Since the answer sheet will be dropped in a slot in the scoring machine, be careful not to bend the corners or get the paper crumpled.

The answer sheet normally has five vertical columns of numbers, with 30 numbers to a column. These numbers correspond to the question numbers in your test booklet. After each number, going across the page are four or five pairs of dotted lines. These short dotted lines have small letters or numbers above them. The first two pairs may also have a "T" or "F" above the letters. This indicates that the first two pairs only are to be used if the questions are of the true-false type. If the questions are multiple choice, disregard the "T" and "F" and pay attention only to the small letters or numbers.

Answer your questions in the manner of the sample that follows:

32. The largest city in the United States is
    A. Washington, D.C.
    B. New York City
    C. Chicago
    D. Detroit
    E. San Francisco

1) Choose the answer you think is best. (New York City is the largest, so "B" is correct.)
2) Find the row of dotted lines numbered the same as the question you are answering. (Find row number 32)
3) Find the pair of dotted lines corresponding to the answer. (Find the pair of lines under the mark "B.")
4) Make a solid black mark between the dotted lines.

VI. BEFORE THE TEST

Common sense will help you find procedures to follow to get ready for an examination. Too many of us, however, overlook these sensible measures. Indeed, nervousness and fatigue have been found to be the most serious reasons why applicants fail to do their best on civil service tests. Here is a list of reminders:

- Begin your preparation early – Don't wait until the last minute to go scurrying around for books and materials or to find out what the position is all about.
- Prepare continuously – An hour a night for a week is better than an all-night cram session. This has been definitely established. What is more, a night a week for a month will return better dividends than crowding your study into a shorter period of time.
- Locate the place of the exam – You have been sent a notice telling you when and where to report for the examination. If the location is in a different town or otherwise unfamiliar to you, it would be well to inquire the best route and learn something about the building.
- Relax the night before the test – Allow your mind to rest. Do not study at all that night. Plan some mild recreation or diversion; then go to bed early and get a good night's sleep.
- Get up early enough to make a leisurely trip to the place for the test – This way unforeseen events, traffic snarls, unfamiliar buildings, etc. will not upset you.
- Dress comfortably – A written test is not a fashion show. You will be known by number and not by name, so wear something comfortable.

- Leave excess paraphernalia at home – Shopping bags and odd bundles will get in your way. You need bring only the items mentioned in the official notice you received; usually everything you need is provided. Do not bring reference books to the exam. They will only confuse those last minutes and be taken away from you when in the test room.
- Arrive somewhat ahead of time – If because of transportation schedules you must get there very early, bring a newspaper or magazine to take your mind off yourself while waiting.
- Locate the examination room – When you have found the proper room, you will be directed to the seat or part of the room where you will sit. Sometimes you are given a sheet of instructions to read while you are waiting. Do not fill out any forms until you are told to do so; just read them and be prepared.
- Relax and prepare to listen to the instructions
- If you have any physical problem that may keep you from doing your best, be sure to tell the test administrator. If you are sick or in poor health, you really cannot do your best on the exam. You can come back and take the test some other time.

VII. AT THE TEST

The day of the test is here and you have the test booklet in your hand. The temptation to get going is very strong. Caution! There is more to success than knowing the right answers. You must know how to identify your papers and understand variations in the type of short-answer question used in this particular examination. Follow these suggestions for maximum results from your efforts:

1) Cooperate with the monitor

The test administrator has a duty to create a situation in which you can be as much at ease as possible. He will give instructions, tell you when to begin, check to see that you are marking your answer sheet correctly, and so on. He is not there to guard you, although he will see that your competitors do not take unfair advantage. He wants to help you do your best.

2) Listen to all instructions

Don't jump the gun! Wait until you understand all directions. In most civil service tests you get more time than you need to answer the questions. So don't be in a hurry. Read each word of instructions until you clearly understand the meaning. Study the examples, listen to all announcements and follow directions. Ask questions if you do not understand what to do.

3) Identify your papers

Civil service exams are usually identified by number only. You will be assigned a number; you must not put your name on your test papers. Be sure to copy your number correctly. Since more than one exam may be given, copy your exact examination title.

4) Plan your time

Unless you are told that a test is a "speed" or "rate of work" test, speed itself is usually not important. Time enough to answer all the questions will be provided, but this does not mean that you have all day. An overall time limit has been set. Divide the total time (in minutes) by the number of questions to determine the approximate time you have for each question.

5) Do not linger over difficult questions

If you come across a difficult question, mark it with a paper clip (useful to have along) and come back to it when you have been through the booklet. One caution if you do this – be sure to skip a number on your answer sheet as well. Check often to be sure that you have not lost your place and that you are marking in the row numbered the same as the question you are answering.

6) Read the questions

Be sure you know what the question asks! Many capable people are unsuccessful because they failed to *read* the questions correctly.

7) Answer all questions

Unless you have been instructed that a penalty will be deducted for incorrect answers, it is better to guess than to omit a question.

8) Speed tests

It is often better NOT to guess on speed tests. It has been found that on timed tests people are tempted to spend the last few seconds before time is called in marking answers at random – without even reading them – in the hope of picking up a few extra points. To discourage this practice, the instructions may warn you that your score will be "corrected" for guessing. That is, a penalty will be applied. The incorrect answers will be deducted from the correct ones, or some other penalty formula will be used.

9) Review your answers

If you finish before time is called, go back to the questions you guessed or omitted to give them further thought. Review other answers if you have time.

10) Return your test materials

If you are ready to leave before others have finished or time is called, take ALL your materials to the monitor and leave quietly. Never take any test material with you. The monitor can discover whose papers are not complete, and taking a test booklet may be grounds for disqualification.

VIII. EXAMINATION TECHNIQUES

1) Read the general instructions carefully. These are usually printed on the first page of the exam booklet. As a rule, these instructions refer to the timing of the examination; the fact that you should not start work until the signal and must stop work at a signal, etc. If there are any *special* instructions, such as a choice of questions to be answered, make sure that you note this instruction carefully.

2) When you are ready to start work on the examination, that is as soon as the signal has been given, read the instructions to each question booklet, underline any key words or phrases, such as *least, best, outline, describe* and the like. In this way you will tend to answer as requested rather than discover on reviewing your paper that you *listed without describing*, that you selected the *worst* choice rather than the *best* choice, etc.

3) If the examination is of the objective or multiple-choice type – that is, each question will also give a series of possible answers: A, B, C or D, and you are called upon to select the best answer and write the letter next to that answer on your answer paper – it is advisable to start answering each question in turn. There may be anywhere from 50 to 100 such questions in the three or four hours allotted and you can see how much time would be taken if you read through all the questions before beginning to answer any. Furthermore, if you come across a question or group of questions which you know would be difficult to answer, it would undoubtedly affect your handling of all the other questions.

4) If the examination is of the essay type and contains but a few questions, it is a moot point as to whether you should read all the questions before starting to answer any one. Of course, if you are given a choice – say five out of seven and the like – then it is essential to read all the questions so you can eliminate the two that are most difficult. If, however, you are asked to answer all the questions, there may be danger in trying to answer the easiest one first because you may find that you will spend too much time on it. The best technique is to answer the first question, then proceed to the second, etc.

5) Time your answers. Before the exam begins, write down the time it started, then add the time allowed for the examination and write down the time it must be completed, then divide the time available somewhat as follows:
    - If 3-1/2 hours are allowed, that would be 210 minutes. If you have 80 objective-type questions, that would be an average of 2-1/2 minutes per question. Allow yourself no more than 2 minutes per question, or a total of 160 minutes, which will permit about 50 minutes to review.
    - If for the time allotment of 210 minutes there are 7 essay questions to answer, that would average about 30 minutes a question. Give yourself only 25 minutes per question so that you have about 35 minutes to review.

6) The most important instruction is to *read each question* and make sure you know what is wanted. The second most important instruction is to *time yourself properly* so that you answer every question. The third most important instruction is to *answer every question*. Guess if you have to but include something for each question. Remember that you will receive no credit for a blank and will probably receive some credit if you write something in answer to an essay question. If you guess a letter – say "B" for a multiple-choice question – you may have guessed right. If you leave a blank as an answer to a multiple-choice question, the examiners may respect your feelings but it will not add a point to your score. Some exams may penalize you for wrong answers, so in such cases *only*, you may not want to guess unless you have some basis for your answer.

7) Suggestions
   a. Objective-type questions
      1. Examine the question booklet for proper sequence of pages and questions
      2. Read all instructions carefully
      3. Skip any question which seems too difficult; return to it after all other questions have been answered
      4. Apportion your time properly; do not spend too much time on any single question or group of questions

5. Note and underline key words – *all, most, fewest, least, best, worst, same, opposite*, etc.
6. Pay particular attention to negatives
7. Note unusual option, e.g., unduly long, short, complex, different or similar in content to the body of the question
8. Observe the use of "hedging" words – *probably, may, most likely*, etc.
9. Make sure that your answer is put next to the same number as the question
10. Do not second-guess unless you have good reason to believe the second answer is definitely more correct
11. Cross out original answer if you decide another answer is more accurate; do not erase until you are ready to hand your paper in
12. Answer all questions; guess unless instructed otherwise
13. Leave time for review

b. Essay questions
  1. Read each question carefully
  2. Determine exactly what is wanted. Underline key words or phrases.
  3. Decide on outline or paragraph answer
  4. Include many different points and elements unless asked to develop any one or two points or elements
  5. Show impartiality by giving pros and cons unless directed to select one side only
  6. Make and write down any assumptions you find necessary to answer the questions
  7. Watch your English, grammar, punctuation and choice of words
  8. Time your answers; don't crowd material

8) Answering the essay question

Most essay questions can be answered by framing the specific response around several key words or ideas. Here are a few such key words or ideas:

M's: manpower, materials, methods, money, management
P's: purpose, program, policy, plan, procedure, practice, problems, pitfalls, personnel, public relations

  a. Six basic steps in handling problems:
    1. Preliminary plan and background development
    2. Collect information, data and facts
    3. Analyze and interpret information, data and facts
    4. Analyze and develop solutions as well as make recommendations
    5. Prepare report and sell recommendations
    6. Install recommendations and follow up effectiveness

  b. Pitfalls to avoid
    1. *Taking things for granted* – A statement of the situation does not necessarily imply that each of the elements is necessarily true; for example, a complaint may be invalid and biased so that all that can be taken for granted is that a complaint has been registered

2. *Considering only one side of a situation* – Wherever possible, indicate several alternatives and then point out the reasons you selected the best one
3. *Failing to indicate follow up* – Whenever your answer indicates action on your part, make certain that you will take proper follow-up action to see how successful your recommendations, procedures or actions turn out to be
4. *Taking too long in answering any single question* – Remember to time your answers properly

IX. AFTER THE TEST

Scoring procedures differ in detail among civil service jurisdictions although the general principles are the same. Whether the papers are hand-scored or graded by machine we have described, they are nearly always graded by number. That is, the person who marks the paper knows only the number – never the name – of the applicant. Not until all the papers have been graded will they be matched with names. If other tests, such as training and experience or oral interview ratings have been given, scores will be combined. Different parts of the examination usually have different weights. For example, the written test might count 60 percent of the final grade, and a rating of training and experience 40 percent. In many jurisdictions, veterans will have a certain number of points added to their grades.

After the final grade has been determined, the names are placed in grade order and an eligible list is established. There are various methods for resolving ties between those who get the same final grade – probably the most common is to place first the name of the person whose application was received first. Job offers are made from the eligible list in the order the names appear on it. You will be notified of your grade and your rank as soon as all these computations have been made. This will be done as rapidly as possible.

People who are found to meet the requirements in the announcement are called "eligibles." Their names are put on a list of eligible candidates. An eligible's chances of getting a job depend on how high he stands on this list and how fast agencies are filling jobs from the list.

When a job is to be filled from a list of eligibles, the agency asks for the names of people on the list of eligibles for that job. When the civil service commission receives this request, it sends to the agency the names of the three people highest on this list. Or, if the job to be filled has specialized requirements, the office sends the agency the names of the top three persons who meet these requirements from the general list.

The appointing officer makes a choice from among the three people whose names were sent to him. If the selected person accepts the appointment, the names of the others are put back on the list to be considered for future openings.

That is the rule in hiring from all kinds of eligible lists, whether they are for typist, carpenter, chemist, or something else. For every vacancy, the appointing officer has his choice of any one of the top three eligibles on the list. This explains why the person whose name is on top of the list sometimes does not get an appointment when some of the persons lower on the list do. If the appointing officer chooses the second or third eligible, the No. 1 eligible does not get a job at once, but stays on the list until he is appointed or the list is terminated.

X. HOW TO PASS THE INTERVIEW TEST

The examination for which you applied requires an oral interview test. You have already taken the written test and you are now being called for the interview test – the final part of the formal examination.

You may think that it is not possible to prepare for an interview test and that there are no procedures to follow during an interview. Our purpose is to point out some things you can do in advance that will help you and some good rules to follow and pitfalls to avoid while you are being interviewed.

What is an interview supposed to test?

The written examination is designed to test the technical knowledge and competence of the candidate; the oral is designed to evaluate intangible qualities, not readily measured otherwise, and to establish a list showing the relative fitness of each candidate – as measured against his competitors – for the position sought. Scoring is not on the basis of "right" and "wrong," but on a sliding scale of values ranging from "not passable" to "outstanding." As a matter of fact, it is possible to achieve a relatively low score without a single "incorrect" answer because of evident weakness in the qualities being measured.

Occasionally, an examination may consist entirely of an oral test – either an individual or a group oral. In such cases, information is sought concerning the technical knowledges and abilities of the candidate, since there has been no written examination for this purpose. More commonly, however, an oral test is used to supplement a written examination.

Who conducts interviews?

The composition of oral boards varies among different jurisdictions. In nearly all, a representative of the personnel department serves as chairman. One of the members of the board may be a representative of the department in which the candidate would work. In some cases, "outside experts" are used, and, frequently, a businessman or some other representative of the general public is asked to serve. Labor and management or other special groups may be represented. The aim is to secure the services of experts in the appropriate field.

However the board is composed, it is a good idea (and not at all improper or unethical) to ascertain in advance of the interview who the members are and what groups they represent. When you are introduced to them, you will have some idea of their backgrounds and interests, and at least you will not stutter and stammer over their names.

What should be done before the interview?

While knowledge about the board members is useful and takes some of the surprise element out of the interview, there is other preparation which is more substantive. It *is* possible to prepare for an oral interview – in several ways:

1) Keep a copy of your application and review it carefully before the interview

This may be the only document before the oral board, and the starting point of the interview. Know what education and experience you have listed there, and the sequence and dates of all of it. Sometimes the board will ask you to review the highlights of your experience for them; you should not have to hem and haw doing it.

2) Study the class specification and the examination announcement

Usually, the oral board has one or both of these to guide them. The qualities, characteristics or knowledges required by the position sought are stated in these documents. They offer valuable clues as to the nature of the oral interview. For example, if the job involves supervisory responsibilities, the announcement will usually indicate that knowledge of modern supervisory methods and the qualifications of the candidate as a supervisor will be tested. If so, you can expect such questions, frequently in the form of a hypothetical situation which you are expected to solve. NEVER go into an oral without knowledge of the duties and responsibilities of the job you seek.

3) Think through each qualification required

Try to visualize the kind of questions you would ask if you were a board member. How well could you answer them? Try especially to appraise your own knowledge and background in each area, *measured against the job sought*, and identify any areas in which you are weak. Be critical and realistic – do not flatter yourself.

4) Do some general reading in areas in which you feel you may be weak

For example, if the job involves supervision and your past experience has NOT, some general reading in supervisory methods and practices, particularly in the field of human relations, might be useful. Do NOT study agency procedures or detailed manuals. The oral board will be testing your understanding and capacity, not your memory.

5) Get a good night's sleep and watch your general health and mental attitude

You will want a clear head at the interview. Take care of a cold or any other minor ailment, and of course, no hangovers.

What should be done on the day of the interview?

Now comes the day of the interview itself. Give yourself plenty of time to get there. Plan to arrive somewhat ahead of the scheduled time, particularly if your appointment is in the fore part of the day. If a previous candidate fails to appear, the board might be ready for you a bit early. By early afternoon an oral board is almost invariably behind schedule if there are many candidates, and you may have to wait. Take along a book or magazine to read, or your application to review, but leave any extraneous material in the waiting room when you go in for your interview. In any event, relax and compose yourself.

The matter of dress is important. The board is forming impressions about you – from your experience, your manners, your attitude, and your appearance. Give your personal appearance careful attention. Dress your best, but not your flashiest. Choose conservative, appropriate clothing, and be sure it is immaculate. This is a business interview, and your appearance should indicate that you regard it as such. Besides, being well groomed and properly dressed will help boost your confidence.

Sooner or later, someone will call your name and escort you into the interview room. *This is it.* From here on you are on your own. It is too late for any more preparation. But remember, you asked for this opportunity to prove your fitness, and you are here because your request was granted.

What happens when you go in?

The usual sequence of events will be as follows: The clerk (who is often the board stenographer) will introduce you to the chairman of the oral board, who will introduce you to the other members of the board. Acknowledge the introductions before you sit down. Do not be surprised if you find a microphone facing you or a stenotypist sitting by. Oral interviews are usually recorded in the event of an appeal or other review.

Usually the chairman of the board will open the interview by reviewing the highlights of your education and work experience from your application – primarily for the benefit of the other members of the board, as well as to get the material into the record. Do not interrupt or comment unless there is an error or significant misinterpretation; if that is the case, do not hesitate. But do not quibble about insignificant matters. Also, he will usually ask you some question about your education, experience or your present job – partly to get you to start talking and to establish the interviewing "rapport." He may start the actual questioning, or turn it over to one of the other members. Frequently, each member undertakes the questioning on a particular area, one in which he is perhaps most competent, so you can expect each member to participate in the examination. Because time is limited, you may also expect some rather abrupt switches in the direction the questioning takes, so do not be upset by it. Normally, a board member will not pursue a single line of questioning unless he discovers a particular strength or weakness.

After each member has participated, the chairman will usually ask whether any member has any further questions, then will ask you if you have anything you wish to add. Unless you are expecting this question, it may floor you. Worse, it may start you off on an extended, extemporaneous speech. The board is not usually seeking more information. The question is principally to offer you a last opportunity to present further qualifications or to indicate that you have nothing to add. So, if you feel that a significant qualification or characteristic has been overlooked, it is proper to point it out in a sentence or so. Do not compliment the board on the thoroughness of their examination -- they have been sketchy, and you know it. If you wish, merely say, "No thank you, I have nothing further to add." This is a point where you can "talk yourself out" of a good impression or fail to present an important bit of information. Remember, *you close the interview yourself.*

The chairman will then say, "That is all, Mr. _____, thank you." Do not be startled; the interview is over, and quicker than you think. Thank him, gather your belongings and take your leave. Save your sigh of relief for the other side of the door.

How to put your best foot forward

Throughout this entire process, you may feel that the board individually and collectively is trying to pierce your defenses, seek out your hidden weaknesses and embarrass and confuse you. Actually, this is not true. They are obliged to make an appraisal of your qualifications for the job you are seeking, and they want to see you in your best light. Remember, they must interview all candidates and a non-cooperative candidate may become a failure in spite of their best efforts to bring out his qualifications. Here are 15 suggestions that will help you:

1) **Be natural – Keep your attitude confident, not cocky**

If you are not confident that you can do the job, do not expect the board to be. Do not apologize for your weaknesses, try to bring out your strong points. The board is interested in a positive, not negative, presentation. Cockiness will antagonize any board member and make him wonder if you are covering up a weakness by a false show of strength.

2) **Get comfortable, but don't lounge or sprawl**

Sit erectly but not stiffly. A careless posture may lead the board to conclude that you are careless in other things, or at least that you are not impressed by the importance of the occasion. Either conclusion is natural, even if incorrect. Do not fuss with your clothing, a pencil or an ashtray. Your hands may occasionally be useful to emphasize a point; do not let them become a point of distraction.

3) **Do not wisecrack or make small talk**

This is a serious situation, and your attitude should show that you consider it as such. Further, the time of the board is limited – they do not want to waste it, and neither should you.

4) Do not exaggerate your experience or abilities
In the first place, from information in the application or other interviews and sources, the board may know more about you than you think. Secondly, you probably will not get away with it. An experienced board is rather adept at spotting such a situation, so do not take the chance.

5) If you know a board member, do not make a point of it, yet do not hide it
Certainly you are not fooling him, and probably not the other members of the board. Do not try to take advantage of your acquaintanceship – it will probably do you little good.

6) Do not dominate the interview
Let the board do that. They will give you the clues – do not assume that you have to do all the talking. Realize that the board has a number of questions to ask you, and do not try to take up all the interview time by showing off your extensive knowledge of the answer to the first one.

7) Be attentive
You only have 20 minutes or so, and you should keep your attention at its sharpest throughout. When a member is addressing a problem or question to you, give him your undivided attention. Address your reply principally to him, but do not exclude the other board members.

8) Do not interrupt
A board member may be stating a problem for you to analyze. He will ask you a question when the time comes. Let him state the problem, and wait for the question.

9) Make sure you understand the question
Do not try to answer until you are sure what the question is. If it is not clear, restate it in your own words or ask the board member to clarify it for you. However, do not haggle about minor elements.

10) Reply promptly but not hastily
A common entry on oral board rating sheets is "candidate responded readily," or "candidate hesitated in replies." Respond as promptly and quickly as you can, but do not jump to a hasty, ill-considered answer.

11) Do not be peremptory in your answers
A brief answer is proper – but do not fire your answer back. That is a losing game from your point of view. The board member can probably ask questions much faster than you can answer them.

12) Do not try to create the answer you think the board member wants
He is interested in what kind of mind you have and how it works – not in playing games. Furthermore, he can usually spot this practice and will actually grade you down on it.

13) Do not switch sides in your reply merely to agree with a board member
Frequently, a member will take a contrary position merely to draw you out and to see if you are willing and able to defend your point of view. Do not start a debate, yet do not surrender a good position. If a position is worth taking, it is worth defending.

14) Do not be afraid to admit an error in judgment if you are shown to be wrong

The board knows that you are forced to reply without any opportunity for careful consideration. Your answer may be demonstrably wrong. If so, admit it and get on with the interview.

15) Do not dwell at length on your present job

The opening question may relate to your present assignment. Answer the question but do not go into an extended discussion. You are being examined for a *new* job, not your present one. As a matter of fact, try to phrase ALL your answers in terms of the job for which you are being examined.

Basis of Rating

Probably you will forget most of these "do's" and "don'ts" when you walk into the oral interview room. Even remembering them all will not ensure you a passing grade. Perhaps you did not have the qualifications in the first place. But remembering them will help you to put your best foot forward, without treading on the toes of the board members.

Rumor and popular opinion to the contrary notwithstanding, an oral board wants you to make the best appearance possible. They know you are under pressure – but they also want to see how you respond to it as a guide to what your reaction would be under the pressures of the job you seek. They will be influenced by the degree of poise you display, the personal traits you show and the manner in which you respond.

ABOUT THIS BOOK

This book contains tests divided into Examination Sections. Go through each test, answering every question in the margin. We have also attached a sample answer sheet at the back of the book that can be removed and used. At the end of each test look at the answer key and check your answers. On the ones you got wrong, look at the right answer choice and learn. Do not fill in the answers first. Do not memorize the questions and answers, but understand the answer and principles involved. On your test, the questions will likely be different from the samples. Questions are changed and new ones added. If you understand these past questions you should have success with any changes that arise. Tests may consist of several types of questions. We have additional books on each subject should more study be advisable or necessary for you. Finally, the more you study, the better prepared you will be. This book is intended to be the last thing you study before you walk into the examination room. Prior study of relevant texts is also recommended. NLC publishes some of these in our Fundamental Series. Knowledge and good sense are important factors in passing your exam. Good luck also helps. So now study this Passbook, absorb the material contained within and take that knowledge into the examination. Then do your best to pass that exam.

EXAMINATION SECTION

EXAMINATION SECTION
TEST 1
Synonyms (Spanish/Spanish)

DIRECTIONS: Below is a list of key words in Spanish, each of which is followed by four other Spanish words, one of which is a synonym of the key word. Select the synonym. *PRINT THE LETTER OF THE CORRECT ANSWER IN THE SPACE AT THE RIGHT.*

1. furibundo
    - A. mortecino
    - B. clandestino
    - C. colérico
    - D. manso

2. efímero
    - A. duradero
    - B. indestructible
    - C. transitorio
    - D. intransigente

3. antifaz
    - A. máscara
    - B. espejuelo
    - C. carilla
    - D. fachada

4. belicoso
    - A. engreído
    - B. precioso
    - C. marcial
    - D. pacífico

5. carestía
    - A. escasez
    - B. plenitud
    - C. rebosamiento
    - D. ternura

6. procer
    - A. heredero
    - B. héroe
    - C. desfile
    - D. pleito

7. lechón
    - A. camilla
    - B. buey
    - C. nata
    - D. cerdo

8. lelo
    - A. flor
    - B. sabio
    - C. purista
    - D. tonto

9. faena
    - A. harina
    - B. labor
    - C. trigo
    - D. don

10. umbrío
    - A. dintel
    - B. estrepitoso
    - C. risueño
    - D. sombrío

KEY (CORRECT ANSWERS)

1. C
2. C
3. A
4. C
5. A

6. B
7. D
8. D
9. B
10. D

TEST 2
Vocabulary (English/Spanish)

DIRECTIONS: Below is a list of English words, each of which is followed by four Spanish words, one of which is a correct translation of the English word. Select the CORRECT translation. *PRINT THE LETTER OF THE CORRECT ANSWER IN THE SPACE AT THE RIGHT.*

1. carrot
   A. guisante B. zanahoria C. espinaca D. remolacha

   1.____

2. apricot
   A. durazno B. ciruela
   C. toronja D. albaricoque

   2.____

3. alligator
   A. tiburón B. caracol C. caimán D. anguila

   3.____

4. hiccough
   A. tos B. estornudo C. hipo D. ahogo

   4.____

5. bat
   A. murciélago B. cuervo
   C. gavilán D. buho

   5.____

6. damage
   A. hurto B. lástima
   C. desperdicio D. estropeo

   6.____

7. freckles
   A. ojeras B. lunares C. pecas D. arrugas

   7.____

8. corkscrew
   A. tirante B. tirabuzón
   C. martillo D. destornillador

   8.____

9. lily
   A. azucena B. lila C. margarita D. jazmín

   9.____

10. measles
    A. sarampión B. viruelas C. tisis D. papera

    10.____

KEY (CORRECT ANSWERS)

1. B
2. D
3. C
4. C
5. A

6. D
7. C
8. B
9. A
10. A

TEST 3
Sentence Completion (English/Spanish)

DIRECTIONS: Below is a series of English sentences, each of which has been translated into Spanish with the omission of a word or expression. Four choices are listed from which you are to choose the MOST appropriate one to complete the Spanish sentence CORRECTLY. *PRINT THE LETTER OF THE CORRECT ANSWER IN THE SPACE AT THE RIGHT.*

1. He had been traveling for two months when he met his friends.
   _____ cuando se encontró con sus amigos.

   A. Hace dos meses que viajó
   B. Hace dos meses qui viajó
   C. Viajó dos meses
   D. Hacia dos meses que viajaba

2. Is there anyone who writes well?
   ¿Hay _____ que escriba bien?

   A. nadie
   B. alguien
   C. ninguno
   D. ninguna persona

3. This secret is only between you and me.
   Este secreto es sólo entre _____ .

   A. Vd. y mí
   B. vosotros y mi
   C. tú y yo
   D. nos

4. You cannot imagine how intelligent those children are. No puede imaginarse _____ que son esos niños.

   A. cuanto inteligentes
   B. lo inteligentes
   C. los inteligentes
   D. cómo inteligentes

5. They will take any books whatsoever.
   Tomarán _____ .

   A. no importan los libros
   B. cuales libros
   C. cualesquier libros
   D. cualquier libro

6. There have been many revoluciones in that country.
   _____ muchas revoluciones en ese pais.

   A. Hubo   B. Hay   C. Han habido   D. Ha habido

7. One learns a great deal by reading.
   Se aprende mucho _____ .

   A. leer
   B. por leer
   C. leyendo
   D. con leyendo

8. For a beginner, he does it well.
   _____ principiante, lo hace bien.

   A. como   B. de   C. para   D. por

9. I saw him coming down the path.
   _____ por el sendero.

   A. Lo vi
   B. Lo vi venir
   C. Lo vi viniendo
   D. Lo veía viniendo

10. It"s true that you never told us to do it.
    Es cierto que Vd. nunca nos dijo _____.

    A. hacerlo
    B. que lo hiciéramos
    C. que lo hagamos
    D. que lo hayamos hecho

KEY (CORRECT ANSWERS)

1. D
2. B
3. C
4. B
5. C

6. C
7. C
8. C
9. B
10. B

TEST 4
Antonyms (Spanish/Spanish)

DIRECTIONS: Below is a list of key words in Spanish, each of which is followed by four other Spanish words, one of which is an antonym of the key word. Select the antonym. *PRINT THE LETTER OF THE CORRECT ANSWER IN THE SPACE AT THE RIGHT.*

1. madrugada
   A. alba B. amanuense C. amanecer D. anochecer
   1.____

2. pulido
   A. pelado B. peloso C. desaseado D. limpio
   2.____

3. regocijarse
   A. entristecerse B. mejorarse
   C. apoderarse D. quejarse
   3.____

4. septentrional
   A. oriental B. meridional
   C. occidental D. tropical
   4.____

5. hogaño
   A. antaño B. hoguera C. hogareño D. huraño
   5.____

6. sencillo
   A. candido B. perplejo C. ingenuo D. enredado
   6.____

7. apaciguar
   A. sosegar B. calmar
   C. alborotar D. arruinar
   7.____

8. dulzura
   A. esfuerzo B. vehemencia
   C. quietud D. zozobra
   8.____

9. apócrifo
   A. animoso B. placentero
   C. cuajado D. auténtico
   9.____

10. escampar
    A. llover B. dormirse C. pasearse D. ocultar
    10.____

7

KEY (CORRECT ANSWERS)

1. D
2. C
3. A
4. B
5. A

6. D
7. C
8. B
9. D
10. A

TEST 5
Reading Comprehension (Spanish/Spanish)

DIRECTIONS: The following passage is followed by five incomplete statements or questions. Four choices are usted from which you are to choose the MOST appropriate one to complete the statement or answer the question. Indícate the CORRECT answer. *PRINT THE LETTER OF THE CORRECT ANSWER IN THE SPACE AT THE RIGHT.*

PASSAGE

Antes de que discutieran los detalles del contrato, Hernando de Luque tuvo ana serie de preocupaciones. Todo seria más fácil si se tratara de otros socios. Porque estos que le habían tocado lo tenían lleno de dudas. Cierto que eran valientes y decididos hasta la temeridad. De eso no le cabía la menor duda. Más inteligente, o mas astuto, Diego de Almagro; con más carácter y decisión, Francisco Pizarra. Buenos soldados, cumplidores de su deber y su palabra, siempre que no estuviesen de por medio grandes intereses y ordenes superiores. Por otra parte, ¿sabia lo suficiente acerca de ellos? Ambos eran analfabetas. Ni siquiera podían, escribir su nombre. Y sus historias eran dudosas, difíciles de comprobar.

Diego de Almagro, natural de la villa castellana de su nombre, contaba que había salido de España por motivos sentimentales. Galán afortunado, habíase visto sorprendido por un rival ante la reja de una guapa moza, De allí a las palabras descomedidas y al cruce de espadas no había mediado mucho tiempo. Al final, el rival había quedado en el suelo, iluminado por la luz mortecina de un farol. Don Diego había tenido que poner pies en polvorosa. Lenguas ajenas afirmaban que todo era producto de la imaginación del narrador.

Don Francisco Pizarra, en cambio, nunca hablada de si mismo. Cuando se le preguntaba acerca de su infancia, respondía con monosílabos. O agriaba el gesto y permanecía en silencio. Trujillanos que lo conocian desde sus años mozos, referían una serie de hechos y de anécdotas. ¿Serian verdad? ¿No lo serian? Lo cierto es que era hijo de doña Francisca Mateos y de don Gonzalo Pizarro; que tenia algunos medio hermanos de distintos padres y otros de distintas madres; que cuidaba cerdos en terrenos colindantes a su villa nativa; que alguna vez perdió uno de ellos, y para evitar la severa sanción que le esperaba, huyó, enrolándoseen los tercios que partían hacia Italia.

1. ¿Qué cualidad, ventajosa para la empresa, tenían los socios de Luque?   1._____

    A. Era muy prudentes.
    B. Tenian mucha audacia.
    C. Eran filosóficos.
    D. Tenían mucho entusiasmo.

2. ¿Cual era el nivel académico de estos socios?   2._____

    A. Eran muy doctos en religión.
    B. Eran muy instruidos en navegación.
    C. No sabían leer.
    D. Les faltaban conocimientos geográficos.

3. Según Almagro mismo, ¿por qué se había marchado de su país natal?

   A. Le había dado calabazas su novia.
   B. No había podido defenderse en un duelo.
   C. Había peleado en un asunto del corazón.
   D. Había fracasado en los negocios.

4. De joven. ¿qué causó la huida de Pizarro?

   A. Tenia tanta ambicion de hacerse rico.
   B. No habia sitio para él en su casa.
   C. No le gustaba trabajar tan duramente.
   D. Le faltaba un día un puerco.

5. Con referencia a su juventud, ¿que revelaba Pizarro?

   A. Era bastante taciturno.
   B. Se jactaba de su linaje.
   C. Solia narrar anécdotas de su vida en Trujillo.
   D. Se describía como muy diestro con la espada.

KEY (CORRECT ANSWERS)

1. B
2. C
3. C
4. D
5. A

TEST 6
Translation (English/Spanish)

DIRECTIONS: Below is a list of English expressions translated into Spanish. From the four choices given, select the Spanish expression which approximates the English in meaning. *PRINT THE LETTER OF THE CORRECT ANSWER IN THE SPACE AT THE RIGHT.*

1. Mary puts on the airs of a great lady.
   Maria _____ de gran persona.

   A. se da tono   B. se describe
   C. hace el papel   D. actúa

   1._____

2. Charles left without rhyme or reason.
   Carlos salio sin _____.

   A. despedirse de nadie
   B. ton ni son
   C. explicación ni rima
   D. un quitame alla esas pajas

   2._____

3. The boat made a stop at London.
   El vapor _____ en Londres.

   A. hizo escala   B. se instaló
   C. se hizo a la mar   D. se desplegó

   3._____

4. He fell on his face.

   A. Se cayó de rodillas.
   B. Cayó de bruces.
   C. Cayó exanime.
   D. Cayó perdiendo los estribos.

   4._____

5. I have nothing at stake.

   A. A mi no me va nada en ello.
   B. No me hace falta nada.
   C. No tengo inconveniente alguno.
   D. Eso no me importa.

   5._____

6. The boy looked askance at his teacher.
   El muchacho miró _____ a su maestro.

   A. con malos ojos   B. con ojos reventones
   C. a cierra ojos   D. de reojo

   6._____

7. She stood me up.

   A. Se dio de cabezazos.   B. Me dejó sin sentido.
   C. Me dejó plantado.   D. Me dio de alta.

   7._____

11

8. The sun <u>will set</u> at six o'clock.
A las seis _____ el sol.

   A. saldrá   B. hará   C. se pondrá   D. aparecerá

9. Diligent pupils do not <u>play hooky</u>.
Los alumnos aplicados no _____.

   A. malgastan el tiempo jugando
   B. matan el tiempo
   C. hacen novillos
   D. se alejan de sus libros

10. We had not room <u>to stand</u>.
No cabíamos _____.

   A. levantados   B. en los asientos
   C. en el paradero   D. ni parados

KEY (CORRECT ANSWERS)

1. A
2. B
3. A
4. B
5. A

6. D
7. C
8. C
9. C
10. D

TEST 7
Translation (Spanish/English)

DIRECTIONS: Below is a series of Spanish idiomatic expressions translated into English. From the four choices given, select the English expression which approximates the Spanish in meaning. *PRINT THE LETTER OF THE CORRECT ANSWER IN THE SPACE AT THE RIGHT.*

1. Tienen que andar a gatas.
   They have to go _____.

   A. on all fours
   B. slowly
   C. on tiptoes
   D. as quietly as mice

   1.____

2. Le dije cuatro verdades.

   A. I gave him a piece of my mind.
   B. I told him the real truth.
   C. I told him the whole story.
   D. I gave him four reasons for my decision.

   2.____

3. Le sacaron de sus casillas.

   A. They drove him crazy.
   B. They helped him move.
   C. They got him out of his predicament.
   D. They got him a better job.

   3.____

4. A la sazón eran buenos amigos.
   They were good friends _____.

   A. for a short time
   B. for years
   C. at that time
   D. from the moment they met

   4.____

5. Está durmiendo la mona.

   A. He's sleeping like a baby.
   B. He's putting the monkey to sleep.
   C. He's thinking it over.
   D. He's sleeping it off.

   5.____

6. Le puse como hoja de perejil y se lo merecía.

   A. I gave him an award.
   B. I gave him a tongue lashing.
   C. I played a trick on him.
   D. I left him in the lurch.

   6.____

7. Han cortado la electricidad.

   A. They replaced the light switch.
   B. They shut off the electricity.
   C. They reduced the cost of electricity.
   D. They dimmed the light.

   7.____

8. No siga tratando de evadir el tema.

    A. shirk responsibility
    B. get away with writing on the given topic
    C. dodge the issue
    D. prevent us from reaching an agreement

9. El portero está de servicio toda la noche.

    A. is being inducted into the service
    B. guards the servants' entrance only
    C. supervises the servants
    D. is on duty

10. El niño se hacía entender a duras penas.

    A. easily
    B. rather eloquently
    C. sorrowfully
    D. hardly

KEY (CORRECT ANSWERS)

1. C
2. A
3. A
4. D
5. D

6. B
7. B
8. C
9. D
10. D

TEST 8
Vocabulary (Spanish/English)

DIRECTIONS: Below is a list of Spanish words, each of which is followed by four English words, one of which is a CORRECT translation of the Spanish word. Select the CORRECT translation. *PRINT THE LETTER OF THE CORRECT ANSWER IN THE SPACE AT THE RIGHT.*

1. acometer

    A. accommodate B. commit
    C. intrust   D. attack

    1._____

2. destreza

    A. havoc B. repair
    C. skill D. destitution

    2._____

3. valentón

    A. arrogant B. courageous
    C. worthy   D. esteemed

    3._____

4. agasajar

    A. entertain B. crouch
    C. grasp   D. strangle

    4._____

5. lindar

    A. border B. beautify C. loan D. sketch

    5._____

6. inmundo

    A. unworldly B. immune
    C. unclean   D. unchangeable

    6._____

7. pericia

    A. laziness B. skill C. danger D. fragility

    7._____

8. imprescindible

    A. impressionable B. indispensable
    C. unnecessary   D. unprecedented

    8._____

9. tacaño

    A. stamping B. stingy C. nailed D. discreet

    9._____

10. apearse

    A. match B. furnish C. dismount D. attend

    10._____

15

KEY (CORRECT ANSWERS)

1. D
2. C
3. A
4. A
5. A

6. C
7. B
8. B
9. B
10. C

TEST 9
Selection (Spanish/Spanish)

DIRECTIONS: Below is a series of sentences in Spanish, each of which can be correctly completed by adding to it one of the four choices which follow it. Select the CORRECT choice. *PRINT THE LETTER OF THE CORRECT ANSWER IN THE SPACE AT THE RIGHT.*

1. *Volverán las oscuras golondrinas*
   En tu balcón sus nidos a colgar,
   Y otra vez con el ala a sus cristales
   Jugando llamarán
   es el principio de una poesía de

   A. Gustavo Adolfo Bécquer
   B. José de Espronceda
   C. Juan Ramón Jiménez
   D. Antonio Machado

   1.____

2. La realidad histórica de España fue escrita por

   A. Dámaso Alonso
   B. Federico de Onís
   C. Salvador de Madariaga
   D. Américo Castro

   2.____

3. El endecasílabo es

   A. un alejandrino
   B. un poema de la Edad Media
   C. un verso de once sílabas
   D. una palabra esdrújula

   3.____

4. El estudiante de Salamanca y El diablo mundo son obras de

   A. Enrique Gil y Carrasco
   B. José de Espronceda
   C. Mariano José de Larra
   D. Gertrudis Gómez de Avellaneda

   4.____

5. Un notable poeta andaluz cuyas obras tienen temas folklóricos y tradicionales es

   A. León Felipe
   B. Ciro Alegría
   C. García Gutiérrez
   D. Federico Garcia Lorca

   5.____

6. *Recuerde el alma dormida,*
   avive el seso y despierte,
   contemplando
   cómo se pasa la vida,
   cómo se viene la muerte
   tan callando
   son los primeros versos de

   A. una Elegia de Garcilaso de la Vega
   B. el Cancionero de Baena
   C. las Coplas de Jorge Manrique
   D. una cántica de Juan Ruiz

   6.____

7. Antonio Buero Vallejo, Miguel Mihura y Joaquin Calvo Sotelo son

   A. dramaturgos
   B. ensayistas
   C. novelistas
   D. historiadores

8. Los personajes principales en un drama de Lope de Vega son

   A. Perlimplín y Belisa
   B. Calixto y Melibea
   C. Diego e Isabel
   D. Peribánez y Casilda

9. Los cantos de Martín Fierro describen la existencia llena de peligros y de inseguridad del

   A. indio mejicano
   B. gaucho argentino
   C. pescador chileno
   D. llanero venezolano

10. El autor de La colmena y La familia de Pascual Duarte es

    A. Camilo José Cela
    B. Ignacio Agusti
    C. Carmen Laforet
    D. Eulalia Galvarriato

KEY (CORRECT ANSWERS)

1. A
2. D
3. C
4. B
5. D
6. C
7. A
8. D
9. B
10. A

EXAMINATION SECTION
TEST 1
Synonyms (Spanish/Spanish)

DIRECTIONS: Below is a list of key words in Spanish, each of which is followed by four other Spanish words, one of which is a synonym of the key word. Select the synonym. *PRINT THE LETTER OF THE CORRECT ANSWER IN THE SPACE AT THE RIGHT.*

1. bufete 1.____
   - A. escritura
   - B. escritorio
   - C. golpe
   - D. bufón

2. peregrinación 2.____
   - A. giro
   - B. golosina
   - C. percha
   - D. romería

3. atónito 3.____
   - A. asombrado
   - B. áspero
   - C. atrasado
   - D. atómico

4. tartamudear 4.____
   - A. mimar
   - B. pecar
   - C. fruncir
   - D. balbucear

5. presagio 5.____
   - A. aguador
   - B. trueno
   - C. agüero
   - D. empresa

6. desfallecer 6.____
   - A. volcar
   - B. desvanecer
   - C. desmayarse
   - D. morir

7. lozanía 7.____
   - A. luciérnaga
   - B. opulencia
   - C. ramillete
   - D. frondosidad

8. conmovido 8.____
   - A. enternecido
   - B. férreo
   - C. esclarecido
   - D. chato

9. embustero 9.____
   - A. ilógico
   - B. rasgador
   - C. mentiroso
   - D. emérito

10. muchedumbre 10.____
    - A. gentileza
    - B. gentío
    - C. gemelo
    - D. multiplicidad

KEY (CORRECT ANSWERS)

1. B
2. D
3. A
4. D
5. C

6. C
7. D
8. A
9. C
10. B

TEST 2
Vocabulary(English/Spanish)

DIRECTIONS: Below is a list of English words, each of which is followed by four Spanish words, one of which is a correct translation of the English word. Select the CORRECT translation. *PRINT THE LETTER OF THE CORRECT ANSWER IN THE SPACE AT THE RIGHT.*

1. passer-by

    A. transeúnte
    B. pasarela
    C. jornalero
    D. ambulante

    1.____

2. short cut

    A. cortadura
    B. abrevadero
    C. atajo
    D. abreviación

    2.____

3. shrimp

    A. cámbaro   B. camarón   C. cangrejo   D. langosta

    3.____

4. stork

    A. cisne   B. ganso   C. avestruz   D. cigüeña

    4.____

5. land

    A. enterrar
    B. aterrizar
    C. aterrorizar
    D. despegar

    5.____

6. dew

    A. aguacate
    B. manantial
    C. cascada
    D. rocío

    6.____

7. to yawn

    A. pellizcar
    B. estornudar
    C. bostezar
    D. encadenar

    7.____

8. expert

    A. perito
    B. genio
    C. dignitario
    D. autoridad

    8.____

9. puppet

    A. muñeca   B. títere   C. payaso   D. juguete

    9.____

10. lace

    A. encage
    B. aguja
    C. costura
    D. bordadura

    10.____

KEY (CORRECT ANSWERS)

1. A
2. C
3. B
4. D
5. B
6. D
7. C
8. A
9. B
10. A

TEST 3
Sentence Completion (English/Spanish)

DIRECTIONS: Below is a series of English sentences, each of which has been translated into Spanish with the omission of a word or expression. Four choices are listed from which you are to choose the MOST appropriate one to complete the Spanish sentence CORRECTLY. *PRINT THE LETTER OF THE CORRECT ANSWER IN THE SPACE AT THE RIGHT.*

1. John was always very kind <u>to his mother</u>.
   Juan siempre fue muy amable _____ .

   A. a su madre
   B. de su madre
   C. para con su madre
   D. por su madre

   1.____

2. <u>If it were not</u> so far, I would walk.
   _____ tan lejos, iría a pie.

   A. Si no fuera
   B. Si no sea
   C. Si no seria
   D. Si no estaba

   2.____

3. She walks as if <u>she were sick</u>.
   Camina como si _____.

   A. estuviera enferma
   B. está inferma
   C. esté enferma
   D. se enfermase

   3.____

4. She was looking for <u>a teacup</u>.
   Ella buscaba una taza _____ té.

   A. para   B. de   C. con   D. por

   4.____

5. I like this hat better <u>than any other one</u>.
   Me gusta este sombrero mas qué _____.

   A. alguno
   B. el otro
   C. otros
   D. ningún otro

   5.____

6. Bolívar is revered in South America.
   _____ Bolivar en Sud America.

   A. Está venerado
   B. Se veneraba a
   C. Se venera a
   D. Fue venerado

   6.____

7. The party <u>will be</u> at Mary's house.
   La fiesta _____ en casa de María.

   A. habrá   B. está   C. estará   D. será

   7.____

8. <u>No matter how difficult it may be</u>, I know he will try to do it.
   _____ , sé que se esforzará por hacerlo.

   A. Por difícil que sea
   B. No importa lo rudo
   C. Por difícil que esté
   D. No es importante la dificultad

   8.____

9. **I wish I had** their courage and their daring!
   _____ su valor y su atrevimiento!

   A. Quién tuviera
   B. Ay si tengo
   C. Ojalá tendría
   D. Espero tener

10. After having **taught** the lesson, the teacher permitted pupils to ask questions.
    Después que _____ la lección, el profesor permitió que los alumnos le hicieran preguntas.

    A. había presentado
    B. hubo, enseñado
    C. haber enseñado
    D. habrá enseñado

KEY (CORRECT ANSWERS)

1. A
2. A
3. A
4. A
5. D
6. C
7. D
8. A
9. A
10. B

TEST 4
Antonyms (Spanish/Spanish)

DIRECTIONS: Below is a list of key words in Spanish, each of which is followed by four other Spanish words, one of which is an antonym of the key word. Select the ANTONYM. *PRINT THE LETTER OF THE CORRECT ANSWER IN THE SPACE AT THE RIGHT.*

1. alabar

    A. encomiar
    C. dispensar
    B. censurar
    D. disputar

    1.____

2. esmero

    A. amparo B. desdicha C. esmalte D. descuido

    2.____

3. manso

    A. indómito B. febril C. indolente D. femenil

    3.____

4. sosegar

    A. ungir B. mecer C. inquietar D. vendar

    4.____

5. insólito

    A. sacrilego
    C. repentino
    B. razonable
    D. acostumbrado

    5.____

6. misericordioso

    A. lastimoso
    C. parsimonioso
    B. incompasivo
    D. tacaño

    6.____

7. regocijo

    A. abatimiento
    C. desaprobación
    B. felicidad
    D. deleite

    7.____

8. atrevido

    A. intrépido
    C. postizo
    B. ingrato
    D. temeroso

    8.____

9. cautela

    A. imprudencia
    C. astucia
    B. advertencia
    D. cautivo

    9.____

10. torpe

    A. afortunado
    C. diestro
    B. afable
    D. terco

    10.____

25

KEY (CORRECT ANSWERS)

1. B
2. D
3. A
4. C
5. D

6. B
7. A
8. D
9. A
10. C

TEST 5
Reading Comprehension (Spanish/Spanish)

DIRECTIONS: The following passage is followed by five incomplete statements or questions. Four choices are listed from which you are to choose the MOST appropriate one to complete the statement or answer the question. *PRINT THE LETTER OF THE CORRECT ANSWER IN THE SPACE AT THE RIGHT.*

No sin dificultades, emprendieron el regreso al vallecillo donde momentos antes descansaron. El jefe de los expedicionarios, dirigiéndose a los suyos, les mostró el vasto panorama que tenían a la vista, todo hecho de cumbres, pues la barrera que les flanqueaba del lado del precipicio les impedía ver el valle e impedía también que se les viera desde el rancho. El gesto del líder no podía ser mas desesperado. Era como la rectificación a la voluntad que mostró cuando organizaba el viaje, cuando aseguraba que ni el recodo mas escondido de la sierra se escaparía a su ojo en busca de lo que el considero siempre como su tesoro. A distancia, esas caminatas parecen fáciles, pero que distintas cuando las piernas se doblan de cansancio, cuando el sol pica en la espalda y las rugosidades del terreno parecen no tener fin!

Colérico, ordenó al intérprete que preguntara al guia sobre la causa verdadera de la expedición. Que con toda franqueza le expresara que no eran hierbas medicinales las que buscaban, sino minas y el escondite del oro en polvo, el de los tributos recibidos por los antecesores. El intérprete interrogo al indígena y este apenas sonreía sin decir nada. El intérprete insistió, diciendo que las tradiciones eran puestas en los labios de los niños y que el, ya un hombre, sabría sin duda alguna toda la tradición. El indígena volvió a mostrar sus dientes de blancura herbívora y dijo no saber nada.

¿Por indicación del jefe, el intérprete agregó que, de hallar los tesoros, el disfrutaría de una buena parte, pero el joven repitió con el mismo acento y con la misma sonrisa, no saber nada¿ Ya dominado completamente por la ira, el lider se alzo de done estaba sentado y, antes que el indígena pudiera moverse, le puso en el pecho el revolver.

1. ¿Por qué no se les podía ver desde el rancho?

    A. Había mucha distancia entre ellos y el rancho.
    B. Había una muralla en medio.
    C. Lo impedía la oscuridad en aquel lugar funesto.
    D. Nadie se había quedado en el pueblo.

2. ¿Que le causo desesperación al lider?

    A. Le faltaba tiempo para hacer todo lo que quería.
    B. Estaba en busca de oro.
    C. Había revelado la causa verdadera de su expedicion.
    D. Le resultaba muy difícil el viaje.

3. ¿Qué había jurado el jefe al emprender el viaje?

    A. Que nunca se cansaría
    B. Que exploraría detenidamente
    C. Que no volvería sin un hallazgo
    D. Que buscaría valiosas hierbas medicinales

1.____

2.____

3.____

4. ¿Por qué esperaba que el guía pudiera conducirle al tesoro?

    A. Todos los naturales sabían estos secretos.
    B. Era un guía muy perito y de mucha experiencia.
    C. El guía conocía íntimamente a los expedicionarios.
    D. El guía quería regresar lo más pronto posible a su familia.

5. ¿Cómo le tentó el jefe al indígena?

    A. Le ofreció un revólver
    B. Le recordó su deber de guía oficial
    C. Prometió darle oro
    D. Concordó en poner fin a la expedición cuanto antes

KEY (CORRECT ANSWERS)

1. B
2. D
3. C
4. A
5. C

TEST 6
Translation (English/Spanish)

DIRECTIONS: Below is a list of English expressions translated into Spanish. From the four choices given, select the Spanish expression which approximates the English in meaning. *PRINT THE LETTER OF THE CORRECT ANSWER IN THE SPACE AT THE RIGHT.*

1. Pedro acts as general.
   Pedro _____ general.

   A. hace de   B. se da por   C. se hace   D. trata de

   1._____

2. He became a doctor.
   _____ médico.

   A. Se puso
   C. Se volvió
   B. Llegó a ser
   D. Se metió

   2._____

3. from a reliable source

   A. de buena gana
   C. de buena tinta
   B. de buen grado
   D. de buenas a primeras

   3._____

4. He felt like crying.
   _____ llorar.

   A. Se le antojaba
   C. Sintió como
   B. Experimentó
   D. Se le ocurrió

   4._____

5. Mary is going to take a nap.
   Maria va a _____ una siesta.

   A. hacer   B. echar   C. dar   D. tomar

   5._____

6. He boasts of his intelligence.
   _____ de inteligente.

   A. Se los echa
   C. Se echa
   B. Se las echa
   D. Se le echa

   6._____

7. A student should take notes.
   Un alumno debe _____.

   A. sacar notas
   C. sacar informes
   B. hacer puntos
   D. hacer apuntes

   7._____

8. They have nothing left over.

   A. Nada los sobra.
   C. No les sobra nada.
   B. Nada sobra.
   D. No les sobran nada.

   8._____

9. He finally came to the point.
   Al fin, vino _____.

   A. al pelo
   C. al grano
   B. a las manos
   D. a menos

   9._____

29

10. The waiter had to clear the table.
    El mozo tuvo que _____ la mesa.

    A. levantar   B. despejar   C. lavar   D. limpiar

KEY (CORRECT ANSWERS)

1. A
2. B
3. C
4. A
5. B

6. B
7. D
8. C
9. C
10. A

TEST 7
Translation (Spanish/English)

DIRECTIONS: Below is a series of Spanish idiomatic expressions translated into English. From the four choices given, select the English expression which approximates the Spanish in meaning. *PRINT THE LETTER OF THE CORRECT ANSWER IN THE SPACE AT THE RIGHT.*

1. La miro con fastidio.
   He looked at her _____.

   A. with affection
   B. angrily
   C. with annoyance
   D. anxiously

   1.____

2. Se hizo a la vela.

   A. He became a watchman.
   B. He set sail.
   C. He seized the opportunity.
   D. He made his way to the candle.

   2.____

3. Maria no tiene pelos en la lengua.
   Mary _____.

   A. is fluent
   B. is not tongue-tied
   C. is discourteous
   D. speaks her mind

   3.____

4. Se le mando a paseo.

   A. He was sent to the stockade.
   B. He was ordered to patrol.
   C. He was sent about his business.
   D. He was ordered to go on foot.

   4.____

5. En todas partes cuecen habas.

   A. It's the same everywhere.
   B. It's breaking out unexpectedly.
   C. They are all impatient.
   D. It's a sure thing.

   5.____

6. Lo llevaron a cuestas.
   They carried it _____.

   A. to the shores
   B. on their backs
   C. sideways
   D. to the markets

   6.____

7. Se sentó en el acto.

   A. He sat in the middle.
   B. He got into the affair.
   C. He took to the stage.
   D. He sat down at once.

   7.____

8. Eso cae de su peso.

   A. That is too heavy.
   B. That is self-reducing.
   C. That is time-consuming.
   D. That is self-evident.

   8.____

9. Veinte mil dolares contantes y sonantes.
   Twenty thousand dollars _____.

   A. outstanding
   C. on deposit
   B. in cold cash
   D. debits and credits

10. Esta vez se hallaba cortada.
    This time _____.

    A. she was confused
    C. she was laconic
    B. she was short-tempered
    D. she was cut off

KEY (CORRECT ANSWERS)

1. C
2. B
3. D
4. C
5. A

6. B
7. D
8. D
9. B
10. A

TEST 8
Vocabulary (Spanish/English)

DIRECTIONS: Below is a list of Spanish words, each of which is followed by four English words, one of which is a correct translation of the Spanish word. Select the CORRECT translation. *PRINT THE LETTER OF THE CORRECT ANSWER IN THE SPACE AT THE RIGHT.*

1. desperezarse

    A. despair   B. clear   C. crave   D. stretch

    1._____

2. sañoso

    A. healthy   B. hygienic   C. prudent   D. furious

    2._____

3. deleznable

    A. pleasing   B. poisonous   C. tardy   D. fragile

    3._____

4. taladrar

    A. hum   B. pave   C. engrave   D. pierce

    4._____

5. semblante

    A. similar   B. face   C. pretending   D. sowing

    5._____

6. umbral

    A. threshold   B. shade tree
    C. intoxicated   D. parsley

    6._____

7. barandilla

    A. bargain   B. small hut
    C. railing   D. trinket

    7._____

8. delantal

    A. stage   B. forward   C. apron   D. advance

    8._____

9. aserrin

    A. affirmation   B. chain
    C. knife   D. sawdust

    9._____

10. suela

    A. floor   B. sole   C. loose   D. salary

    10._____

KEY (CORRECT ANSWERS)

1. D
2. D
3. D
4. D
5. B

6. A
7. C
8. C
9. D
10. B

TEST 9
Selection (Spanish/Spanish)

DIRECTIONS: Below is a series of sentences in Spanish, each of which can be CORRECTLY completed by adding to it one of the four choices which follow it. Select the CORRECT choice. *PRINT THE LETTER OF THE CORRECT ANSWER IN THE SPACE AT THE RIGHT.*

1. Manuel Gutiérrez Najera y Amado Nervo son poetas 1.____
    - A. nicaragüenses
    - B. mejicanos
    - C. cubanos
    - D. venezolanos

2. Son ganadores del Premio Nobel de Literatura Juan Ramón Jiménez, Jacinto Benavente, Gabriela Mistral y 2.____
    - A. Pío Baroja
    - B. Benito Pérez Galdos
    - C. Antonio Machado
    - D. José Echegaray

3. El uso de alusiones, mitológicas, la abundancia de cultismos y neologismos, y la riqueza de metáforas son caracteres del estilo 3.____
    - A. realista
    - B. clásico
    - C. cervantino
    - D. gongorista

4. El autor de la obra titulada LOS PERROS HAMBRIENTOS es 4.____
    - A. Romulo Gallegos
    - B. Antonio Alatorre
    - C. Ciro Alegria
    - D. Alonso Ercilla

5. Fernán Caballero escribió 5.____
    - A. Doña Perfecta
    - B. Los Pazos de Ulloa
    - C. Sotileza
    - D. La gaviota

6. Los hermanos Quintero escribieron 6.____
    - A. EN ANDES SE HA PUESTO EL SOL
    - B. EL ABOLENGO
    - C. LA MALQUERIDA
    - D. LA MALVALOCA

7. Alcanzó renombre Domingo Sarmiento como presidente de su pais y como 7.____
    - A. militar
    - B. educador
    - C. arquitecto
    - D. poeta

8. El autor de JOSÉ también escribió 8.____
    - A. PLATERO Y YO
    - B. MARTA Y MARÍA
    - C. EL SEÑOR DE BEMBRIBE
    - D. CANTOS DE VIDA Y ESPERANZA

9. Las Sonatas de otoño, de estío, de la primavera y del invierno son obras de 9.____
    - A. Valle Inclan
    - B. Leopoldo Alas
    - C. Rubén Dario
    - D. Azorin

10. Recibió el premio Nadal por sus novelas   10.____
    A. Concha Espina   B. Lucila Godoy
    C. Carmen Laforet   D. Cecilia Bohl von Faber

KEY (CORRECT ANSWERS)

1. B
2. D
3. D
4. C
5. D
6. D
7. B
8. B
9. A
10. C

EXAMINATION SECTION
TEST 1

Synonyms (Spanish/Spanish)

DIRECTIONS: Below is a list of key words in Spanish, each of which is followed by four other Spanish words, one of which is a synonym of the key word. *PRINT THE LETTER OF THE CORRECT ANSWER IN THE SPACE AT THE RIGHT.*

1. hacendoso   1.____
   A. finquero   B. diligente   C. lloroso   D. rico

2. harto   2.____
   A. dificil   B. duro   C. satisfecho   D. cómico

3. durazno   3.____
   A. melocotón   B. ciruela
   C. albaricoque   D. pina

4. maña   4.____
   A. manta   B. habilidad   C. tejido   D. árbol

5. arrimar   5.____
   A. alejar   B. echar   C. acercar   D. llegar

6. loor   6.____
   A. honor   B. olor   C. gusto   D. alabanza

7. medrar   7.____
   A. merecer   B. temer   C. mejorar   D. relucir

8. fallecer   8.____
   A. colgar   B. morir   C. fracasar   D. faltar

9. hogaza   9.____
   A. hoguera   B. carne   C. holgura   D. pan

10. pesadumbre   10.____
    A. tristeza   B. densidad
    C. humedad   D. oscuridad

KEY (CORRECT ANSWERS)

1. B
2. C
3. A
4. B
5. C

6. D
7. C
8. B
9. D
10. A

TEST 2
Vocabulary (English/Spanish)

DIRECTIONS: Below is a list of English words, each of which is followed by four Spanish words, one of which is a correct translation of the English word. Select the CORRECT translation. *PRINT THE LETTER OF THE CORRECT ANSWER IN THE SPACE AT THE RIGHT.*

1. to boast 1.____

   A. sobornar B. esparcir
   C. jactarse D. bosquejar

2. eyelash 2.____

   A. ceja B. latigazo
   C. pestaña D. frente

3. legal 3.____

   A. leíble B. leal C. lego D. lícito

4. duel 4.____

   A. desafi'o B. contienda
   C. desacuerdo D. competencia

5. frying pan 5.____

   A. caldera B. sarta C. olla D. sartén

6. parchment 6.____

   A. cuero B. pergamino
   C. testamento D. jadeo

7. inexhaustible 7.____

   A. inaguantable B. inagotable
   C. inaudito D. inacabado

8. harvest 8.____

   A. slega B. siembra
   C. semilla D. agricultor

9. mortgage 9.____

   A. arrendamiento B. morador
   C. hipoteca D. hoguera

10. sparrow 10.____

    A. ave B. golondrina
    C. águila D. gorrión

39

KEY (CORRECT ANSWERS)

1. C
2. C
3. D
4. A
5. D

6. B
7. B
8. A
9. C
10. D

TEST 3
Sentence Completion (English/Spanish)

DIRECTIONS: Below is a series of English sentences, each of which has been translated into Spanish with the omission of a word or expression. Four choices are usted from which you are to choose the MOST appropriate one to complete the Spanish sentence CORRECTLY. *PRINT THE LETTER OF THE CORRECT ANSWER IN THE SPACE AT THE RIGHT.*

1. As long as there is freedom, we will live happily. Mientras _____ libertad, viviremos felices.

    A. hay B. habrá C. haya D. está

    1.____

2. As soon as they finished the reading, they would begin to write the exercises. Luego que _____ la lectura, empezaban a escribir los ejercicios.

    A. terminaban B. terminen
    C. terminaron D. terminasen

    2.____

3. If they had studied, they would have known more. Si _____ estudiado, hubieran sabido mas.

    A. habrían B. hayan C. habían D. hubiesen

    3.____

4. She was heard singing in the garden. _____ en el jardin.

    A. Fue oída cantar B. Se la oyeron cantando
    C. Se la oyó cantar D. La oyó cantar

    4.____

5. I begged him to write those words to his mother. Le rogue _____ esas palabras a su madre.

    A. escribir B. que escriba
    C. que escribe D. que escribió

    5.____

6. She insists on buying a great many dresses, which displeases me very much. Ella se empeña en comprarse una cantidad de vestidos; _____ me disgusta muchísimo.

    A. el que B. la cual C. lo cual D. los cuales

    6.____

7. What a man!
   ¡_____ Qué hombre!

    A. Un B. B. Vaya C. Cuán D. Cuál

    7.____

8. We learned the news yesterday. _____ la noticia ayer.

    A. Aprendimos B. Enteramos
    C. Conocimos D. Supimos

    8.____

9. The majority of the inhabitants must have believed that politician. La mayor parte denlos habitantes _____ a ese político.

    A. hubieran creído B. habría creído
    C. creería D. habrán creído

    9.____

10. They ought not to treat the poor boy in that way. No _____ tratar al pobre muchacho de esa manera. 10.____

    A. deben de   B. debieran
    C. han de   D. tenían que

KEY (CORRECT ANSWERS)

1. C
2. A
3. D
4. C
5. A

6. C
7. B
8. D
9. D
10. B

TEST 4
Antonyms (Spanish/Spanish)

DIRECTIONS: Below is a list of key words in Spanish, each of which is followed by four other Spanish words, one of which is an antonym of the key word. Select the antonym. *PRINT THE LETTER OF THE CORRECT ANSWER IN THE SPACE AT THE RIGHT.*

1. enhiesto

    A. encorvado B. descuidado
    C. enfriado   D. enojado

    1._____

2. enano

    A. poblado   B. honrado
    C. rico   D. gigantesco

    2._____

3. mugriento

    A. aseado   B. miedoso   C. lodoso   D. lioso

    3._____

4. torpe

    A. laico   B. listo   C. laja   D. lamentoso

    4._____

5. grosero

    A. grande   B. grumoso   C. fino   D. ordinario

    5._____

6. estrépito

    A. estruendo   B. sebo
    C. selección   D. silencio

    6._____

7. holgazanería

    A. ociosidad   B. sentimentalidad
    C. homeopatía D. actividad

    7._____

8. ablandar

    A. censurar   B. endurecer
    C. negar   D. callar

    8._____

9. hogaño

    A. este año   B. cada *ocho* años
    C. antaño   D. un año si otro no

    9._____

10. recio

    A. endeble   B. pobre
    C. defraudado D. engañado

    10._____

43

KEY (CORRECT ANSWERS)

1. A
2. D
3. A
4. B
5. C

6. D
7. D
8. B
9. C
10. A

———

TEST 5
Reading Comprehension (Spanish/Spanish)

DIRECTIONS: The passage below is followed by five incomplete statements or questions. Four choices are listed from which you are to choose the MOST appropriate one to complete the statement or answer the question. Indicate the CORRECT answer. *PRINT THE LETTER OF THE CORRECT ANSWER IN THE SPACE AT THE RIGHT.*

Se casaron y fuéronse a vivir a la corte. Las relaciones y amistades de Alejandro eran merced a su fortuna, muchas, pero algo extrañas. Los más de los que frecuentaban su casa, aristócratas de blasón no pocos, antojabas ele a Julia que debían ser deudores de su marido, que daba dinero a prestamos con sólidas hipotecas. Pero nada sabía de los negocios de el ni éste le hablada nunca de ellos. A ella no le faltaba nadas podía satisfacer hasta sus menores capri-choss pero le faltaba lo que más podía faltarle. No ya el amor de aquel hombre a quien se sentía subyugada y como por el hechizada, sino la certidumbre de aquel amor.

--¿Me quiere, o no me quiere? -- se preguntaba. Me colma de atenciones, me trata con el mayor respeto, aunque algo como a una criatura voluntariosas hasta me mima; ¿pero me quiere?

Y era inútil querer hablar de amor, de cariño, con aquel hombre.

-- Solamente los tontos hablan de esas cosas -- solía decir Alejandro.

-- "Encanto..., rica...., hermosa...., queria..." ¿Yo? ¿lo esas cosas? ¿Con esas cosas a mí? ¿A mí? Esas son cosas de novela. Y ya sé que a ti te gustaba leerlas.

-- Y me gusta todavía.

-- Pues lee cuantas quieras. Mira, si te empeñas, luego hago construir en ese solar que hay ahí al lado un gran pabellón para biblioteca y te la lleno de todas, la novelas que se han escrito desde Adán acá.
-- ¡Qué cosas dices...!

1. En esta selección se trata de

    A. un matrimonio a punto de divorciarse
    B. una señora que dudaba del afecto de su esposo
    C. una regia fiesta nupcial en un palacio
    D. un matrimonio dedicada a indagaciones bíblicas

1._____

2. El matrimonio estableció su hogar en

    A. un pueblo pequeño
    B. un campo remoto
    C. la capital
    D. un castillo en el extranjero

2._____

3. Venían a ver a los nuevos esposos

   A. personas de abolengo que habían hecho empréstitos
   B. muchos comerciantes y políticos socios del matrimonio
   C. amistades de ambos
   D. los parientes políticos de ambos

4. ¿Cómo trataba el esposo a su mujer?

   A. La trataba con hipocresía y engaño.
   B. Le colmaba de regalos.
   C. La trataba de igual en todo.
   D. Le era excesivamente cruel.

5. Jocosamente, el esposo se comprometió a

   A. mandar fabricar una cancha de equitación
   B. llevar a su esposa en un viaje extenso
   C. darle a su esposa todo lo que se le antojase
   D. conseguirle todo lo que quisiera para satisfacer su gran afición

---

KEY (CORRECT ANSWERS)

1. B
2. C
3. A
4. B
5. D

TEST 6
Translation (English/Spanish)

DIRECTIONS: Below is a list of English idiomatic expressions translated into Spanish. From the four choices given, select the Spanish expression which approximates the English in meaning. *PRINT THE LETTER OF THE CORRECT ANSWER IN THE SPACE AT THE RIGHT.*

1. The bomb <u>went off</u> in the air. La bomba ___ en el aire. 1.____

   A. estalló   B. se alejó   C. desinfló   D. derrumbó

2. The two horses were running <u>wild</u>. Los dos caballos corrían _____. 2.____

   A. sin moderación   B. con rapidez
   C. a rienda suelta   D. como si fueran venenosas

3. They don't get along well. No se _____ bien. 3.____

   A. llevan   B. van
   C. ven   D. arrastran

4. His constant whistling drives me out of my mind. Su constante silbar _____. 4.____

   A. me echa a perder
   B. me saca da mis casillas
   C. me arrastra a loco
   D. me vuelve la mente

5. You have to wind the watch regularly. Tiene que _____ siempre. 5.____

   A. volver el reloj   B. hacer cuerda al reloj
   C. darle cuerda al reloj   D. girar el reloj

6. He looked over the new book. _____ el nuevo libro. 6.____

   A. Pasó por alto   B. Miró sobre
   C. Dio vueltas   D. Hojeó

7. I caught him <u>red-handed</u> 7.____
   Lo agarré _____.

   A. con las manos abiertas   B. con los manos desnudas
   C. con las manos en alto   D. con las manos en la masa

8. We didn't leave because it rained cats and dogs. No salimos porque _____. 8.____

   A. llovía a cántaros   B. llovía gatos y perros
   C. llovía a rios   D. llovía a pucheros

9. My brother is a student who <u>burns the midnight oil.</u> Mi hermano es un estudiante que _____. 9.____

   A. tarda en dormirse   B. se quema las pestañas
   C. se quema los ojos   D. quema la lámpara

47

10. Mary always has it her own way. Maria siempre _____.

    A. lleva la derecha
    B. tiene razón
    C. se sale con la suya
    D. mantiene su voluntad

KEY (CORRECT ANSWERS)

1. A
2. C
3. A
4. B
5. C

6. D
7. D
8. A
9. B
10. C

TEST 7
Translation (Spanish/English)

DIRECTIONS: Below is a series of Spanish idiomatic expressions translated into English. From the four choices given, select the English expression which approximates the Spanish in meaning.

1. Este muchacho <u>me da la lata.</u>
   This boy _____.

   A. keeps me broke
   B. is giving me a *rush act*
   C. bores me to death
   D. is in love with me

   1.____

2. No lo dude usted porque él lo sabe de buena tinta. Don't doubt it because _____.

   A. he knows it thoroughly
   B. he knows it on good authority
   C. he has always known it
   D. he knows it by heart

   2.____

3. El lo leyó todo sin pasar nada por alto. He read it all without _____.

   A. hesitating at all
   B. changing anything
   C. denying anything
   D. skipping anything

   3.____

4. Se me hace cuesta arriba madrugar. _____ to get up early.

   A. I find it invigorating
   B. I am expected
   C. I find it hard
   D. I need an alarm

   4.____

5. Ana está completamente <u>en ayunas.</u>
   Anna is completely _____.

   A. on a diet
   B. in the dark
   C. in agreement
   D. fed up

   5.____

6. Está en el cuento de todo lo que pasa allí.
   _____ of everything that is happening there.

   A. He is informed
   B. He takes advantage
   C. He keeps a record
   D. He keeps count

   6.____

7. No salió bien en el examen por haber hecho demasiados novillos.
   He failed the examination because _____.

   A. he played truant too often
   B. he was too careless
   C. he made too many mistakes
   D. he forgot too much

   7.____

8. Este sábado <u>vamos de parranda.</u>
   This Saturday we _____.

   A. are going on a double date
   B. are going to get down to brass tacks

   8.____

49

C. are going on a spree
D. are going to play cards

9. No le busque tres pies al gato.

    A. Don't look for the impossible.
    B. Don't look too closely.
    C. Don't be superstitious.
    D. Don't look for trouble.

10. Está durmiendo la mona.

    A. He is sleeping soundly.
    B. He is sleeping it off.
    C. He is sleeping noisily.
    D. He is making believe that he is sleeping.

KEY (CORRECT ANSWERS)

1. C
2. B
3. D
4. C
5. B

6. A
7. A
8. C
9. D
10. B

TEST 8
Vocabulary (Spanish/English)

DIRECTIONS: Below is a list of Spanish words, each of which is followed by four English words, one of which is a correct translation of the Spanish word. Select the CORRECT translation. *PRINT THE LETTER OF THE CORRECT ANSWER IN THE SPACE AT THE RIGHT.*

1. indumentaria

    A. clothing B. indulgence
    C. tax D. amnesty

2. estafar

    A. stuff B. staff C. staplé D. swindle

3. quinqué

    A. game B. hardware C. peddler D. lamp

4. espeluznante

    A. hair-raising B. extraordinary
    C. repugnant D. hopeful

5. increpar

    A. thicken B. scold C. doubt D. darken

6. escarmiento

    A. ladder B. frost
    C. warning D. escarpment

7. sediento

    A. silky B. sedentary
    C. mutinous D. thirsty

8. yunque

    A. yoke B. forest C. anvil D. ox

9. mote

    A. landmark B. nickname C. dimple D. riot

10. azorar

    A. to frighten B. to beat
    C. to deceive D. to guess

KEY (CORRECT ANSWERS)

1. A
2. D
3. D
4. A
5. B

6. C
7. D
8. C
9. B
10. A

TEST 9
Selection (Spanish/Spanish)

DIRECTIONS: Below is a series of sentences in Spanish, each of which can be correctly completad by adding to it one of the four choices which follow it. Select the CORRECT cholee. *PRINT THE LETTER OF THE CORRECT ANSWER IN THE SPACE AT THE RIGHT.*

1. La obra de Mateo Alemán es

    A. Guzmán de Alfarache
    B. La vida del Buscón
    C. Lazarillo de Tormes
    D. Rinconete y Cortadillo

2. Entre los eruditos principales del siglo veinte en España figura

    A. Julio Cejador
    B. Fray Luis de León
    C. Feijoo
    D. Gracián

3. La obra titulada *Malvaloca* fue escrita por

    A. Linares Rivas
    B. Los hermanos Quintero
    C. Jacinto Benavente
    D. Eduardo Marquina

4. Zunzunegui, autor de *El camión justiciero,* figura entre los novelistas

    A. clasicos
    B. románticos
    C. modernos
    D. centroamericanos

5. Juan Valera escribió la novela cuyos protagonistas son el padre Enrique y

    A. dona Perfecta
    B. dona Luz
    C. dona Clarines
    D. dona Maria la Brava

6. Una de las novelas ejemplares de Cervantes es

    A. El coloquio de los perros
    B. Rimas del Licenciado Burguillos
    C. La hermosura de Angélica
    D. El castigo sin venganza

7. Ortega y Gasset escribió

    A. Del sentimiento trágico de la cida
    B. Ariel
    C. Idearium español
    D. La rebelión de las masas

8. José Maria de Pereda escribió

    A. Dona Perfecta
    B. La madre naturaleza
    C. Sotileza
    D. La gaviota

9. Camilo José Cela es el autor de

    A. La gafas del diablo
    B. La colmena
    C. La trepadora
    D. Cita con el pasado

10. *Nada menos que todo un hombre* es de
    - A. Unamuno
    - B. Ortega y Gasset
    - C. Pío Baroja
    - D. Carmen Laforet

KEY (CORRECT ANSWERS)

1. A
2. A
3. B
4. C
5. B

6. A
7. D
8. C
9. B
10. A

EXAMINATION SECTION
TEST 1
Vocabulary (English/Spanish)

DIRECTIONS: Below is a list of English words, each of which is followed by four Spanish words, one of which is a correct translation of the English word. Select the CORRECT translation. *PRINT THE LETTER OF THE CORRECT ANSWER IN THE SPACE AT THE RIGHT.*

1. little finger   1.____
   A. pulgar   B. dedal   C. uña   D. meñique

2. to spend the night   2.____
   A. adormecer   B. trasnochar
   C. dormitar   D. madrugar

3. to dwell   3.____
   A. demorar   B. albergar   C. morar   D. hostigar

4. mire   4.____
   A. polvo   B. barro   C. heno   D. cieno

5. frivolous   5.____
   A. liviano   B. pesado   C. friolero   D. nimio

6. daring   6.____
   A. mudez   B. denuedo
   C. ceguera   D. pusilanimidad

7. ice box   7.____
   A. nevisca   B. nevasca   C. nevera   D. nevada

8. arrow   8.____
   A. alfiler   B. aguja   C. sonda   D. saeta

9. steep   9.____
   A. puntiagudo   B. tieso
   C. escabroso   D. pino

10. magnet   10.____
    A. tamaño   B. imán   C. idilio   D. manga

55

KEY (CORRECT ANSWERS)

1. D
2. B
3. C
4. D
5. A
6. B
7. C
8. D
9. D
10. B

Sentence Completion (English/Spanish)

DIRECTIONS: Below is a series of English sentences, each of which has been translated into Spanish with the omission of a word or expression. Four choices are listed from which you are to choose the MOST appropriate one to complete the Spanish sentence correctly. *PRINT THE LETTER OF THE CORRECT ANSWER IN THE SPACE AT THE RIGHT.*

1. I have two pesos left.
   _____ dos pesos.

   A. Me quedan B. Se me queda
   C. Se me le quedan D. Me quedo

2. How learned she is!
   ¡_____ docta es!

   A. Cuan B. Cuanto C. Cuánta D. Cuánto

3. The thief entered <u>without our knowing it.</u>
   El ladrón entró_____.

   A. sin nuestro saberlo B. sin sabiéndolo nosotros
   C. sin que lo supimos D. sin que lo supiésemos

4. How long is the canal?
   ¿Cuánto tiene _____ el canal?

   A. por longitud B. de largueza
   C. a lo largo D. de largo

5. Whose watch did they steal?
   ¿_____ quién le robaron el reloj?

   A. Por B. Para C. A D. De

6. He denied that he had lost his watch.
   Negó _____ su reloj.

   A. había perdido B. haber perdido
   C. haya perdido D. hubo perdido

7. Are you the mother of the child? I am.
   ¿Es Ud. la madre de la niña? _____.

   A. La soy B. Soy C. La estoy D. Lo soy

8. It feels like silk.
   Parece _____ seda.

   A. por B. para C. de D. cerca de

9. I am not forgetting that we are eleven thousand feet above sea level.
   No _____ que estamos a once mil pies sobre el nivel del mar.

   A. me te olvide B. se me olvida
   C. se me olvido D. me olvida

10. She said she would tell me when she carne.
   Dijo que me lo diría cuando_____.

   A. viniera   B. vino   C. venía   D. vendría

KEY (CORRECT ANSWERS)

1. A
2. A
3. D
4. D
5. C

6. B
7. D
8. C
9. B
10. A

Reading Comprehension (Spanish/Spanish)

DIRECTIONS: The reading passage below is followed by five incomplete statements or questions. Four choices are listed from which you are to choose the MOST appropriate one to complete the statement or answer the question. Indicate the CORRECT answer. *PRINT THE LETTER OF THE CORRECT ANSWER IN THE SPACE AT THE RIGHT.*

PASSAGE

La asamblea se inició en las últimas horas de la tarde, cuando ya el sol tendía sobre la plaza la sombra de los eucaliptos que crecían junto a la capilla.

El alcalde y los regidores estaban sentados, en bancos de maguey, al filo del corredor de la casa del primero. Habían planeado construir un cabildo, después de la escuela, pero ahora no querían ni recordar el proyecto. Fueron llegando los comuneros -- hombres, mujeres, niños --, y acuclillándose o sentándose sobre el suelo. Muchos se paraban formando una especie de óvalo que encerraba a los otros. Los niños no iban a hablar ni votar, pero se les llevaba para que oyeran y les fuera entrando el juicio.

Rosendo tenía la cara contraída en un gesto severo y triste ... Parecía muy viejo. Tanto como un tronco batido por vendavales tenaces. El mismo se sentía cansado. Los últimos tiempos lo habían azotado implacablemente, diezmando su cuerpo y estrujando su corazón. Los comuneros escrutaban la faz rugosa y encrespada sintiendo, unos, que habia hecho todo lo posible y, otros, que seria dificil encontrar las palabras necesarias contra ese hombre.

1. ¿Que se verifica aqui?

   A. Un juicio
   B. Una sesión parlamentaria
   C. Una reunión política
   D. Una junta legislativa

2. ¿Por qué parecía rendido Rosendo?

   A. Había recibido una paliza.
   B. Había sido atropellado por el viento.
   C. Habia pasado muchos tormentos en su vida.
   D. Acababa de llegar de su trabajo.

3. Estaban presentes los menores porque

   A. no podían quedarse en casa
   B. iban a dar su opinión
   C. se trataba de construir una escuela
   D. habia que darles cuenta de la importancia del asunto

4. Se reunieron en casa del alcalde porque

   A. era tarde
   B. querían escaparse del calor de la plaza
   C. había amplio sitio para sentarse
   D. el pueblo carecia de casa de ayuntamiento

5. Se le veía a Rosendo
   A. fuerte y robusto
   B. lleno de vigor
   C. completamente abatido
   D. de rostro liso

KEY (CORRECT ANSWERS)

1. A
2. C
3. D
4. D
5. C

Vocabulary (Spanish/English)

DIRECTIONS: Below is a list of Spanish words, each of which is followed by four English words, one of which is the correct translation of the Spanish word. Select the CORRECT translation. *PRINT THE LETTER OF THE CORRECT ANSWER IN THE SPACE AT THE RIGHT.*

1. buhardilla

    A. attic B. lamp C. lie D. owl

    1._____

2. disparate

    A. shot
    C. foolishness
    B. diversity
    D. surprise

    2._____

3. piar

    A. to swear
    C. to confess
    B. to chirp
    D. to pat

    3._____

4. esquivar

    A. to shear
    C. to avoid
    B. to square
    D. to swindle

    4._____

5. picarse

    A. to primp
    C. to pride oneself
    B. to be offended
    D. to be deceived

    5._____

6. isleño

    A. islander
    C. islet
    B. Islamite
    D. Icelandic

    6._____

7. pormenor

    A. retail B. purse C. detail D. prodigy

    7._____

8. sarmiento

    A. itch B. seed bed C. image D. twig

    8._____

9. podar

    A. to prune B. to rot C. to shame D. to lodge

    9._____

10. albedrío

    A. pensión B. asylum C. apricot D. will

    10._____

KEY (CORRECT ANSWERS)

1. A
2. C
3. B
4. C
5. B

6. A
7. C
8. D
9. A
10. D

Selection (Spanish/Spanish)

DIRECTIONS: Below is a series of sentences in Spanish, each of which can be correctly completed by adding to it one of the four choices which follow it. Select the CORRECT choice. *PRINT THE LETTER OF THE CORRECT ANSWER IN THE SPACE AT THE RIGHT.*

1. El Pico de Orizaba es el más alto de   1._____

    A. Ecuador   B. Guatemala   C. Perú   D. Méjico

2. Tenerife es una de las Islas   2._____

    A. Canarias   B. Baleares
    C. Juan Fernández   D. Filipinas

3. La ciudad de Salamanca ofrece una inolvidable perspectiva desde la margen del   3._____

    A. Tajo   B. Tormes   C. Guadiana   D. Ebro

4. Las tres Provincias Vascongadas son Guipúzcoa, Álava y   4._____

    A. Murcia   B. Vizcaya   C. Navarra   D. León

5. El rio Amazonas está navigable hasta Iquitos en   5._____

    A. Perú   B. Bolivia   C. Ecuador   D. Colombia

6. Don Juan de Austria fue jefe de   6._____

    A. la Mashorca
    B. la batalla de Ayacucho
    C. la flota española en la batalla de Lepante
    D. las tropas españolas en 1808

7. Se halla en Chile   7._____

    A. la sierra de Guadarrama   B. el desierto de Atacama
    C. la Giralda   D. el Teatro Colon

8. Torremolinos se encuentra   8._____

    A. en las Islas Baleares   B. en Galicia
    C. en el sur de España   D. cerca de Madrid

9. Ibiza escuna isla del   9._____

    A. Pacifico   B. Atlántico
    C. Caribe   D. Mediterráneo

10. De estas ciudades, todas son capitales de pais menos   10._____

    A. Asunción   B. Barranquilla
    C. Managua   D. Santiago

KEY (CORRECT ANSWERS)

1. B
2. A
3. D
4. B
5. A

6. B
7. C
8. C
9. C
10. A

TEST 2
Vocabulary (English/Spanish)

DIRECTIONS: Below is a list of English words, each of which is followed by four Spanish words, one of which is a correct translation of the English word. Select the CORRECT translation. *PRINT THE LETTER OF THE CORRECT ANSWER IN THE SPACE AT THE RIGHT.*

1. tissue paper
   A. papel secante   B. tejido
   C. papel de seda   D. papelito

1._____

2. abyss
   A. apogeo   B. sima   C. sótano   D. tajo

2._____

3. to empty
   A. vaciar   B. vagar   C. inundar   D. derramar

3._____

4. baldness
   A. calavera   B. melena   C. peladillo   D. calvicie

4._____

5. tape
   A. tapón   B. cinta   C. cerilla   D. encaje

5._____

6. short cut
   A. lío   B. breva   C. atajo   D. cortadura

6._____

7. rogue
   A. grano   B. granuja   C. embuste   D. granjero

7._____

8. to eye
   A. ojear   B. olear   C. hollar   D. ocluir

8._____

9. to chew
   A. tragar   B. condenar   C. chupar   D. masticar

9._____

10. strike
   A. huelga   B. huella   C. juerga   D. esgrima

10._____

KEY (CORRECT ANSWERS)

1. C
2. B
3. A
4. D
5. B
6. C
7. B
8. A
9. D
10. A

Sentence Completion (English/Spanish)

DIRECTIONS: Below is a series of English sentences, each of which has been translated into Spanish with the omission of a word or expression. Four choices are listed from which you are to choose the MOST appropriate to complete the Spanish sentence CORRECTLY. *PRINT THE LETTER OF THE CORRECT ANSWER IN THE SPACE AT THE RIGHT.*

1. It is ten degrees below zero.
   La temperatura está a 10 grados _____ cero.

   A. bajo　　　B. debajo de　　　C. menos de　　　D. menos que

2. There is no one who can say what will happen tomorrow.
   No hay nadie que _____ decir qué pasará mañana.

   A. puede　　　B. pudiera　　　C. sepa　　　D. pueda

3. The pupils have less time than they need.
   Los alumnos tienen menos tiempo _____ necesitan.

   A. que　　　B. de lo que　　　C. del que　　　D. de los que

4. It is often humid here.
   A menudo _____ humedad en ésta.

   A. hace　　　B. hay　　　C. es　　　D. está

5. Well, sirs, to bed!
   ¡ Pues a _____, caballeros!

   A. acuéstense　　　B. dormir
   C. dormios　　　D. acostaos

6. If you had been there, you would have witnessed this triumph.
   Si _____ alli, hubieras presenciado esta victoria.

   A. hubieras estado　　　B. habias estado
   C. hubiese estado　　　D. hubiste estado

7. Today's liners are veritable floating palaces.
   Los transatlánticos de hoy son verdaderos palacios_____.

   A. flotando　　　B. flotados　　　C. flotantes　　　D. flotillas

8. While she is sleeping, the children went out of the house.
   Mientras_____, salieron de la casa los niños.

   A. durmió　　　B. se dormia
   C. estuvo durmiendo　　　D. dormia

9. I had nobody to help me. Yo no tenía persona_____.

   A. que me ayudara　　　B. a ayudarme
   C. que me ayude　　　D. que me ayudaba

10. After they returned, we saw the leaders.
    Luego de_____ vimos a los jefes.

    A. hubieron vuelto
    B. vueltos
    C. hubieran vuelto
    D. volvieron

KEY (CORRECT ANSWERS)

1. A
2. D
3. C
4. A
5. B

6. A
7. C
8. D
9. A
10. B

Reading Comprehension (Spanish/Spanish)

DIRECTIONS: The reading passage below is followed by five incomplete statements or questions. Four choices are listed from which you are to choose the MOST appropriate one to complete the statement or answer the question. Indicate the CORRECT answer. *PRINT THE LETTER OF THE CORRECT ANSWER IN THE SPACE AT THE RIGHT.*

PASSAGE

Resurgir, renacer, regenerarse, son procesos dinámicos que implican estado anterior de agotamiento, decadencia o regresión. Importa, pues, desde luego dilucidar este importante punto: ¿Es exacto que, en orden a la filosofía y a la ciencia, hemos decaído verdaderamente? Como productores de civilización en su más amplio sentido, ¿es lícito afirmar que hemos degenerado con relación a nuestros antepasados de los siglos XVI y XVII?

España es un país intelectualmente atrasado, no decadente. Estudiando imparcialmente la historia de la producción científica y filosófica española durante la Edad Media, durante el siglo XVI (considerado con alguna exageración, a nuestro juicio, como la cima de nuestra intelectualidad) y en fin, durante las últimas centurias; comparando, con absoluta sinceridad, intensiva y estensivamente, la ciencia española forjada en cada uno de esos períodos (descontando las alzas y bajas causadas por fortuitos accidentes, quiero decir, el avance cultural producido por el descubrimiento de América, queabrió de repente a nuestros sabios espléndido campo de investigación, y la postración mental provocada por las guerras desastrosas y errores políticos de la época de Felipe IV); si cotejamos, en fin, en cada una de las citadas épocas, las conquistas intelectuales positivas hechas por españoles con las debidas a sabios extranjeros, nos veremos obligados a reconocer que ni la raza ni la ciencia española han decaído ni se han estacionado por completo. Sobre poco mas o menos, su rendimiento científico se mantuvo siempre al mismo nivel.

La imparcialidad obliga, empero, a confesar que, apreciado globalmente, dicho rendimiento ha sido pobre y discontinué, mostrando, con relación al resto de Europa, un atraso y, sobre todo, una mezquindad teórica deplorable.

1. Según el escritor,

    A. la ciencia española ha sufrido una gran decadencia
    B. ha habido una degeneración intelectual en España
    C. el estado intelectual de España ha quedado algo inactivo
    D. el descubrimiento de América cambió por completo el desarrollo intelectual de España

2. Según el autor, ¿qué época se podría considerar con exactitud como apogeo de la sabiduría española?

    A. el siglo XVI
    B. el siglo XV
    C. la época de Felipe IV
    D. ninguna

3. Conviene declarar que

   A. España se jacta de una historia filosóficamente fecunda
   B. la época de Felipe IV ha dejado una marca indeleble en España
   C. hay marcas de cierto florecimiento intelectual en cada período de la historia española
   D. muchos extranjeros han contribuido a la intelectualidad de España

4. Se puede demostrar que

   A. los científicos españoles se aprovecharon del descubrimiento de América
   B. la ciencia española se ha estancado del todo
   C. los antecedentes españoles de los siglos XVI y XVII se habían decaído por completo
   D. unos sucesos en España fueron causa de su decadencia

5. Como se puede caracterizar a España?

   A. Su producción científica está al mismo nivel que de las otras naciones.
   B. Su producción científica carece de volumen.
   C. Ha rendido al mundo suficientes contribuciones científicas.
   D. La raza española ha aceptado las innovaciones de los otros países.

KEY (CORRECT ANSWERS)

1. C
2. D
3. C
4. A
5. B

Vocabulary (Spanish/English)

DIRECTIONS: Below is a list of Spanish words, each of which is followed by four English words, one of which is the correct translation of the Spanish word. Select the CORRECT translation. *PRINT THE LETTER OF THE CORRECT ANSWER IN THE SPACE AT THE RIGHT.*

1. rezongar 1.____
   - A. to fret
   - B. to grumble
   - C. to frisk
   - D. to encourage

2. acatamiento 2.____
   - A. purchase
   - B. exhaustion
   - C. esteem
   - D. command

3. trastornar 3.____
   - A. to fret
   - B. to stutter
   - C. to sheer
   - D. to upset

4. sinrazón 4.____
   - A. wrong
   - B. insanity
   - C. carelessness
   - D. shamelessness

5. hartar 5.____
   - A. to tire
   - B. to cajole
   - C. to loathe
   - D. to satiate

6. colmena 6.____
   - A. fang
   - B. zenith
   - C. beehive
   - D. incisor

7. rozar 7.____
   - A. to gnaw
   - B. to romp
   - C. to rub
   - D. to surround

8. ordenar 8.____
   - A. to milk
   - B. to command
   - C. to arrange
   - D. to ordain

9. picaflor 9.____
   - A. vase
   - B. hummingbird
   - C. butterfly
   - D. honeysuckle

10. guardabarro 10.____
    - A. closet
    - B. cover
    - C. windshield
    - D. fender

KEY (CORRECT ANSWERS)

1. B
2. C
3. D
4. A
5. D

6. C
7. C
8. A
9. B
10. D

Selection (Spanish/Spanish)

DIRECTIONS: Below is a series of sentences in Spanish, each of which can be correctly completed by adding to it one of the four choices which follow it. Select the CORRECT choice and indicate it in each case. *PFINT THE LETTER OF THE CORRECT ANSWER IN THE SPACE AT THE RIGHT.*

1. La Vispera Del Ano Nuevo, los madrileños van a la Puerta del Sol con   1._____

    A. un racimo de doce uvas   B. un ramillete de rosas
    C. cascabeles de cristal   D. sus regalos de Navidad

2. El Ñanduti de los guaraníes es   2._____

    A. una bebida alcohólica   B. un poncho de lana
    C. un encage muy fino   D. un instrumento musical

3. En julio muchos turistas van a Pamplona para ver   3._____

    A. el Tribunal de las Aguas
    B. los juegos de béisbol
    C. los torneos de los llaneros
    D. la fiesta de San Fermín

4. El Día de los Difuntos cae el   4._____

    A. primero de noviembre   B. dos de noviembre
    C. treinta de mayo   D. dos de mayo

5. *La gallina ciega* es   5._____

    A. el título de una canción popular
    B. un juego de niños
    C. un juego de naipes
    D. un plato gallego

6. En la corrida de toros pelea a caballo el   6._____

    A. mono sabio   B. banderillero
    C. picador   D. matador

7. La buhardilla es   7._____

    A. un animal
    B. un ave
    C. la ventana en el tejado de una casa
    D. el zaguán de una casa

8. A los nacidos en España los tildan los mexicanos de   8._____

    A. Galgos   B. Gachupines
    C. Griegos   D. Peluquines

9. El calzado llevado por el campesino en Chile se llama   9._____

    A. el zueco   B. la cueca
    C. la alpargata   D. el huarache

10. El aeropuerto internacional de Madrid es el de

    A. Campeón   B. Maiquetia   C. Júcar   D. Barajas

KEY (CORRECT ANSWERS)

1. A
2. C
3. B
4. D
5. C
6. B
7. B
8. D
9. A
10. D

TEST 3
Vocabulary (English/Spanish)

DIRECTIONS: Below is a list of English words, each of which is followed by four Spanish words, one of which is a correct translation of the English word. Select the CORRECT translation. *PRINT THE LETTER OF THE CORRECT ANSWER IN THE SPACE AT THE RIGHT.*

1. steep
   A. empanada   B. empinada   C. empuñada   D. empañada
1.____

2. needle
   A. aguja   B. dedal   C. alfiler   D. hilo
2.____

3. cheek
   A. carilla   B. mandíbula   C. mejilla   D. pescuezo
3.____

4. cavity
   A. muela hueca   B. muela picada
   C. muela hayada   D. muela cavernosa
4.____

5. windshield
   A. limpiador   B. ventanilla
   C. palanca   D. parabrisas
5.____

6. to purify
   A. lucir   B. averiguar   C. apurar   D. puntar
6.____

7. fraud
   A. símbolo   B. embeleco   C. sello   D. hurto
7.____

8. typist
   A. estilográfico   B. episgrafista
   C. caligráfico   D. mecanógrafo
8.____

9. idiom
   A. índole   B. modernismo
   C. idiotismo   D. mecanismo
9.____

10. hinge
   A. gozne   B. rendija   C. gozque   D. pulla
10.____

KEY (CORRECT ANSWERS)

1. B
2. A
3. C
4. B
5. D

6. C
7. B
8. D
9. C
10. A

Sentence Completion (English/Spanish)

DIRECTIONS: Below is a series of English sentences, each of which has been translated into Spanish with the omission of a word or expression. Four choices are listed from which you are to choose the MOST appropriate to complete the Spanish sentence CORRECTLY. *PRINT THE LETTER OF THE CORRECT ANSWER IN THE SPACE AT THE RIGHT.*

1. We spent a whole summer there.
   Pasamos allí_____.

   A. todos los veranos
   B. todo verano
   C. un todo verano
   D. todo un verano

2. The grandfather was a well-read man.
   El abuelo fue hombre muy _____.

   A. leíble
   B. conocido
   C. leído
   D. leyendo

3. Our firm imported two hundred thousand pounds of tobáceo. Nuestra compañía importó_____ mil libras de tabaco.

   A. doscientas
   B. dos cien
   C. doscientos
   D. ciento dos

4. Every sphere has a single center.
   _____ tiene un solo centro.

   A. Toda la esfera
   B. Todas esferas
   C. Toda esfera
   D. Cierta

5. Would that it were tomorrow!
   ¡Ojalá_____ ya mañana!

   A. sería
   B. sea
   C. estuviera
   D. fuese

6. After he dies, you will inherit the house. En _____ él, heredarás la casa.

   A. morir
   B. muriendo
   C. fallecido
   D. muera

7. I have two newspapers. That's one too many. Take one.
   Tengo dos periódicos. _____ uno. Aquí lo tiene Ud.

   A. Me sobran
   B. No me falta
   C. Me sobra
   D. Me basta

8. The leader ordered that the rebels be shot.
   El caudillo mandó que _____ los rebeldes.

   A. se fusilen
   B. se fusilase a
   C. sé fusilaran a
   D. se fusile a

9. There is a good breeze.
   _____ mucho aire.

   A. Está
   B. Hace
   C. Susurra
   D. Corre

10. She always has a beautiful garden, the flowers of which perfume the air.   10.____
Siempre tiene un jardín hermoso, _____ perfuman al aire.

    A. cuyas flores   B. cuyo flores
    C. cuyos flores   D. las flores de quien

KEY (CORRECT ANSWERS)

1. D   6. B
2. C   7. C
3. A   8. B
4. C   9. D
5. D   10. A

Reading Comprehension (Spanish/Spanish)

DIRECTIONS: The reading passage below is followed by five incomplete statements or questions. Four choices are listed from which you are to choose the MOST appropriate one to complete the statement or answer the question. Indicate the CORRECT answer.

PASSAGE

—Está muerto - dijo la gitana después de contemplarle.

—No, está dormido. ¿Qué le daré para que despierte? - dijo Marichu.

—Te digo que está muerto; pero si quieres, haré un cocimiento de siete plantas....

—Gitana - dijo el hombre decrépito - lo que vas a hacer no servirá de nada.

—Si quieres despertar a tu hijo, no tienes más que un remedio: que te albergues en una casa en donde la familia que viva bajo su techo no recuerde una desgracia próxima. Anda, ve a buscarla.

Marichu salió de la casa con el niño en brazos y fue recorriendo los caseríos de los alrededores. En uno acababa de morir el padre; en otro volvía el hijo del servicio, declarado inútil, con los pulmones llenos de tubérculos; aquí se moría una madre, dejando cinco niños abandonados; allá, un enfermo marchaba a un asilo de la capital, porque ninguno de sus hermanos, que estaban en holgada posición, quería recogerle.

Del campo, Marichu fue a la aldea, y de la aldea pasó a una gran ciudad, y en todas partes reinaban la tristeza y el dolor. Cada pueblo era un inmenso hospital lleno de carne enferma.

El remedio del viejo era imposible de emplear. A todas partes llegaba la desgracia. No, no había remedio; era necesario vivir con el corazón apenado. Marichu lloró, y luego, con una desesperación tranquila, volvió a su casa a vivir al lado de su marido.

1. ¿Qué remedio sugirió el viejo?

    A. Que tomara Marichu un cocimiento de 7 plantas
    B. Que no le sirviera nada
    C. Que fuera la madre a las gitanas
    D. Que buscara alojamiento en casa de una familia feliz

2. ¿Por qué volvía el soldado?

    A. Su padre había muerto.
    B. Su esposa había muerto y tuvo que cuidar a sus cinco hijos.
    C. Estaba enfermo.
    D. Deseaba ayudar a Marichu.

3. ¿Por qué tuvo que ir al asilo el enfermo?

    A. Le habían declarado inútil.
    B. Sus hermanos no podían ayudarle siendo muy pobres.
    C. Sus hermanos no podían ayudarle a causa de la huelga.
    D. Sus hermanos no querían ayudarle.

4. ¿En dónde encontró Marichu el remedio?

    A. No lo encontró en ninguna parte.
    B. Lo encontró en un hospital.
    C. Lo encontró en casa.
    D. Lo encontró en todas partes.

5. Al fin, ¿qué hizo Marichu?

    A. Sufrió un achaque de corazón.
    B. Se resignó a seguir viviendo con su esposo.
    C. Se casó
    D. Se dio cuenta de que es necesario tener compañeros.

KEY (CORRECT ANSWERS)

1. D
2. C
3. D
4. A
5. B

7 (#3)

Vocabulary (Spanish/English)

DIRECTIONS: Below is a list of Spanish words, each of which is followed by four English words, one of which is the correct translation of the Spanish word. Select the CORRECT translation. *PRINT THE LETTER OF THE CORRECT ANSWER IN THE SPACE AT THE RIGHT.*

1. ufanía 1.____

   A. strip   B. grease   C. sound   D. pride

2. finado 2.____

   A. farm-like   B. quintupled
   C. deceased   D. interrupted

3. muslo 3.____

   A. Mohammedian   B. thigh
   C. neck   D. muslin

4. muralla 4.____

   A. wall   B. mural
   C. plaster wall   D. beaver board

5. torvo 5.____

   A. turned   B. torn
   C. upside down   D. grim

6. avestruz 6.____

   A. quill   B. trinket   C. damage   D. ostrich

7. pelotón 7.____

   A. game   B. squad   C. hairy   D. creóle

8. quinto 8.____

   A. room   B. note   C. draftee   D. avenue

9. baldío 9.____

   A. untilled   B. unemployed
   C. damaged   D. paved

10. barbiespeso 10.____

    A. having a protruding chin
    B. having a sparse beard
    C. gray-bearded
    D. heavy-bearded

KEY (CORRECT ANSWERS)

1. D
2. C
3. B
4. A
5. D

6. D
7. B
8. C
9. A
10. D

Selection (Spanish/Spanish)

DIRECTIONS: Below is a series of sentences in Spanish, each of which can be correctly completed by adding to it one of the four choices which follow it. Select the CORRECT choice. *PRINT THE LETTER OF THE CORRECT ANSWER IN THE SPACE AT THE RIGHT.*

1. Es autor de un excelente diccionario en el siglo XVII, TESORO DE LA LENGUA CASTELLANA O ESPAÑOLA

    A. Vicente Espinel
    B. Sebastián de Covarrubias y Orozco
    C. Diego de Saavedra Fajardo
    D. Andrés Bello

2. Es auto del POEMA DE OTOÑO que comienza
   TÚ, que estás la barba en la mano meditabundo
   ¿ has dejado pasar, hermano la flor del mundo?...

    A. Amado Ñervo
    B. Leopoldo Lugones
    C. Ricardo Jaimes Freyre
    D. Rubén Dario

3. Sobresalen como autores de comedias del siglo de oro, Lope Félix de Vega, Calderón de la Barca, Gabriel Téllez y

    A. Baltasar Gracián y Morales
    B. Guillen de Castro y Bellvís
    C. Juan de Mariana
    D. Florián de Ocampo

4. TUÉRCELE EL CUELLO AL CISNE es el título de un poema de

    A. Julio Herrera y Reissig
    B. José Santos Chocano
    C. José M. Egareu
    D. Enrique González Martinez

5. El personaje de CELESTINA tiene su origen en la obra de Alfonso Martínez de Toledo titulada

    A. CORBACHO o REPROBACIÓN DEL AMOR MUNDANO
    B. LIBRO DE LOS EJEMPLOS POR A.B.C.
    C. LIBRO DE LOS GATOS
    D. HISTORIA DEL GRAN TAMOLÁN

6. La obra, GIL BLAS DE SANTILLANA por Alain Rene Lesage fue traducida al español por

    A. Diego de Torres Villarroel
    B. Nicolás Fernández de Moratin
    C. José Francisco de Isla
    D. Vicente García de la Huerta

7. Cultivaron el género de la poesía durante el período llamado *romántico* en el siglo XIX Ángel de Saavedra, José Zorrilla, José de Espronceda y

    A. Manuel Fernández y González
    B. Enrique Pérez Escrich
    C. Rosalía de Castro
    D. Juana de Ibarbourou

7.____

8. Hernando del Pulgar fue el autor de la obra histórica

    A. CLAROS VARONES DE CASTILLA
    B. CRÓNICA DE ESPAÑA ABREVIADA
    C. CRÓNICA DE ENRIQUE IV
    D. SUMARIO DE LOS REYES DE ESPAÑA

8.____

9. Fernando de Herrera, el *divino* autor de CANCIÓN A LA VICTORIA DE LEPANTO escribió también

    A. SOLEDADES
    B. CANCIÓN A LAS RUINAS DE ITÁLICA
    C. ERÓTICAS
    D. POR LA PERDIDA DEL REY DON SEBASTIÁN

9.____

10. El famoso madrigal que comienza:
Ojos claros, serenos...
es la obra de

    A. Francisco de Figueroa   B. Diego Hurtado de Mendoza
    C. Garcilaso de la Vega   D. Gutierre de Cetina

10.____

KEY (CORRECT ANSWERS)

1.	B	6.	C
2.	D	7.	C
3.	B	8.	A
4.	D	9.	D
5.	A	10.	D

EXAMINATION SECTION
TEST 1

DIRECTIONS: Each question or incomplete statement is followed by several suggested answers or completions. Select the one that BEST answers the question or completes the statement. *PRINT THE LETTER OF THE CORRECT ANSWER IN THE SPACE AT THE RIGHT.*

Questions 1-20.

DIRECTIONS: Below is a series of English sentences, each of which has been translated into Spanish with the omission of a word or expression. Four choices are Usted from which you are to choose the MOST appropriate one to complete the Spanish sentence CORRECTLY.

1. The woman, aided by her companion, boarded the train with difficulty.
   La mujer, _____ su compañero, subió al tren penosamente.

   A. asistida por
   B. alentada por
   C. atendida por
   D. ayudada de

2. They have killed the thief.
   _____ al ladrón.

   A. Han muerto
   B. Ha fenecido
   C. Agotaron
   D. Hubieron matado

3. Many believe that Granada is one of the world's wonders and it is.
   Muchos creen que Granada es una de las maravillas del mundo y _____.

   A. la está   B. lo es   C. es ello   D. la es

4. I fell asleep. I believe my companions must have done likewise.
   Me dormí. Creo que mis compañeros debieron hacer _____.

   A. otro tanto
   B. lo parecido
   C. lo semejante
   D. igualmente

5. The girls are half dead from so much traveling. Las niñas están _____ muertas de tanto viajar.

   A. las mitades
   B. medias
   C. medio
   D. apenas

6. If you had been there, you would have witnessed this triumph.
   Si _____ allí, hubieras presenciado esta victoria.

   A. hubieras estado
   B. habías estado
   C. hubiese estado
   D. hubiste estado

7. Today's liners are veritable floating palaces.
   Los transatlánticos de hoy son verdaderos palacios _____.

   A. flotando   B. flotados   C. flotantes   D. flotillas

85

8. While she was sleeping, the children went out of the house.
   Mientras_____,salieron de la casa los niños.

   A. durmió
   B. se dormía
   C. estuvo durmiendo
   D. dormía

9. I had nobody to help me.
   Yo no tenía persona _____ .

   A. que me ayudara
   B. a ayudarme
   C. que me ayude
   D. que me ayudaba

10. After they returned, we saw the leaders.
    Luego de _____ vimos a los jefes.

    A. hubieron vuelto
    B. vueltos
    C. hubieran vuelto
    D. volvieron

11. I have two pesos left.
    _____ dos pesos.

    A. Me quedan
    B. Se me queda
    C. Se me le quedan
    D. Me quedo

12. How learned she is!
    _____ docta es!

    A. Cuan   B. Cuanto   C. Cuánta   D. Cuánto

13. The thief entered without our knowing it.
    El ladrón entró_____.

    A. sin nuestro saberlo
    B. sin sabiéndolo nosotros
    C. sin que lo supimos
    D. sin que lo supiésemos

14. How long is the canal?
    Cuánto tiene _____ el canal?

    A. por longitud
    B. de largueza
    C. a lo largo
    D. de largo

15. Whose watch did they steal?
    ¿_____ quién le robaron el reloj?

    A. Por   B. Para   C. A   D. De

16. He needs many things.
    _____ muchas cosas.

    A. Le faltan
    B. El falta
    C. Se le faltan
    D. Le necesitan

17. I went to bed early without anyone knowing it.
    Me acosté temprano sin saberlo _____.

    A. cualquiera
    B. ningunos
    C. nadie
    D. alguien

18. John's daughter, who is young, is very pretty.
    La hija de Juan, _____ es joven, es muy bonita.

    A. quién   B. la cual   C. que   D. cual

19. I will stay home if you will also stay (home).
    Yo me quedaré en casa si Ud. también_____.

    A. se quedara   B. se quedará
    C. se quede   D. se queda

20. I have five hundred and thirty-one pesetas.
    Tengo _____ pesetas.

    A. quinientas treinta y una
    B. quinientas treinta y unas
    C. quinientos y treinta y unas
    D. quinientas y treinta y una

Questions 21-45.

DIRECTIONS: Below is a list of Spanish words, each of which is followed by four English words, one of which is the correct translation of the Spanish word. Select the CORRECT translation.

21. agacharse

    A. squat   B. grapple   C. fondle   D. fame

22. deleite

    A. finesse   B. delight
    C. crime   D. denunciation

23. sumir

    A. sink   B. add   C. resume   D. summon

24. caimán

    A. caliph   B. magnet   C. alligator   D. islet

25. trapo

    A. pitfall   B. trapeze   C. tackle   D. rag

26. esmero

    A. jewel   B. great care   C. scarcity   D. grinder

27. reo

    A. criminal   B. prayer   C. creek   D. lattice

28. medida

    A. fear   B. average
    C. arbitration   D. measure

29. presidio

    A. chair
    B. grounds
    C. penitentiary
    D. capital

30. titubear

    A. protect
    B. stagger
    C. treat familiarly
    D. whisper

31. rezongar

    A. to fret
    B. to grumble
    C. to frisk
    D. to encourage

32. acatamiento

    A. purchase
    B. exhaustion
    C. esteem
    D. command

33. trastornar

    A. to fret
    B. to stutter
    C. to shear
    D. to upset

34. sinrazón

    A. wrong
    B. insanity
    C. carelessness
    D. shamelessness

35. hartar

    A. to tire
    B. to cajole
    C. to loathe
    D. to satiate

36. bosquejo

    A. woods   B. yawn   C. buttress   D. sketch

37. esclusas

    A. locks
    B. exclusions
    C. locksmiths
    D. leaks

38. copa

    A. crown   B. cuff   C. gorget   D. tavern

39. arredrar

    A. rent   B. frighten   C. rip   D. involve

40. agostado

    A. summery   B. narrow   C. parched   D. anxious

41. trepador

    A. tremulous   B. slippery   C. climbing   D. fearful

42. desvío

    A. vigilance
    B. raving
    C. garret
    D. aversión

43. ultraje

    A. last
    B. fashionable
    C. insult
    D. exaggerated

44. derruir

    A. pour
    B. destroy
    C. melt
    D. derive

45. piropo

    A. flattery
    B. pyromaniac
    C. wardrobe
    D. oration

Questions 46-70.

DIRECTIONS: Below is a list of English words, each of which is followed by four Spanish words, one of which is a correct translation of the English word. Select the CORRECT translation.

46. cheek

    A. quijada
    B. pómulo
    C. mandíbula
    D. mejilla

47. bat

    A. murciélago
    B. bata
    C. mirlo
    D. ruiseñor

48. harvest

    A. segadera
    B. sembrada
    C. vendimia
    D. vendaje

49. barley

    A. avena
    B. cebada
    C. heno
    D. centeno

50. appear

    A. surcar
    B. apear
    C. surgir
    D. surtir

51. paved

    A. empedrado
    B. empedernido
    C. empinado
    D. emparedado

52. sunset

    A. acaso
    B. sonsonete
    C. solsticio
    D. ocaso

53. move

    A. trasladar
    B. trastornar
    C. transcurrir
    D. transigir

54. theft   54.____
    A. roble   B. harto   C. ladrillo   D. hurto

55. propeller   55.____
    A. propalador   B. hélice
    C. heladero   D. empuñador

56. tissue paper   56.____
    A. papel secante   B. tejido
    C. papel de seda   D. papelito

57. abyss   57.____
    A. apogeo   B. sima   C. sótano   D. tajo

58. to empty   58.____
    A. vaciar   B. vagar   C. inundar   D. derramar

59. baldness   59.____
    A. calavera   B. melena   C. peladillo   D. calvicie

60. tape   60.____
    A. tapón   B. cinta   C. cerilla   D. encaje

61. fertile   61.____
    A. feroz   B. fiero   C. feral   D. feraz

62. downpayment   62.____
    A. pago bajo   B. anterior
    C. anticipo   D. importe

63. faucet   63.____
    A. grifo   B. lavadero   C. vajilla   D. plumero

64. ticklish   64.____
    A. rencoroso   B. estrafalario
    C. arriesgado   D. cosquilloso

65. spend the night   65.____
    A. trasnochar   B. pernoctar
    C. nocturnar   D. ennochecer

66. pawn   66.____
    A. empeñar   B. apremiar
    C. entrecoger   D. premiar

67. trick   67.____
    A. atraco   B. ardid   C. desgano   D. juerga

68. conceited

   A. ensimismado
   B. congraciado
   C. acertado
   D. engreído

69. dive

   A. hundirse
   B. abatirse
   C. zambullirse
   D. agobiarse

70. flood

   A. corriente
   B. afluencia
   C. aguacero
   D. riada

Questions 71-80.

DIRECTIONS: Below is a list of key words in Spanish, each of which is followed by four other Spanish words, one of which is a synonym of the key word. Select the synonym.

71. garbo

   A. ropa
   B. guisante
   C. basura
   D. gracia

72. certamen

   A. concurso
   B. acierto
   C. resolución
   D. seguridad

73. abarcar

   A. navegar
   B. empezar
   C. comprender
   D. subir

74. recelo

   A. odio
   B. sospecha
   C. zarpazo
   D. chistera

75. encuademación

   A. maquillaje
   B. cobertera
   C. pasta
   D. pasquín

76. yerro

   A. pariente
   B. hierba loca
   C. amonestación
   D. extravío

77. medrar

   A. merecer
   B. temer
   C. mejorar
   D. relucir

78. fallecer

   A. colgar
   B. morir
   C. fracasar
   D. faltar

79. insondable

   A. insólito
   B. profundo
   C. lejano
   D. increíble

80. importunar

   A. imponer   B. importar   C. influir   D. incomodar

Questions 81-90.

DIRECTIONS: Below is a list of key words in Spanish, each of which is followed by four other Spanish words, one of which is an antonym of the key word. Select the antonym.

81. soso

   A. expresivo   B. superior   C. excesivo   D. ancho

82. llaneza

   A. montaña   B. vacío
   C. ostentación   D. traición

83. soltar

   A. asir   B. estarse quieto
   C. separar   D. llorar

84. borrasca

   A. desbrozo   B. zonda   C. ripio   D. calma

85. mordaz

   A. dulce   B. sanguíneo   C. incauto   D. rufo

86. atirantar

   A. amenguar   B. amedrentar
   C. aflojar   D. amilanar

87. holgazanería

   A. ociosidad   B. sentimentalidad
   C. homeopatía   D. actividad

88. ablandar

   A. censurar   B. endurecer
   C. negar   D. callar

89. cuidadoso

   A. descuido   B. descomunal
   C. cuitado   D. descuidado

90. atildado

   A. afeitado   B. esmerado
   C. desaseado   D. elegante

Questions 91-100.

DIRECTIONS: Below is a list of English idiomatic expressions trans-lated into Spanish. From the four choices given, select the Spanish expression which approximates the English in meaning.

91. This boy likes to play truant.
    A este niño le gusta _____.

    A. jugar a la ausencia
    B. hacer el papel de haragán
    C. hacer novillos
    D. presenciar novilladas

92. She exclaimed, *That was the last straw!*
    Exclamó;¡_____!

    A. Era el límite
    B. No faltaba más
    C. Fue la misma idea
    D. No le quedó paja

93. Let's come to the point.

    A. Andémonos por las ramas.
    B. Vengamos en punto.
    C. Vengamos al punto.
    D. Vamos al grano.

94. Susie dropped her handkerchief when she stood up.
    Al levantarse, Susanita _____.

    A. tumbó el pañuelo al suelo
    B. cayó el pañuelo
    C. dejó caer el pañuelo
    D. tiró el pañuelo al suelo

95. We bought our tickets for the play beforehand.
    Compramos nuestros billetes para la comedia_____.

    A. de antemano
    B. de por medio
    C. adelante
    D. de hecho

96. By the way, have you read EL ÁRBOL DE LA CIENCIA?
    _____¿ has leído EL ÁRBOL DE LA CIENCIA?

    A. de paso
    B. a propósito
    C. en camino
    D. de propósito

97. I caught him red-handed.
    Lo agarré _____.

    A. con las manos abiertas
    B. con los manos desnudas
    C. con las manos en alto
    D. con las manos en la masa

98. We didn't leave because it rained cats and dogs.
    No salimos porque_____.

    A. llovía a cántaros
    B. llovía gatos y perros
    C. llovía a rios
    D. llovía a pucheros

99. These tourists like to go through the fields.
    Les gusta _____ a estos turistas.

A. correr por los campos
B. recorrer los campos
C. inspeccionar los rincones del campo
D. registrar el campo

100. That company is rated among the outstanding.
Esa compañia _____ las sobresalientes.

   A. figura entre
   B. lleva marca de
   C. es clasificada por entre
   D. lleva fama de

Questions 101-110.

DIRECTIONS: Below is a series of Spanish idiomatic expressions trans-lated into English. From the four choices given, select the English expression which approximates the ?panish in meaning.

101. Pedro está de buen talante.
Peter is _____.

   A. clever
   B. in a good humor
   C. talented
   D. in an ugly frame of mind

102. Pasaron el día al raso.
They spent the day _____.

   A. indoors
   B. rashly
   C. in the open air
   D. searching

103. Lleva el bulto a cuestas.
He is carrying the package_____.

   A. at his expense
   B. on the hill
   C. at his side
   D. on his shoulders

104. No vale la pena leer ese libro.
_____ to read that book.

   A. It doesn't cost much
   B. It isn't difficult
   C. It isn't worthwhile
   D. It isn't easy

105. Después de una discusión acalorada, vineron a las manos.
After a heated discussion, they_____.

   A. shook hands
   B. came to an agreement
   C. came to blows
   D. came home together

106. El día menos pensado, volverán los gorriones a sus nidos.
_____ the sparrows will return to their nests.

   A. any day now
   B. on the appointed day
   C. some day soon
   D. when least expected

107. No salió bien en el examen por haber hecho demasiados novillos.
He failed the examination because_____.

A. he played truant too often
B. he was too careless
C. he made too many mistakes
D. he forgot too much

108. Este sábado vamos de parranda.
This Saturday we _____.

   A. are going on a double date
   B. are going to get down to brass tacks
   C. are going on a spree
   D. are going to play cards

109. Piensa hacer su agosto.
He intends to _____.

   A. be on vacation
   B. take the sun
   C. take advantage of his opportunities
   D. be well off

110. A otro perro con ese hueso.

   A. Feed the dog.
   B. Throw a scrap to someone.
   C. There's enough for all.
   D. Tell it to the marines.

Questions 111-200.

DIRECTIONS: Below is a series of sentences in Spanish, each of which can be correctly completed by adding to it one of the four choices which follow it. Select the CORRECT choice.

111. Los amores de Caliste y Melibea constituyen el argumento de

   A. la Cárcel de Amor
   B. el Libro de Buen Amor
   C. el Libro de Kalila et Digma
   D. la Celestina

112. Los nobles de Carrión figuran en

   A. el Poema del Cid   B. Las Siete Partidas
   C. Libro de Apolonio   D. Libro de Alexandre

113. *Juventud, divino tesoro,*
ya te vas para no volver;
cuando quiero llorar, no lloro...
y a veces lloro sin querer
Esto fue escrito por

   A. Antonio Machado   B. Rubén Darío
   C. José Martí   D. José Asunción Silva

114. La historia de Segismundo, hijo único del rey de Polonia, constituye el argumento de

    A. El mágico prodigioso
    B. El principe constante
    C. El escondido y la tapada
    D. La vida es sueño

115. *Las Moradas y Noche Serena* son ejemplos del género

    A. místico   B. culterano   C. romántico   D. modernista

116. La hermosa elegia, *Coplas por la muerte de su padre* es obra de

    A. el Marqués de Santillana
    B. Juan Alfonso de Baena
    C. Jorge Manrique
    D. Juan de Mena

117. Un soldado de Cortés que luego escribió sobre la conquista de Méjico fue

    A. Garcilaso de la Vega
    B. Alvaro Núñez Cabeza de Vaca
    C. Diego de Almagro
    D. Bernal Díaz del Castillo

118. *Morada de grandeza,*
templo de claridad y hermosura,
mi alma que a tu alteza
nació, ¿ qué desventura
la tiene en esta cárcel baja, oscura?
Estos renglones son obra de

    A. Zorrilla   B. Luis de León
    C. Bécquer   D. Espronceda

119. PRECIOSA es el nombre de la heroína de

    A. la Gitanilla
    B. La ilustre Fregona
    C. El licenciado de Vidriera
    D. La Calatea

120. *El chico fue de mal en peor, pues si el mendigo la habia matado de hambre, y el clérigo le habia casi enterrado, a su nuevo dueño tuvo que mantenerlo a él pordioseando.*
Esto se refiere a

    A. Sancho Panza   B. Gil Blas
    C. Guzmán de Alfarache   D. Lazarillo de Tormes

121. La leyenda toledena en que la imagen del Cristo de la Vega baja el brazo es el tema de la obra de Zorrilla titulada

    A. Ira de Dios
    B. A buen juez, mejor testigo
    C. Traidor, inconfeso y mártir
    D. Margarita la Tornera

122. El drama célebre del Duque de Rivas se titula DON ÁLVARO O

   A. la Fuerza del Sino
   B. el Moro Expósito
   C. la Conjuración de Venecia
   D. los Amantes de Teruel

123. Es maestro y la máxima autoridad en el campo de la fonética española del siglo veinte

   A. Bonilla y San Martín   B. Navarro Tomás
   C. de Onís   D. Menéndez Pidal

124. La palabra *dolora* para designar cierto tipo de poema breve fue inventada por

   A. Núñez de Arce   B. Espronceda
   C. Campoamor   D. Bécquer

125. El gran pen?ador de la generación del 98, autor de NIEBLA, y de ABEL SANCHEZ, fue

   A. Unamuno   B. Ortega y Gasset
   C. Ganivet   D. Rodríguez Marín

126. La historia de la seña Frasquita (la molinera), el tío lucas, y el corregidor se encuentra en

   A. El capitán Veneno   B. El libro talonario
   C. El niño de la bola   D. El sombrero de tres picos

127. La famosa novela de José Eustacio Rivera, que trata de la vida trágica de los caucheros, es

   A. Valle negro   B. la Vorágine
   C. Jornadas de Agonía   D. Doña Bárbara

128. La obra maestra de la poesía gauchesca es

   A. el Hombre de Oro   B. Tradiciones argentinas
   C. Amalia   D. Martín Fierro

129. LA DÉCIMA MUSA MEXICANA, la destacada escritora mejicana del siglo diecisiete, fue

   A. Gertrudis Gómez de Avellaneda
   B. Cecilia Bohl de Faber
   C. Sor Juana Inés de la Cruz
   D. Santa Teresa de Jesús

130. A Sarmiento le ha dado mucha fama su libro, FACUNDO O

   A. la civilización y la barbarie
   B. los Mellizos de la Flor
   C. los amores del payador
   D. el himno de Santos Vega

131. Una constitución liberal fue promulgada por

   A. Fernando VII   B. Carlos IV
   C. Las Cortes de Cádíz   D. La Cámara de Castilla

132. Se retiró al monasterio de Yuste

   A. Alfonso XIII
   B. Fray Luis de León
   C. Carlos V
   D. Primo de Rivera

133. Los moros beatizados que se quedaron en España después de la reconquista se llamaban

   A. mozárabes
   B. mudejares
   C. abencerrajes
   D. moriscos

134. La región mas inquieta de España, ahora lo mismo que en el siglo XVII, es

   A. Galicia
   B. Vizcaya
   C. Cataluña
   D. Castilla la Nueva

135. El Valle de los Caidos es un monumento erigido en memoria de

   A. los que fallecieron en la última Guerra Civil
   B. los héroes de la Guerra de la Independencia
   C. las victimas de la Guerra de la Sucesión de España
   D. los que fallecieron en la Revolución

136. *El Grito de Delores* marca el principio de la Guerra de Independencia de

   A. Cuba   B. el Perú   C. Méjico   D. Colombia

137. El *Protector del Perú* fue el nombre que se le dió a

   A. Simón Bolívar
   B. José de San Martin
   C. José Sucre
   D. José Morelos

138. El último rey de la Casa de Borbón en España fue

   A. Felipe V
   B. Carlos I
   C. Fernando III
   D. Alfonso XIII

139. Fue presidente de la Argentina

   A. Bartolomé Mitre
   B. Bartolomé de las Casas
   C. Bartolomé de los Ríos
   D. Barolomé Hidalgo

140. A invitación del Presidente Kennedy Pablo Casáis dió un recital recientemente en Casa Blanca en honor de

   A. don Federico de Onís
   B. Konrad Adenauer
   C. Luis Muñoz Marin
   D. Jawaharlal Nehru

141. Domingo Faustino Sarmiento, amigo de Horace Mann, estableció escuelas al estilo estaounidense en

   A. Chile
   B. la Argentina
   C. el Paraguay
   D. el Perú

142. El aniversario del levantamiento del pueblo español contra las fuerzas de Napoleón se celebra en España el

   A. 25 de mayo
   B. el 19 de noviembre
   C. el 16 de julio
   D. el 2 de mayo

143. El presidente actual del Perú es 143.____

    A. Mateo Alemán B. Manuel Prado
    C. Victor Arosemena D. Rómulo Gallegos

144. El embajador cubano ante la Organización de Naciones Unidas es 144.____

    A. José María Colon B. Raúl Roa (padre)
    C. *Ché* Guevara D. José Antonio Moreno

145. Carlos Julio Arosemena representa el elemento izquierdista en el gobierno del 145.____

    A. Paraguay   B. Salvador   C. Uruguay   D. Ecuador

146. Durante el otoño de 1961, se estreno en Broadway la versión cinematográfica de la historia de 146.____

    A. El Greco
    B. Francisco Goya y Lucientes
    C. El Cid
    D. El Quijote

147. Pelayo conquisto a los musulmanes en 718 en la batalla de 147.____

    A. Guadalete B. Covadonga
    C. Clavijo D. las Navas de Tolosa

148. La primera universidad española fue fundada en Palencia por 148.____

    A. Alfonso VIII, el Bueno B. Fernando III, el Santo
    C. Pedro I, el Cruel D. Alfonso X, el Sabio

149. Con la muerte de Carlos II, termino en España el reinado de la Casa de 149.____

    A. Borbón B. Hapsburgo
    C. Windsor D. Hohenzollern

150. El General Sucre conquisto a los españoles en el 1824 en la batalla de 150.____

    A. Aconcagua B. Junín C. Bailen D. Ayacucho

151. En el año 1960 en el Museo de Guggenheim de Nueva York, hubo una exhibición del arte moderno de 151.____

    A. España B. Méjico C. Chile D. Colombia

152. El mejor ejemplo del estilo plateresco en la arquitectura es la fachada de la Universidad de 152.____

    A. Burgos B. Oviedo C. Salamanca D. Alcalá

153. El escultor cuyo monumento a Alfonso XII está en el Parque del Retiro en Madrid es 153.____

    A. Benlliure B. Blay C. Berruguete D. Querol

154. SAN ANTONIO DE PADUA, EL MILAGRO DE SAN DIEGO, DOS MUCHACHOS COMIENDO MELÓN son obras de 154.____

    A. Ribera B. Zurbarán C. Murillo D. Pacheco

155. La obra culminante del arte románico español es la Catedral de

    A. León   B. Santiago   C. Toledo   D. Burgos

156. Chichén Itzá es ejemplo de la arquitectura de los

    A. aztecas   B. incas   C. mayas   D. toltecas

157. El cuadro *Guérnica*, hecho en protesta contra el bombardeo de un pueblo indefenso, fue pintado por

    A. Dalí   B. Fortuny   C. Miró   D. Picasso

158. Puede verse el arte de la España primitiva en las Cuevas de Altamira en

    A. Santander   B. Valencia   C. Cádiz   D. la Coruña

159. El famoso pintor mejicano que sigue encarcelado por su gobierno es

    A. Orozco   B. Rivera
    C. Siqueiros   D. Covarrubias

160. El Escorial es ejemplo de arquitectura del estilo llamado

    A. estilo Cisneros   B. estilo Isabel
    C. churrigueresco   D. herreriano

161. Una playa famosa de Chile es

    A. Viña del Mar   B. Copacabana
    C. Arequipa   D. Tacna

162. Chamberí es un barrie en

    A. Barcelona   B. Toledo   C. Madrid   D. Bilbao

163. En Puerto Rico se halla la famosa playa de

    A. Barranquitas   B. Luquillo
    C. Rió Piedras   D. El Yunque

164. El desierto del norte de Chile que produce una gran variedad de minerales es

    A. El Atacama   B. Antofagasta
    C. Arequipa   D. La Noria

165. El éuskaro es el idioma

    A. gallego   B. andaluz   C. catalán   D. vasco

166. La Sierra Nevada se halla entre

    A. Navarra y Francia   B. Galicia y Portugal
    C. Castilla y Andalucía   D. Castilla y Extremadura

167. La ciudad más grande de Mallorca es

    A. Palma   B. Mahón   C. Ibiza   D. Santa Cruz

168. En la Albufera, cerca de la ciudad de Valencia, se cultiva

    A. la guanábana   B. la piña
    C. el mango   D. el arroz

169. Todas tienen costa marítima menos

    A. Castilla la Vieja   B. Extremadura
    C. Galicia   D. Asturias

170. Uno de los lagos del sistema del Canal de Panamá es el Lago

    A. Gatún   B. Culebra   C. Goethals   D. Amapola

171. El teatro guiñol es un teatro de

    A. ópera   B. conciertos
    C. muñecos   D. zarzuelas

172. En los salones de concierto se ha demonstrado la vitalidad de las obras para el órgano de

    A. Vicente Gómez   B. Antonio Soler
    C. Pablo de Sarasate   D. Roberto Iglesias

173. Una de las piezas más conocidas para el violín es el *Zigeunerweisen* de

    A. Pablo de Sarasate   B. Antonio de Cabezón
    C. Pablo Casáis   D. Augustín Nieves

174. En el ballet *El sombrero de Tres Pieos,* el tema de la *Jota navarra* se inicia cada vez que aparece en escena

    A. el Corregidor   B. la molinera
    C. el molinero   D. Garduña

175. La música en forma de cantigas formaba parte fundamental en la corte de

    A. Carlos V   B. Fernando e Isabel
    C. Alfonso X   D. Carlos IV

176. La gran cantante de ópera es

    A. Teresa Carreño   B. Elisa Brabante
    C. María Barrientes   D. Teresa Berganza

177. Ernesto Halffter y Escriche es mundialmente conocido como

    A. escritor   B. arquitecto   C. músico   D. pintor

178. Cantante popular que ganó fama mundial por su producción y su papel en la versión mejicana de MY FAIR LADY es

    A. Manolo Fábregas   B. José Wences
    C. Ricardo Montalbán   D. Cantinflas

179. Todos los siguientes son bailes de la Argentina menos

    A. el pericón   B. la chacarera
    C. el gato   D. la laucha

180. La Atlántida, que se representará en Barcelona, fue la última obra de

    A. Bretón de los Herreros
    B. Manuel de Falla
    C. Enrique Granados
    D. Felipe Pedrell

181. Un nuevo desarrollo arquitectónico que floreció en el siglo XVII es el estilo

    A. barroco   B. románico   C. gótico   D. mozárabe

182. *Los desastres de la guerra* es una colección de aguafuertes de

    A. Zuloaga   B. Fortany   C. Goya   D. Picasso

183. El pintor español del siglo XIX cuyos cuadros llenan una sala del Museo Hispánico en Nueva York es

    A. Joan Miró
    B. Juan Gris
    C. José de Madrazo
    D. Joaquin Sorolla

184. Velázquez pinto

    A. LA RENDICIÓN DE BREDA
    B. LA TAUROMAQUIA
    C. TOLEDO
    D. LOS BAÑISTAS

185. El notable caricaturista mejicano es

    A. Orozco
    B. Covarrubias
    C. Siqueiros
    D. Atl

186. El arquitecto de Felipe II que edificó el Escorial fue

    A. Pedro Berruguete
    B. San Lorenzo
    C. Juan de Herrera
    D. Alonso Cano

187. Obra culminante del arte ibérico es

    A. la Torre de Hércules
    B. el Doncel de Simienza
    C. La Dama de Elche
    D. el castillo de Ávila

188. Un ejemplo notable de la pintura primitiva lo tenemos en

    A. el circo de Mérida
    B. los baños de Alange
    C. la cueva de Altamira
    D. la necrópolis de Cilla

189. El famoso pintor argentino de los gauchos es

    A. Quirós   B. Pabón   C. Magariños   D. Berrocal

190. Un ejemplo notable de la arquitectura r?mana en España es

    A. la mezquita de Córdoba
    B. la Basilica de San Vicente
    C. la Puerta del Sol
    D. el acueducto de Segovia

191. *Pelar la pava* es costumbre de

    A. los gitanos
    B. los jóvenes
    C. los campesinos
    D. los carniceros

192. El baquiano es un

   A. baile de influencia árabe
   B. tipo argentino
   C. juego
   D. tipo de la clase media madrileña

193. En Bolivia el sombrero cónico y adornado que usan los indios se llama

   A. montera
   B. boina
   C. barretina
   D. sombrero calañes

194. Todos los años, en muchos teatros de España se representa DON JUAN TENORIO el

   A. 1 de noviembre
   B. 25 de junio
   C. 24 de diciembre
   D. Sábado de Gloria

195. El Tribunal de la Aguas es

   A. un impuesto que pagan los aldeanos
   B. titulo de una comedia de Hartzenbusch
   C. un sistema de justicia popular
   D. una reunión de mujeres en las fuentes de los pueblos

196. Se celebra una verbena

   A. en honor del cumpleaños de un niño
   B. en honor de un santo
   C. la vispera del 2 de mayo
   D. después del estreno de un auto sacramental

197. Durante la Semana Santa en Sevilla se sacan en procesión

   A. fallas   B. pasas   C. cabezudos   D. pasos

198. En la corrida de toros, el que lleva la muleta es el

   A. matador
   B. banderillo
   C. picador
   D. muletero

199. En España generalmente se sirve la comida en los restaurantes

   A. a eso de las seis
   B. a la hora de la siesta
   C. muy tarde por la noche
   D. a cualquier hora de la tarde

200. Se llama gazpacho

   A. un niño malcriado
   B. un género de sopa fria
   C. un tipo peruano
   D. una enfermedad de los viejos

KEY (CORRECT ANSWERS)

1. D	41. C	81. A	121. B	161. A
2. A	42. D	82. C	122. A	162. C
3. B	43. C	83. A	123. B	163. B
4. A	44. B	84. D	124. C	164. A
5. C	45. A	85. A	125. A	165. D
6. A	46. D	86. C	126. D	166. C
7. C	47. A	87. D	127. B	167. A
8. D	48. C	88. B	128. D	168. D
9. A	49. B	89. D	129. C	169. B
10. B	50. C	90. C	130. A	170. A
11. A	51. A	91. C	131. C	171. C
12. A	52. D	92. B	132. C	172. B
13. D	53. A	93. D	133. D	173. A
14. D	54. D	94. C	134. C	174. B
15. C	55. B	95. A	135. A	175. C
16. A	56. C	96. B	136. C	176. D
17. C	57. B	97. D	137. B	177. C
18. B	58. A	98. A	138. D	178. A
19. D	59. D	99. B	139. A	179. D
20. A	60. B	100. A	140. C	180. B
21. A	61. D	101. B	141. B	181. A
22. B	62. C	102. C	142. D	182. C
23. A	63. A	103. D	143. B	183. D
24. C	64. D	104. C	144. B	184. A
25. D	65. B	105. C	145. D	185. B
26. B	66. A	106. D	146. C	186. C
27. A	67. B	107. A	147. B	187. C
28. D	68. D	108. C	148. A	188. C
29. C	69. C	109. C	149. B	189. A
30. B	70. D	110. D	150. D	190. D
31. A	71. D	111. D	151. A	191. B
32. C	72. A	112. A	152. C	192. B
33. D	73. C	113. B	153. A	193. A
34. A	74. B	114. D	154. C	194. A
35. D	75. C	115. A	155. B	195. C
36. D	76. D	116. C	156. C	196. B
37. A	77. C	117. D	157. D	197. D
38. A	78. B	118. B	158. A	198. A
39. B	79. B	119. A	159. C	199. C
40. C	80. D	120. D	160. D	200. B

EXAMINATION SECTION
TEST 1

DIRECTIONS: Each question or incomplete statement is followed by several suggested answers or corapletions. Select the one that BEST answers the question or completes the statement. *PRINT THE LETTER OF THE CORRECT ANSWER IN THE SPACE AT THE RIGHT.*

Questions 1-40.

DIRECTIONS: Below is a series of English sentences, each of which has been translated into Spanish with the omission of a word or expression. Four choices are listed from which you are to choose the MOST appropriate to complete the Spanish sentence correctly. Indicate your cholee.

1. There nave been many meetings here.
   Aqui _____ muchas reuniones.

   A. han estado B. han habido
   C. ha habido   D. ha sido

2. As a student he works hard.
   _____ trabaja mucho.

   A. Como un estudiante   B. De estudiante
   C. De un estudiante   D. Estando estudiante

3. Don't you think she is intelligent?
   ¿ No cree Vd. que ella _____ inteligente?

   A. sea   B. es   C. esté   D. está

4. I shall write him to send them to me.
   Le escribiré _____.

   A. que me los envia   B. enviármelos
   C. que me los envíe   D. que me los envié

5. He doubts whether she will be back on time.
   Duda si ella _____ a tiempo.

   A. estará de vuelta   B. llegue
   C. esté de vuelta   D. vuelva

6. They did the work easily, which surprised me. Hicieron fácilmente el trabajo, _____ me sorprendió.

   A. que   B. el que   C. cual   D. lo cual

7. It is true that he wrote the letter last night. Es verdad que él _____ la carta anoche.

   A. haya escrito   B. escribió
   C. escribiese   D. escribiria

8. You see how high the mountains are.
   Vd. ve_____ que son las montanas.

   A. como altas
   B. lo altas
   C. las altas
   D. la alta

9. We hope that he is coming today.
   Esperamos que _____ hoy.

   A. venga
   B. viene
   C. vendrá
   D. esta viniendo

10. All héroes are admired.
    _____ a todos los héroes.

    A. Se los admiran
    B. Se les admira
    C. Se les admiran
    D. Se los admira

11. I am sorry that you have seen it.
    Siento que Vd. lo _____.

    A. vió
    B. haya veido
    C. haya visto
    D. ha visto

12. Are the girls pretty? They are.
    ¿ Son bonitas las muchachas? _____.

    A. Lo son
    B. La son
    C. Las son
    D. Que son

13. He quarreled with his brother.
    _____ con su hermano.

    A. Reñió
    B. Reñó
    C. Riñió
    D. Riñó

14. We have exercises to write.
    Tenemos ejercicios _____.

    A. para escribir
    B. por escribir
    C. de escribir
    D. escribir

15. The man has an agreeable face.
    El hombre tiene _____.

    A. la cara agradable
    B. su cara agradable
    C. una cara agradable
    D. una agradable cara

16. I like this novel better than any other.
    Esta novela me gusta más que _____.

    A. alguna otra
    B. nada
    C. ninguna
    D. algo

17. Do you intend to return to the city?
    ¿ _____ volver a la ciudad?

    A. Intenta Vd. de
    B. Piensa Vd. de
    C. Piensa Vd.
    D. Cree Vd. a

18. The teacher always explained so that the class understood him.
El profesor siempre explicaba de manera que la clase la _____.

    A. comprendiera
    B. comprendía
    C. hubo comprendide
    D. hubiera comprendido

19. The lady, whose parents were French, speaks well. La dama, _____ padres eran franceses, habla bien.

    A. cuya
    B. cuyos
    C. de quien
    D. cuales

20. The mother said to her children, *Dress quickly!*
La madre dijo a sus hijos - _____ vosotros pronto!

    A. Vestidos
    B. Vístanse
    C. Vistos
    D. Vistós

21. He promised to be home by five o'clock.
Prometió estar en casa _____ las cinco.

    A. para
    B. por
    C. a eso de
    D. acerca de

22. They took the toys from the child.
Le quitáronlos juguetes _____.

    A. del niño
    B. al niño
    C. desde el niño
    D. de niño

23. He succeeded in finishing the work.
_____ terminar el trabajo.

    A. Sucedió en
    B. Sucedió
    C. Logró en
    D. Logró

24. Is it an interesting film? Yes, very.
¿Es una película interesante? Sí, _____.

    A. mucho
    B. mucha
    C. muy
    D. tanto

25. As soon as I had seen him, I left.
Luago que le _____, salí.

    A. hube visto
    B. hubiese visto
    C. había visto
    D. ví

26. The thief was running down the street.
El ladrón corría _____.

    A. bajo la calle
    B. abaja la calle
    C. calle abajo
    D. a bajar la calle

27. I heard her repeat it.

    A. Se lo oí repetir.
    B. La oí repetirlo.
    C. Oí repetírselo.
    D. Oí la repetirlo.

28. I wonder if it was eight o'clock when he arrived.
¿_____ las ocho cuando llego?

    A. Eran a
    B. Serían a

C. Serían   D. Eran

29. This wood is very hard.
    Esta madera es _____.

    A. muy duro   B. durísima
    C. dúrrima   D. duérima

30. Have you ever seen such a thing?
    ¿ _____ tal cosa?

    A. Jamás ha visto Vd.   B. No ha visto Vd. jamás
    C. Ha jamás visto Vd.   D. Ha visto Vd. jamás

31. I do not believe that the coffee is hot.
    No creo que el café _____.

    A. sea caliente   B. esté caliente
    C. tenga calor   D. es cálido

32. All you say is true.
    _____ Vd. dice es verdad.

    A. Todo lo que   B. Cuantos
    C. Todo que   D. Cuánto

33. Because of his efforts he earned a great deal of money.
    _____ sus esfuerzos gano mucho dinero.

    A. Porque   B. Porque de
    C. Por   D. A medio de

34. All of us wish for peace.
    _____ deseamos la paz.

    A. Todos de nosotros   B. Nos todos
    C. Cuantos nosotros   D. Nosotros todos

35. The men often became tired.
    A menudo los hombres _____ cansados.

    A. llegaban a ser   B. se hacían
    C. se volvían   D. se ponían

36. He is afraid I'll laugh at him.
    Teme que yo _____.

    A. me ria de el   B. me le rio
    C. me le reiré   D. me le ria

37. I have a pencil, but I do not have paper.
    Tengo lápiz _____ no tengo papel.

    A. mas   B. sino   C. sino que   D. pero

38. He told me he could speak French.
    Me dijo que _____ hablar francés.

    A. pudiese   B. sabía   C. podía   D. supiese

39. At the university studying is always necessary.
    En la universidad _____ es siempre necesario.

    A. a estudiar   B. estudiando
    C. el estudiar   D. el estudiando

40. How long have John and I been friends?
    ¿Desde cuando _____ amigos Juan y yo?

    A. son   B. han sido   C. fueron   D. somos

Questions 41-60.

DIRECTIONS: Below is a list of key words in Spanish, each of which is followed by four other Spanish words, one of which is an antonym of the key word. Select the ANTONYM.

41. esperanza

    A. coraje   B. abatimiento
    C. displicencia   D. despernada

42. fresco

    A. refresco   B. tosco   C. marchito   D. chato

43. osado

    A. dotado   B. libre   C. esquivo   D. desposado

44. odio

    A. intrepidez   B. temor
    C. valor   D. simpatía

45. previo

    A. postrero   B. segundo   C. siguiente   D. proviso

46. porvenir

    A. proveer   B. pasado   C. advenir   D. posadero

47. ufano

    A. mero   B. jactancioso
    C. humilde   D. mercero

48. varón

    A. vara   B. hombre   C. desagravio   D. balde

49. estival

    A. destiempo   B. tibio   C. nocturno   D. frigido

50. grosero

    A. miniatura   B. ingenio   C. pulido   D. corto

6 (#1)

51. escaso   51.____
    A. caso   B. común   C. cortés   D. escapo

52. feraz   52.____
    A. suave   B. febril   C. infecundo   D. doméstico

53. alabanza   53.____
    A. balanza   B. censura   C. elegía   D. ebúrnea

54. enredado   54.____
    A. difuso   B. rumbo   C. sentido   D. sencillo

55. parecido   55.____
    A. aparecido   B. difunto   C. diverso   D. suplico

56. apagar   56.____
    A. alumbrar   B. luminar   C. licenciar   D. desalentar

57. sagaz   57.____
    A. feroz   B. necio   C. timidez   D. feral

58. venturoso   58.____
    A. afortunado   B. malhecho
    C. desgraciado   D. tímido

59. pesar   59.____
    A. mejorar   B. regocijo   C. despezar   D. recogida

60. derecho   60.____
    A. siniestro   B. retiro   C. directo   D. franco

Questions 61-80.

DIRECTIONS: Below is a list of key words in Spanish, each of which is followed by four other Spanish words, one of which is a synonym of the key word. Select the SYNONYM.

61. famélico   61.____
    A. faltante   B. famular
    C. hambriento   D. fase

62. bracero   62.____
    A. bramido   B. braco   C. broche   D. peón

63. morigerar   63.____
    A. morir   B. moderar   C. morar   D. teñir

7 (#1)

64. alnado 64.____

　　A. aliento　　B. hijastro　　C. almohada　　D. camarero

65. recoveco 65.____

　　A. redil　　B. recorte　　C. curva　　D. calderón

66. caletre 66.____

　　A. botón　　B. calendario　　C. borrasca　　D. tino

67. macota 67.____

　　A. vaso　　B. magia　　C. sitio　　D. ráiz

68. fantoche 68.____

　　A. coche　　B. baile　　C. títere　　D. fantasma

69. borinqueño 69.____

　　A. puertorriqueño　　B. pequeño
　　C. bastonero　　D. documento

70. derramar 70.____

　　A. criticar　　B. verter　　C. alabar　　D. cortar

71. escarapela 71.____

　　A. escena　　B. escarabajo
　　C. sable　　D. riña

72. jacarandoso 72.____

　　A. torpe　　B. harapiento
　　C. enfermizo　　D. alegre

73. ecuménico 73.____

　　A. universal　　B. ecuestre
　　C. eficaz　　D. *tenaz*

74. cenceño 74.____

　　A. pagano　　B. cenizoso　　C. delgado　　D. sólido

75. acendrado 75.____

　　A. ácido　　B. asoleado　　C. amargo　　D. puro

76. propinar 76.____

　　A. asombrar　　B. recetar　　C. propagar　　D. hechizar

77. ludir 77.____

　　A. frotar　　B. huir　　C. lucir　　D. cavar

78. verdugo

    A. reo B. ejecutor C. legumbre D. origen

79. abrevar

    A. reducir B. regar C. ceñir D. abdicar

80. incuria

    A. negligencia B. enfermedad
    C. fuero D. tribunal

Questions 81-90.

DIRECTIONS: Below is a list of key words in Spanish, each of which is followed by four other Spanish words, one of which is related in derivation to the key word. Select the RELATED word.

81. apertura

    A. abridor B. perturbar C. apercibir D. perdurable

82. reloj

    A. relaxión B. horario C. elogio D. alojar

83. don

    A. donde B. dotar C. onda D. adueñar

84. integral

    A. entero B. interés C. estirar D. engendrar

85. sínfonia

    A. música B. orquesta C. cenefa D. zampona

86. prisión

    A. aprehender B. prisma
    C. primo D. premio

87. echar

    A. aclamar B. aclarar C. jactancia D. chal

88. igual

    A. iguana B. ecuador C. guiar D. gualda

89. juez

    A. juego B. ajedrez C. ajimez D. adjudicar

90. animar

    A. alma B. marina
    C. aminorar D. encorazonar

Questions 91-130.

DIRECTIONS: Below is a list of Spanish words, each of which is followed by four English words, one of which is a correct translation of the Spanish word. Select the CORRECT translation.

91. empañar 91.____
    A. bake   B. deceive   C. dim   D. endose

92. reto 92.____
    A. challenge   B. net   C. globe   D. syllable

93. jurar 93.____
    A. swear   B. judge   C. drain   D. adore

94. bodega 94.____
    A. bottle   B. wine cellar
    C. great-grandmother   D. groceries

95. mohín 95.____
    A. moths   B. grimace   C. Indian   D. skirt

96. fusil 96.____
    A. futile   B. ball   C. gun   D. cracker

97. padrastro 97.____
    A. kick   B. stepfather
    C. rake   D. quarrel

98. abrasar 98.____
    A. rub   B. file   C. burn   D. embrace

99. culebra 99.____
    A. snake   B. ditch   C. disease   D. cut

100. garra 100.____
    A. grab   B. war   C. claw   D. garage

KEY (CORRECT ANSWERS)

1. C	21. A	41. B	61. C	81. A
2. B	22. B	42. C	62. D	82. B
3. B	23. D	43. C	63. B	83. D
4. C	24. A	44. D	64. B	84. A
5. A	25. A	45. C	65. C	85. D
6. D	26. C	46. B	66. D	86. A
7. B	27. A	47. C	67. A	87. C
8. B	28. C	48. B	68. C	88. B
9. A	29. B	49. D	69. A	89. D
10. B	30. D	50. C	70. B	90. A
11. C	31. B	51. B	71. D	91. C
12. A	32. A	52. C	72. D	92. A
13. D	33. C	53. B	73. A	93. A
14. B	34. D	54. D	74. C	94. B
15. A	35. D	55. C	75. D	95. B
16. C	36. A	56. A	76. B	96. C
17. C	37. D	57. B	77. A	97. B
18. B	38. B	58. C	78. B	98. C
19. B	39. C	59. B	79. B	99. A
20. D	40. D	60. A	80. A	100. C

TEST 2

DIRECTIONS: Each question or incomplete statement is followed by several suggested answers or corapletions. Select the one that BEST answers the question or completes the statement. *PRINT THE LETTER OF THE CORRECT ANSWER IN THE SPACE AT THE RIGHT.*

1. indulto 1.____
   A. pardon   B. unharmed   C. mature   D. bag

2. acre 2.____
   A. measure   B. sour   C. chest   D. peak

3. gremio 3.____
   A. union   B. grey   C. unkempt   D. feneing

4. acecho 4.____
   A. bush   B. couch   C. attitude   D. ambush

5. abono 5.____
   A. subscription   B. native
   C. volume   D. lesson

6. osar 6.____
   A. dare   B. climb   C. rattle   D. ogle

7. gorro 7.____
   A. goal   B. cap   C. horrible   D. greasy

8. cuero 8.____
   A. candle   B. cattle   C. cord   D. leather

9. abejorro 9.____
   A. stream   B. jug   C. abacus   D. bumblebee

10. delantal 10.____
    A. apron   B. previous   C. delicious   D. wagón

11. liso 11.____
    A. smooth   B. ready   C. firm   D. unharmed

12. nivel 12.____
    A. nut   B. saw   C. level   D. avalanche

13. abarcar 13.____
    A. embark   B. strip   C. include   D. shut up

115

14. cadalso
    A. scaffold   B. container   C. false   D. lie

15. crepúsculo
    A. growth   B. whisper   C. twilight   D. caress

16. callejón
    A. highway   B. wart   C. idiot   D. alley

17. potro
    A. kettle   B. rotten   C. pallid   D. colt

18. jubilación
    A. retirement   B. dance
    C. surrender   D. courtesy

19. cascabeleo
    A. peel   B. jingling
    C. altercation   D. vacation

20. lagarto
    A. legacy   B. slow   C. uneven   D. lizard

21. labranza
    A. liquor   B. bronze   C. etching   D. farming

22. náufrago
    A. broken   B. shipwrecked man
    C. deck   D. nausea

23. chancleta
    A. chandelier   B. china
    C. slipper   D. pudding

24. charco
    A. comed beef   B. puddle
    C. suspicion   D. coal

25. zalamería
    A. flattery   B. Venetian blind
    C. jealousy   D. jewelry store

26. yerto
    A. white of egg   B. stiff
    C. shovel   D. painful

27. usurero

    A. dictator
    B. secretary
    C. moneylender
    D. user

28. uña

    A. nail
    B. meeting
    C. raccoon
    D. rug

29. trapo

    A. rag
    B. carriage
    C. net
    D. device

30. planchar

    A. plant
    B. widen
    C. iron
    D. guess

Questions 31-50.

DIRECTIONS: Below is a series of English phrases translated into Spanish. The correct translation will be found among the four choices given in each question. Select the CORRECT translation.

31. to regain consciousness

    A. volver a ganar la conciencia
    B. volver a ver
    C. volver en sí
    D. decir que si

32. to tease

    A. buscar las cosquillas
    B. buscar la risa
    C. prender las teas
    D. hacer reír

33. in a squatting position

    A. en cuclillas
    B. en posición baja
    C. con los pies cruzados
    D. sentado

34. on all fours

    A. boca arriba
    B. en cuatro manos
    C. a gatas
    D. a los pies

35. stealthily

    A. al robe
    B. a manera de robo
    C. a hurtadillas
    D. a las hurtadillas

36. to pick a quarrel

    A. recoger el cuarto
    B. buscar sitio
    C. hacerse maña
    D. meterse con

37. behind

    A. en zaga
    B. en balde
    C. en vano
    D. en trapos

38. to act to no purpose   38.____

    A. hacer por hacer   B. hacer y hacer
    C. hacer y deshacer   D. hacer y no hacer

39. to know a thing or two   39.____

    A. conocer lo que se debe   B. ser listo
    C. ser conocido   D. estar al tanto

40. I mean what I say   40.____

    A. lo quiero decir   B. quiero decirlo
    C. lo dicho dicho   D. lo dicho bien

41. suddenly   41.____

    A. en llegando   B. a dos por tres
    C. a la una   D. a la bartola

42. He played one of his pranks   42.____

    A. Hizo una de las suyas   B. Jugó una jugada
    C. Hizo el juego   D. Se salió con una salida

43. to pack a trunk   43.____

    A. llenar el baúl   B. hacer un baúl
    C. cerrar un baúl   D. empacar un baúl

44. to sharpen the pencil   44.____

    A. sacar punta al lápiz   B. sacar punto al lápiz
    C. sacar punta del lápiz   D. sacar punte del lápiz

45. to take a fancy to   45.____

    A. tomar vuelo a   B. echar gusto en
    C. tener gusto en   D. antojarse de

46. to get off   46.____

    A. apearse   B. dejarse   C. abandonar   D. afanarse

47. on purpose   47.____

    A. a propósito   B. adrede
    C. a causa de   D. por instancias de

48. same old story   48.____

    A. llega que llega   B. siempre hablando
    C. dale que dale   D. el cuento sin fin

49. to be obvious   49.____

    A. saltar a la vista   B. saltar a la mar
    C. aparecer   D. parecer visto

50. as usual

    A. sin novedad
    B. como tantos
    C. sin ninguna razón
    D. sin nungún objeto

Questions 51-100.

DIRECTIONS: Below is a series of sentences in Spanish, each of which can be correctly completed by adding to it one of the four expressions which follow it. Select the CORRECT expression.

51. LA ARAUCANA fue escrita por

    A. Garcilaso de la Vega
    B. Alonso de Ercilla
    C. Bernal Diaz del Castillo
    D. Pedro de Ona

52. En el Perú la unidad monetaria es el

    A. balboa   B. peso   C. sol   D. sucre

53. Sor Juana Inés de la Cruz nació en

    A. Cuba   B. España   C. México   D. el Perú

54. EL PERIQUILLO SARMIENTO fue escrito por

    A. José Joaquín Olmedo
    B. José María Heredia
    C. Andrés Bello
    D. Fernandez de Lizardi

55. No fue poeta modernista

    A. Casal
    B. Gutiérrez Najera
    C. Nervo
    D. Sarmiento

56. No es obra gauchesca

    A. SANTOS VEGA
    B. MARTÍN FIERRO
    C. MARTÍN RIVAS
    D. FAUSTO

57. Novela de la selva colombiana es

    A. LA VORÁGINE
    B. EL MONSTRUO
    C. EL MAL METAFÍSICO
    D. CASA GRANDE

58. Fue escritor de los *llanos* -venezolanos

    A. Tomás Carrasquilla
    B. Rómulo Gallegos
    C. Carlos Loveira
    D. Eduardo Barrios

59. Novela que no trata de la revolución mexicana es

    A. LOS DE ABAJO
    B. CATACLARO
    C. EL ÁGUILA Y LA SERPIENTE
    D. TIERRA

60. Una obra escrita por un argentino que describe la España del reino de Felipe II es

    A. LA GLORIA DE DON RAMIRO
    B. EL EMBRUJO DE SEVILLA
    C. EL MUNDO ES ANCHO Y AJENO
    D. LOS HIJOS DEL SOL

61. La Universidad Nacional Mayor de San Marcos se encuentra en   61.____

    A. Bogotá   B. Lima   C. México   D. Santiago

62. El Callao es un puerto   62.____

    A. de Colombia   B. de Honduras
    C. del Perú   D. de Chile

63. Un pico de los Andes del Ecuador es   63.____

    A. Orizaba   B. Chimborazo
    C. Aconcagua   D. El Misti

64. El Magdalena es un río   64.____

    A. de Colombia   B. del Perú
    C. de Venezuela   D. de Honduras

65. Las islas Juan Fernández están situadas frente a la costa de   65.____

    A. México   B. Colombia   C. Venezuela   D. Chile

66. La capital de Honduras es   66.____

    A. Tegucigalpa   B. Managua
    C. Asunción   D. San José

67. En la batalla de Ayacucho salió vencedor   67.____

    A. San Martín   B. O'Higgins
    C. Sucre   D. Belgrano

68. El bambuco es un baile popular en   68.____

    A. Chile   B. Colombia   C. Venezuela   D. Guatemala

69. Los toltecas vivieron en   69.____

    A. Chile   B. el Perú   C. México   D. el Paraguay

70. *La Golondrina* es una canción   70.____

    A. argentina   B. mexicana   C. peruana   D. chilena

71. Muy famosa en la historia por sus minas de plata ha sido   71.____

    A. Buenaventura   B. Montevideo
    C. Potosí   D. Guayaquil

72. Fue capital del antiguo reino de los incas la ciudad de   72.____

    A. Cuzco   B. Guanajuato
    C. Arequipa   D. Trujillo

73. El inca a quien Pizarro dió muerte fue   73.____

    A. Huayna Cápac   B. Atahualpa
    C. Huáscar   D. Toparca

74. La *Casa de Contratación* fue fundada en   74._____

    A. La Coruña   B. Bilbao
    C. Sevilla   D. Málaga

75. Fué el fundador de la nacionalidad española   75._____

    A. Rodrigo   B. Pelayo   C. Carlos   D. El Cid

76. Es la iglesia gótica más grande del mundo cristiano la catedral de   76._____

    A. Burgos   B. Sevilla   C. León   D. Barcelona

77. La Santa Hermandad era   77._____

    A. una orden eclesiástica
    B. un comité de la Inquisición
    C. una especie de policía rural
    D. una confradía

78. Compuso EL AMOR BRUHO   78._____

    A. Granados   B. Albéniz   C. de Falla   D. Pedrell

79. Fué el padre del teatro español   79._____

    A. Lope de Rueda   B. Juan del Encina
    C. Gil Vicente   D. Torres Naharro

80. La obra de Cervantes que nos ofrece descripciones de las costumbres de los ladrones   80._____
    en Sevilla es

    A. LA CALATEA   B. EL VIAJE DEL PARNASO
    C. PINCONETE Y CORTADILLO   D. LA NUMANCIA

81. Los españoles pelearon contra los turcos en la batalla de Lepante en el año 81._____

    A. 1496   B. 1515   C. 1571   D. 1602

82. Las *taifas* eran   82._____

    A. impuestos   B. bailarinas musulmanas
    C. novelas sentimentales   D. pequeños reinos

83. Los ganaderos de la España medieval se organizaron en una asociación llamada 83._____

    A. la *Mesta*   B. la *Asociación Ganadera*
    C. los *Hidalgos*   D. los *Caballeros de Santiago*

84. Compuso GOYESCAS   84._____

    A. Granados   B. Ponce   C. Goya   D. Chávez

85. El La Fontaine español fue   85._____

    A. Ruiz de Alarcón   B. Vélez de Guevara
    C. Pérez de Montalban   D. Tomás de Iriarte

86. Fundó la Universidad de Alcalá de Henares

    A. Fray Luis de León   B. el cardenal Cisneros
    C. Menéndez y Pelayo   D. Recaredo

87. Escribió LAS CONFESIONES DE UN PEQUEÑO FILÓSOFO

    A. José Ortega y Gasset   B. Miguel de Unamuno
    C. José Martínez Ruiz   D. Joaquin Costa

88. Fue el rey de la escena española en el ultimo cuarto del siglo XIX

    A. Martínez de la Rosa   B. Mariano José de Larra
    C. José Zorrilla   D. José Echegaray

89. Durante el reinado de Fernando e Isabel, el comercio con América sólo podía hacerse desde los puertos de Cádiz y

    A. Sevilla   B. La Coruña
    C. Balboa   D. Málaga

90. Fue el fundador de la Compañía de Jesús

    A. Fray Junípero Serra   B. San Juan de la Cruz
    C. San Ignacio de Loyola   D. Fray Luis de Granada

91. Introdujo el naturalismo en España

    A. Valle Inclán   B. Pardo Bazán
    C. Pérez Caldos   D. Fernán Caballero

92. La expedición de Colón salió del puerto de

    A. Valencia   B. Palos   C. Vigo   D. Cádiz

93. Pintó el cuadro llamado LAS MENINAS

    A. Velázquez   B. Goya   C. Zurbarán   D. Sert

94. En las minas de RÍO Tinto, más que otra cosa, se encuentra el

    A. hierro   B. carbón   C. cobre   D. estaño

95. El primero de noviembre los españoles asisten a una función teatral de

    A. O LOCURA O SANTIDAD   B. LAS MORADAS
    C. DON JUAN TENORIO   D. EL MEJER ALCALDE EL REY

96. Fue el último rey moro de España

    A. Abdallá   B. Abderramán III
    C. Almanzor   D. Boabdil

97. La gaita se toca en

    A. Granada   B. Galicia   C. Valencia   D. Andalucía

98. El estilo barroco exagerado es también llamado

    A. plateresco   B. granadino
    C. churrigueresco   D. valenciano

99. La dictadura de Primo de Rivera en España se mantuvo durante _____ años.   99._____

   A. siete
   B. quince
   C. diez y ocho
   D. veinte

100. Fue el poeta moderno que más espléndidamente evocó las tradiciones de la vieja España   100._____

   A. Nuñez de Arce
   B. Ramón de Campoamor
   C. José Zorrilla
   D. José de Espronceda

KEY (CORRECT ANSWERS)

1. A	21. D	41. B	61. B	81. C
2. B	22. B	42. A	62. C	82. D
3. A	23. C	43. B	63. B	83. A
4. D	24. B	44. A	64. A	84. A
5. A	25. A	45. D	65. D	85. D
6. A	26. B	46. A	66. A	86. B
7. B	27. C	47. B	67. C	87. C
8. D	28. A	48. C	68. B	88. D
9. D	29. A	49. A	69. C	89. A
10. A	30. C	50. A	70. B	90. C
11. A	31. C	51. B	71. C	91. B
12. C	32. A	52. C	72. A	92. B
13. C	33. A	53. C	73. B	93. A
14. A	34. C	54. D	74. C	94. C
15. C	35. C	55. D	75. B	95. C
16. D	36. D	56. C	76. B	96. D
17. D	37. A	57. A	77. C	97. B
18. A	38. A	58. B	78. C	98. C
19. B	39. B	59. B	79. B	99. A
20. D	40. C	60. A	80. C	100. C

EXAMINATION SECTION
TEST 1

DIRECTIONS: Each question or incomplete statement is followed by several suggested answers or completions. Select the one that BEST answers the question or completes the statement. *PRINT THE LETTER OF THE CORRECT ANSWER IN THE SPACE AT THE RIGHT.*

Questions 1-40.

DIRECTIONS: Below is a series of English sentences, each of which has been translated into Spanish with the omission of a word or expression. Four choices are listed from which you are to choose the MOST appropriate to complete the Spanish sentence correctly.

1. We studied for two hours.
   Estudiamos_____.

   A. hace dos horas
   B. desde hace dos horas
   C. por dos horas
   D. para dos horas

   1._____

2. She doesnt know how poor they are.
   No sabe _____ pobres que son.

   A. lo   B. qué   C. cómo   D. los

   2._____

3. He speaks as if he were from Madrid.
   Habla como si _____ de Madrid.

   A. era   B. sea   C. esté   D. fuera

   3._____

4. I regret that I didnt do it before.
   Siento _____ antes.

   A. que no lo hice
   B. no haberlo hecho
   C. no hacerlo
   D. que no lo hiciera

   4._____

5. She is richer than they are.
   Ella es más rica _____ son ellos.

   A. que
   B. de las que
   C. de la que
   D. de lo que

   5._____

6. They entered the room; they entered it.
   Entraron en el cuarto; _____.

   A. lo entraron
   B. entraron en él
   C. entraron en ello
   D. entraron en lo

   6._____

7. We paid $151.
   Pagamos_____ dólares.

   A. cien cincuenta y un
   B. ciento y cincuenta y unos
   C. ciento cincuenta y un
   D. ciento cincuenta y anos

   7._____

125

8. She was told that yesterday.
   Ayer _____ eso.

   A. ella fué dicha
   B. se la dijeron
   C. la dijeron
   D. se le dijo

9. He introduced me to her.
   El _____.

   A. me la presentó a ella
   B. me le presentó a ella
   C. me presentó a ella
   D. le me presentó a ella

10. This book is the one I bought.
    Este libro es _____ compré.

    A. el uno que
    B. el que
    C. lo que
    D. el cual

11. Even though he is coming early I wont go out.
    Aunque él _____ temprano, no saldré.

    A. viene
    B. venga
    C. vendrá
    D. está viniendo

12. They told the truth, which pleased him.
    Dijeron la verdad, _____ le gustó.

    A. la que   B. cual   C. la cual   D. lo que

13. I am glad she could go.
    Me alegro de que ella _____ ir.

    A. pueda   B. podría   C. pudiera   D. podía

14. Did you buy a chair that was comfortable?
    ¿Compró Vd. una silla que _____ cómoda?

    A. era   B. estaba   C. fuera   D. estuviera

15. He continued to read.
    El siguió _____.

    A. leyendo   B. leer   C. a leer   D. el leer

16. Marys son, who writes well, has arrived.
    El hijo de María, _____ escribe bien, ha llegado.

    A. el que   B. lo cual   C. quien   D. el cual

17. She did it herself.
    Ello lo hizo _____.

    A. su misma   B. misma   C. sí misma   D. ella misma

18. He promised to eat after they went away.
    Prometió comer después de que ellos _____.

    A. se irían   B. se vayan   C. se iban   D. se fuesen

19. Anyone can do it.
    _____ puede hacerlo.

    A. Alguno   B. Cualquiera
    C. Cualquier   D. Alguien

20. ¿Will there be many doctors there?
    _____ muchos médicos allí?

    A. Habrá   B. Hará   C. Harán   D. Estarán

21. The door was open.
    La puerta _____.

    A. estaba abriendo   B. fue abierta
    C. estaba abierta   D. se abrió

22. When I was a child, I would often cry.
    Cuando era niño a menudo _____.

    A. habría llorado   B. lloraría
    C. lloraba   D. llovería

23. It seems incredible, but it is not.
    Parece increíble, pero no _____.

    A. es   B. está asi   C. lo está   D. lo es

24. He took his hat with him.
    _____ el sombrero.

    A. Se quitó   B. Se tomó
    C. Se llevó   D. Tomó con él

25. He ate more than he brought.
    Comió más _____ trajo.

    A. que   B. como   C. de lo que   D. del cual

26. He gave more presents than he received.
    Dio más regalos _____ recibió.

    A. de los que   B. de que
    C. de lo que   D. que

27. He came before the king.
    Vino _____ el rey.

    A. antes   B. delante   C. enfrente   D. ante

28. It is made by hand.
    Está hecho _____ mano.

    A. en   B. a   C. por   D. para

29. He looks for the book.
    _____ el libro.

A. Busca por		B. Busco para	
C. Busca		D. Mira por	

30. She thinks they should not do it.
    Ella cree que no _____.

    A. lo harían   B. deben hacerlo
    C. lo hagan   D. deban hacerlo

31. He entered without looking at me.
    Entró sin _____.

    A. mirándome   B. buscándome
    C. mirarme   D. verme

32. He lacks the time.
    _____ hace falta el tiempo.

    A. Él   B. Le   C. Lo   D. Se

33. The man whose leg they amputated yesterday is doing well this morning.
    El hombre _____ amputaron ayer la pierna sigue bien esta mañana.

    A. de quien   B. a quien   C. que   D. cuya

34. We do not know how to help them.
    No sabemos _____ ayudarles.

    A. --   B. como   C. a   D. que

35. As soon as I had seen him, I left.
    Luego que le_____, salí.

    A. hubiese visto   B. ví
    C. había visto   D. hube visto

36. He succeeded in finishing the work.
    _____ terminar el trabajo.

    A. Sucedió en   B. Sucedió
    C. Logró en   D. Logro

37. They have four exercises to write.
    Tienen cuatro ejercicios _____.

    A. para escribir   B. por escribir
    C. de escribir   D. escribir

38. They agreed to do it.
    Acordaron _____ hacerlo.

    A. en   B. —   C. de   D. a

39. Don't listen to him. Do it.
    No le escuchéis _____.

    A. Hazlo   B. Hágalo   C. Hacedlo   D. Háganlo

40. I doubt that she cooks well. 40.____
    Dudo que ella _____ bien.

    A. coce   B. cueza   C. cuezca   D. coza

Questions 41-60.

DIRECTIONS: Below is a list of key words, in Spanish, each of which is followed by four other Spanish words, one of which is an antonym of the key word. Select the antonym.

41. acertar 41.____

    A. asegurar   B. temer   C. mentir   D. errar

42. alboroto 42.____

    A. noche   B. silencio   C. tristeza   D. costoso

43. apego 43.____

    A. antipatía   B. cariño
    C. pálido   D. fresco

44. corpulento 44.____

    A. estrecho   B. fino   C. flaco   D. aprisa

45. desgracia 45.____

    A. felicidad   B. orgullo   C. gratitud   D. bondad

46. despejado 46.____

    A. anublado   B. pegajoso   C. sencillo   D. enfadado

47. destapar 47.____

    A. levantar   B. odiar   C. curar   D. cubrir

48. desvelado 48.____

    A. descubierto   B. dudoso
    C. claro   D. soñoliento

49. estirar 49.____

    A. encoger   B. introducir
    C. aceptar   D. echar

50. gastar 50.____

    A. ahorcar   B. ahorrar   C. horadar   D. odiar

51. grosero 51.____

    A. delgado   B. bonito   C. corto   D. cortés

52. lluvia 52.____

    A. séquito   B. sequía   C. nieve   D. lodo

53. macho 53.____

    A. duro   B. vieja   C. hembra   D. poco

54. medroso 54.____

    A. entero   B. valiente   C. válido   D. lleno

55. ocioso 55.____

    A. hostil   B. trabajador
    C. precoz   D. infantil

56. prisa 56.____

    A. espesura   B. espacio   C. lenteja   D. lentitud

57. risueño 57.____

    A. sombrío   B. asombro
    C. despierto   D. silencioso

58. soberbio 58.____

    A. humilde   B. ciudad   C. inferior   D. frío

59. tacaño 59.____

    A. pequeño   B. útil   C. generoso   D. siglo

60. torpe 60.____

    A. hábil   B. adelante   C. abajo   D. triste

Questions 61-80.

DIRECTIONS: Below is a list of key words, in Spanish, each of which is followed by four other Spanish words, one of which is a synonym of the key word. Select the synonym.

61. agasajar 61.____

    A. mantener   B. aguantar   C. renovar   D. festejar

62. ajado 62.____

    A. animado   B. marchito   C. renovado   D. perspicaz

63. apesadumbrado 63.____

    A. deshonrado   B. ligero
    C. afligido   D. denso

64. convenio 64.____

    A. cita   B. fecha   C. contrato   D. comodidad

65. desamparado

    A. afligido
    B. abandonado
    C. inhibido
    D. destripado

66. disimular

    A. fingir   B. aseverar   C. insistir   D. precaver

67. embrollo

    A. sombra
    B. enredo
    C. casualidad
    D. accidente

68. enlace

    A. adorno
    B. encaje
    C. matrimonio
    D. cinta

69. escudrinar

    A. examinar   B. entirpar   C. endosar   D. presumir

70. fastidioso

    A. elegante
    B. molesto
    C. minucioso
    D. remilgado

71. fementido

    A. descompuesto
    B. fracasado
    C. falso
    D. inútil

72. fenecer

    A. ventilar   B. fallecer   C. explorar   D. dimitir

73. galardón

    A. premio   B. elegancia   C. orgullo   D. cortesía

74. garrulidad

    A. desenfado
    B. impaciencia
    C. revoltijo
    D. locuacidad

75. juicioso

    A. enjuto   B. discreto   C. acuoso   D. mojado

76. letal

    A. mortífero   B. lechoso   C. blanco   D. duro

77. opulento

    A. desastroso
    B. inadvertido
    C. malhumorado
    D. lujoso

78. palpar

    A. cosechar B. murmurar
    C. advertir D. tocar

79. patán

    A. zapatero B. apuntador
    C. rústico D. comerciante

80. pusilánime

    A. cobarde B. vanidoso
    C. paciente D. agresivo

Questions 81-90.

DIRECTIONS: Below is a list of key words in Spanish, each of which is followed by four other Spanish words, one of which is related in derivation to the key words. Select the related word.

81. alquilar

    A. inquilino B. quilate
    C. aguileno D. equilibrio

82. dedal

    A. desdorar B. delantal
    C. prestidigitador D. dedicar

83. garganta

    A. sargento B. garantía
    C. guante D. ingurgitar

84. herrero

    A. descarrilarse B. ferrocarril
    C. guardar D. ahorro

85. lumbre

    A. alambre B. iluminar C. columpio D. lámina

86. malsano

    A. gusano B. salvavidas
    C. salubre D. sandía

87. medida

    A. agrimensor B. meditabundo
    C. immediato D. merecido

88. piedra

    A. padrastro B. pedestre
    C. pedigüeño D. petrificado

89. sembrar

   A. sempiterno B. inseminar
   C. semenal   D. símbolo

90. solar

   A. solo   B. soledad   C. suelo   D. consolación

Questions 91-130.

DIRECTIONS: Below is a list of Spanish words, each of which is followed by four English words, one of which is a correct translation of the Spanish word. Select the CORRECT translation.

91. acequia

   A. present   B. obsequiousness
   C. ditch   D. acceptance

92. ademán

   A. request   B. gesture
   C. moreover   D. command

93. alborozo

   A. agitation   B. dawn   C. joy   D. peach

94. añejo

   A. musty   B. seasonal
   C. yearly   D. supplement

95. arrasar

   A. demolish   B. sprinkle   C. drag   D. plant

96. balbucear

   A. enjoy   B. dive   C. stammer   D. balance

97. bandolero

   A. broker   B. tray   C. conductor   D. bandit

98. barranco

   A. leap   B. ravine   C. cheap   D. raucous

99. biombo

   A. swelling   B. screen   C. candy   D. drum

100. botín

   A. booty   B. jug   C. button   D. scraps

101. congoja

   A. crab   B. meeting   C. leak   D. anxiety

102. contratiempo

    A. raincoat
    B. alarm clock
    C. disappointment
    D. umbrella

103. corteza

    A. piece
    B. penknife
    C. gash
    D. bark

104. cuchichear

    A. knife
    B. cut
    C. whisper
    D. hide

105. delatar

    A. delay
    B. accuse
    C. beat
    D. delete

106. derribar

    A. leave
    B. overtake
    C. disembark
    D. throw down

107. desavenencia

    A. loss
    B. disagreement
    C. disparagement
    D. without a future

108. descartar

    A. deal
    B. correspond
    C. reject
    D. mail

109. desfallecer

    A. nightfall
    B. faint
    C. disappoint
    D. disown

110. despedir

    A. depart
    B. take leave of
    C. dismiss
    D. implore

111. desván

    A. scorn
    B. faint
    C. disappearance
    D. attic

112. enredadera

    A. quarrel
    B. vine
    C. untrue
    D. complicated

113. entremetido

    A. meddler
    B. prisoner
    C. jailer
    D. secluded one

114. estornudo

    A. thunderous
    B. stubborn
    C. screw
    D. sneeze

115. faena

   A. flour   B. peacock   C. bonfire   D. task

116. fango

   A. tusk   B. dance   C. mire   D. mercy

117. farol

   A. shoe polish   B. bean
   C. frivolous   D. street light

118. flecha

   A. flicker   B. arrow   C. eyelash   D. mud

119. gatear

   A. act coy   B. spend   C. creep   D. spoil

120. granizo

   A. hail   B. farmland
   C. red   D. prize

121. hinchado

   A. curved   B. crowded   C swollen   D. sunk

122. lustro

   A. five years   B. polish
   C. fame   D. gloomy

123. luto

   A. flute   B. mourning   C. can   D. soiled

124. manojo

   A. bunch   B. handle   C. order   D. anger

125. postizo

   A. comb   B. nincompoop
   C. false   D. hairpin

126. servicial

   A. official   B. servants   C. obliging   D. useful

127. surco

   A. surcharge   B. furrow   C. match   D. search

128. surtido

   A. assortment   B. sordid
   C. ill-fated   D. deaf

129. vistazo 129.____

    A. showy   B. glance
    C. view   D. overdressed

130. zarza 130.____

    A. bramble   B. musical comedy
    C. anchor   D. good-looking

Questions 131-140.

DIRECTIONS: Below is a series of Spanish phrases translated into English. The correct translation will be found among the four choices given in each item. Select the CORRECT translation.

131. desempeñar un papel 131.____

    A. to open a package   B. to order a newspaper
    C. to unroll a paper   D. to play a role

132. echar de ver 132.____

    A. to have just seen   B. to notice
    C. to ignore   D. to cast from sight

133. empeñarse en 133.____

    A. to strike against   B. to regret
    C. to insist on   D. to realize

134. estar en huelga 134.____

    A. to be on strike   B. to be in trouble
    C. to be in good spirits   D. to be on vacation

135. hacer cola 135.____

    A. to make glue   B. to stand in line
    C. to cook cabbage   D. to pout

136. llevarse bien 136.____

    A. to bear up   B. to get along well
    C. to walk well   D. to go straight

137. saber a 137.____

    A. to taste like   B. to resemble
    C. to understand   D. to be expert in

138. sacar a luz 138.____

    A. to give birth
    B. to wear for the first time
    C. to light up
    D. to publish

139. tener en cuenta

- A. to bear in mind
- B. to bear a grudge
- C. to keep account books
- D. to relate

140. tomar la palabra

- A. to swear
- B. to interrupt
- C. to take the floor
- D. to take someones word for

Questions 141-150.

DIRECTIONS: Below is a series of English phrases translated into Spanish. The correct translation will be found among the four choices in each item. Select the CORRECT translation.

141. to break ones promise

- A. quebrar su palabra
- B. faltar a su palabra
- C. romper su promesa
- D. quebrar su promesa

142. Ill get even with him

- A. me las pagará
- B. me las pagaré
- C. me pagará
- D. me lo pagará

143. to go out of style

- A. envejecer
- B. pasar de moda
- C. salir de estilo
- D. pasar de manera

144. to have to do with

- A. tener que hacer con
- B. haber de ver con
- C. tener que ver con
- D. tenérselas con

145. to hit the mark

- A. dar en el blanco
- B. herir el blanco
- C. dar en el marco
- D. herir al marco

146. to miss the train

- A. echar de menos el tren
- B. faltar el tren
- C. no encontrar el tren
- D. perder el tren

147. to put on airs

- A. ponerse aires
- B. hacerse aires
- C. darse tono
- D. dase orgullo

148. say what he will

- A. que diga lo que dirá
- B. diga lo que diga
- C. diga lo que dirá
- D. que diga lo que pueda

149. to spoil

    A. echar a dañar
    B. hacer dañar
    C. hacer perder
    D. echar a perder

150. to wind a clock

    A. torcer el reloj
    B. darle cuerda al reloj
    C. torcerle al reloj
    D. dar el reloj una cuerda

151. Un pintor español del siglo XVIII fue

    A. Velázquez   B. Goya   C. Murillo   D. Picasso

152. No figura en DON QUIJOTE

    A. Ginés de Pasamente
    B. Dorotea
    C. Pedro Crespo
    D. Maritornes

153. EL ESTUDIANTE DE SALAMANCA es una obra de

    A. Zorrilla
    B. Unamuno
    C. Bécquer
    D. Espronceda

154. No es obra de Cervantes

    A. EL LICENCIADO VIDRIERA
    B. LA CALATEA
    C. EL BUSCÓ
    D. RINCONETE Y CORTADILLO

155. Carlos V fue el padre de

    A. Felipe II
    B. Juana la Loca
    C. Isabel la Católica
    D. Alfonso XII

156. No escribió de la pampa argentina

    A. José Hernández
    B. José Rubén Romero
    C. Sarmiento
    D. Güiraldes

157. La primera obra importante de Rubén Darío fue

    A. CANTOS DE VIDA Y ESPERANZA
    B. EL CANTO ERRANTE
    C. AZUL
    D. PROSAS PROFANAS

158. LOS DE ABAJO es una obra de

    A. Azuela   B. Guzmán   C. Rivera   D. Gallegos

159. No limita con el Brasil

    A. Argentina   B. Colombia   C. el Perú   D. el Ecuador

160. Rosas, Solano, López, García Moreno y Juan Vicente Gómez fueron

    A. dictadores sudamericanos
    B. escritores españoles

C. personajes de *Don Segundo sombra*
D. presidentes de la Argentina

161. Ciro Alegría es

    A. el autor de DOÑA BÁRBARA
    B. actual presidente de Chile
    C. delegado panameño a las Naciones Unidas
    D. novelista peruano

162. Ricardo Palma escribió

    A. SÓNGORO COSONGO
    B. TRADICIONES PERUNAS
    C. BARRANCA ABAJO
    D. CUENTOS DE LA PAMPA

163. Se llama *porteño* a un habitante de

    A. Rio de Janeiro
    B. Caracas
    C. Buenos Aires
    D. Lima

164. Se asocia con *los descamisados* el nombre de

    A. Trujillo   B. Bolívar   C. Perón   D. Batista

165. No es un baile

    A. el fandango
    B. el pericón
    C. el jarabe
    D. la zafra

166. Lope de Vega escribió

    A. EL MÉDICO DE SU HONRA
    B. DEL REY ABAJO, NINGUNO
    C. LA DAMA BOBA
    D. LAS PAREDES OYEN

167. Cuando los españoles llegaron al Nuevo Mundo no encontraron

    A. caballos   B. tabaco   C. patatas   D. cacao

168. Una novela romántica de Hispanoamérica es

    A. EL INGLÉS DE LOS GÜESOS
    B. LA MAESTRA RURAL
    C. MARÍA
    D. LA SERPIENTE DE ORO

169. Un pícaro famoso de la literatura española es

    A. Santos Vega
    B. Guzmán de Alfarache
    C. Juan Moreira
    D. Palacio Valdés

170. ES EL PROTAGONISTA DE LAS SONATAS de Valle Inclan

    A. Juan de Manara
    B. Elizabide el vagabundo
    C. Pablos de Segovia
    D. El Marqués de Bradomln

171. Un español famoso recientemente fallecido es

    A. Antonio Machado
    B. Ortega y Gasset
    C. Eduardo Marquina
    D. Pío Baroja

172. Antiguamente los mayas vivieron

    A. en Yucatán
    B. en los Andes
    C. a orillas del rio Marañen
    D. en las selvas de Brasil

173. Un historiador importante fue

    A. Benito Juárez   B. Bernal Díaz del Castillo
    C. Cipriano Castro   D. Alvaro Obregón

174. No está en Andalucía

    A. Cádiz   B. Córdoba
    C. Jerez de la Frontera   D. Valladolid

175. Fedrico García Lorca escribió

    A. ROMANCERO GITANO   B. ZALACAÍN EL AVENTURERO
    C. FLOR DE SANTIDAD   D. ABEL SÁNCHEZ

176. Una poetisa romántica fue

    A. Sor Juana Inés de la Cruz
    B. Delmira Agustini
    C. Gertrudis Gómez de Avellaneda
    D. Emilia Pardo Bazán

177. No pertenece a *la generación del 98*

    A. Pereda   B. Azorín   C. Baroja   D. Unamuno

178. No fué autor romántico

    A. El Duque de Rivas   B. Hartzenbusch
    C. Espronceda   D. Quevedo

179. Terminó la guerra civil de España con el triunfo de Franco en

    A. 1931   B. 1936   C. 1939   D. 1945

180. Los españoles lucharon con los araucanos en lo que es hoy

    A. Chile   B. Argentina   C. Méjico   D. Colombia

181. No escribió obras de inspiración hispánica

    A. Washington Irving   B. Prescott
    C. Hemingway   D. Faulkner

182. La ciudad *mora y gitana* de España es

    A. Barcelona   B. Granada   C. Cuenca   D. Segovia

183. Es novelista de la ciudad

    A. Pereda   B. Pedro Antonio de Alarcón
    C. Fernán Caballero   D. Galdos

184. Los complutenses son de 184.____

　　A. Santiago de Compostela　　B. Alcalá de Henares
　　C. Colombia　　　　　　　　　D. La Plata

185. Son de Chile los 185.____

　　A. llaneros　　B. gauchos　　C. vaqueros　　D. huasos

186. El *género chico* ha sido cultivado por 186.____

　　A. los místicos　　　　　　　　B. Quevedo
　　C. los hermanos Quintero　　　D. los afrancesados

187. *La niche triste* se relaciona con 187.____

　　A. Pizarro　　　B. Cabeza de Vaca
　　C. Balboa　　　D. Cortés

188. Se parece al idioma portugués el 188.____

　　A. catalán　　　B. gallego
　　C. castellano　 D. vascuence

189. Una de las universidades más antiguas de España se encuentra en 189.____

　　A. Toledo　　　B. Granada
　　C. Salamanca　 D. Bilbao

190. No es escritora hispanoamericana 190.____

　　A. Teresa de la Parra　　B. Rosalía de Castro
　　C. Juana de Ibarbourou　 D. Alfonsina Storni

191. *La Huerta* se refiere a 191.____

　　A. Andalucía　　　　　　B. una bailarina española
　　C. una actriz famosa　　D. Valencia

192. Don Juan Tenorio figura en 192.____

　　A. un drama nuevo　　　B. EL BURLADOR DE SEVILLA
　　C. EL GRAN GALEOTO　　D. EL CABALLERO DE OLMEDO

193. Fue un patriota mejicano 193.____

　　A. Hidalgo　　　B. Rosas
　　C. OHiggins　　 D. San Martin

194. Al que vuelve a España rico, de América, se le llama 194.____

　　A. criollo　　B. gringo　　C. indiano　　D. ladino

195. Son obras dramáticas los 195.____

　　A. autos sacramentales　　B. gaiteros
　　C. autos de fé　　　　　　D. cuadros de costumbres

196. Las guerras carlistas fueron guerras
    A. religiosas
    B. de independencia
    C. civiles
    D. entre España e Inglaterra

197. Se trata de la vida de los caucheros en
    A. DOÑA BÁRBARA
    B. EL HOMBRE DE HIERRO
    C. EL MUNDO ES ANCHO Y AJENO
    D. LA VORÁGINE

198. Se llama la perla de las Antillas a
    A. Cuba
    B. Puerto Rico
    C. Haití
    D. Santo Domingo

199. No hay elemento realista en
    A. LA CELESTINA
    B. AMADÍS DE GAULA
    C. LOS PAZOS DE ULLOA
    D. LA BARRACA

200. Está escrita en forma epistolar parte de
    A. LA RANA VIAJERA
    B. PEPITA JIMÉNEZ
    C. EL SOMBRERO DE TRES PICOS
    D. PLATERO Y YO

KEY (CORRECT ANSWERS)

1. C	41. D	81. A	121. C	161. D
2. A	42. B	82. C	122. A	162. B
3. D	43. A	83. D	123. B	163. C
4. B	44. C	84. B	124. A	164. C
5. D	45. A	85. B	125. C	165. D
6. B	46. A	86. C	126. C	166. C
7. C	47. D	87. A	127. B	167. A
8. D	48. D	88. D	128. A	168. C
9. C	49. A	89. B	129. B	169. B
10. B	50. B	90. C	130. A	170. D
11. A	51. D	91. C	131. D	171. B
12. D	52. B	92. B	132. B	172. A
13. C	53. C	93. C	133. C	173. B
14. C	54. B	94. A	134. A	174. D
15. A	55. B	95. A	135. B	175. A
16. D	56. D	96. C	136. B	176. C
17. D	57. A	97. D	137. A	177. A
18. D	58. A	98. B	138. D	178. D
19. B	59. C	99. B	139. A	179. C
20. A	60. A	100. A	140. C	180. A
21. C	61. D	101. D	141. B	181. D
22. C	62. B	102. C	142. A	182. B
23. D	63. C	103. D	143. B	183. D
24. C	64. C	104. C	144. C	184. B
25. C	65. B	105. B	145. A	185. D
26. A	66. A	106. D	146. D	186. C
27. D	67. B	107. B	147. C	187. D
28. B	68. C	108. C	148. B	188. B
29. C	69. A	109. B	149. D	189. C
30. B	70. B	110. C	150. B	190. B
31. C	71. C	111. D	151. B	191. D
32. B	72. B	112. B	152. C	192. B
33. B	73. A	113. A	153. D	193. A
34. A	74. D	114. D	154. C	194. C
35. D	75. B	115. D	155. A	195. A
36. D	76. A	116. C	156. B	196. C
37. B	77. D	117. D	157. C	197. D
38. A	78. D	118. B	158. A	198. A
39. C	79. C	119. C	159. D	199. B
40. B	80. A	120. A	160. A	200. B

BASIC FUNDAMENTALS OF SPOKEN SPANISH

CONTENTS

GRAMMATICAL INTRODUCTION

			Page
I.	Sounds and Spelling		1
	0.1	Vowels	1
	0.2	Consonants	1
	0.3	Syllables	3
	0.4	Stress	3
II.	Forms		3
	1.1	Nouns and Adjectives	4
	1.2	Pronouns	4
	1.3	Prepositions and Conjunctions	7
	1.4	Adverbs	8
	1.5	Diminutives and Augmentatives	9
	1.6	Absolute Superlative	9
	1.7	Verbs	9
	1.8	Special Uses of Some Important Verbs	15
III.	Phrase Structure		18
	2.0	Universal Phrase Types	18
	2.1	Noun Phrases	18
	2.2	Adjective Phrases	19
	2.3	Pronoun Phrases	19
	2.4	Verb Phrases	19
	2.5	Adverb Phrases	21
	2.6	Preposition Phrases	21
	2.7	Conjunction Phrases	21
IV.	Clause Structure		22
	3.0	The Clause	22
	3.1	The Predicate	22
	3.2	The Subject	22
	3.3	Order of Subject and Predicate	22
	3.4	Coordination	22
	3.5	Subordination	23
	3.6	Minor Clauses	24

BASIC FUNDAMENTALS OF SPOKEN SPANISH

GRAMMATICAL INTRODUCTION

I. Sounds and Spelling

Both the sounds and the spelling of Spanish are simple, and will be described together, with the Spanish letters as a starting point.

0.1 Vowels are five in number:

SPELLING	DESCEIPTION	EXAMPLES
i	like English *i* in *machine* or *ee* in *beet*	*fino* "fine"; *mí* "me"
u	like English *oo* in *boot*.	*puro* "pure"; *tú* "you"

These two vowels may occur unstressed before or after a stressed vowel, in which case they are pronounced like English *y* and *w* respectively: *bien* "well"; *bueno* "good"; *automóvil* "automobile".

e	like the *e* of English *they*, if no consonant follows in the same syllable; like *e* in *bed*, if a consonant follows in the same syllable	*pero* "but"; *puesto* "put"
o	like the *o* of English *know*, if no consonant follows in the same syllable; like *au* in *taut*, if a consonant follows in the same syllable	*todo* "all"; *corte* "court"
o	like the *a* of English *father*	*mano* "hand" *parte* "part"

0.2 Consonants are:

p	like English *p*	*Pepe* "Joe"
t	like English *t*, but with tongue against upper teeth instead of güín ridge	*tanto* "so much"
qu	like English *k* or "hard *c*"	*gue* "that"; *carro* "cart"

(before *e, i*),
c (elsewhere)

These three sounds are never pronounced with the puff of breath after them, as the corresponding English sounds often are.

SPELLING	DESCRIPTION	EXAMPLES
b, v	like English *b*	*bebe* "he drinks"
d	like English *d*	*dedo* "finger"
gu (before *e, i*), g (elsewhere)	like English "hard g"	*pague Usted* "(you) pay"; *pagar* "pay"

The above three sounds, when they come between two vowels, are not pronounced with a full closure of lips or tongue (as are English *b, d, g*) but with the breath forcing its way out between the lips, or between the tongue and teeth, or between the tongue and top of the mouth.

m	like English *m*	*mano* "hand"
n	like English *n*, but with the tip of the tongue against the front teeth	*nada* "nothing"
ñ	like *ni* in English *onion*, but a single sound (beginning like *n* and ending like *y*)	*año* "year"
f	like English f	*fuerte* "strong"
c (before *e, i*), z (elsewhere)	like *th* in English *thick*	*cierto* "certain"; *zorra* "fox"; *conozco* "I know"

The above sound is not used by speakers of American Spanish, who replace it by "s".

s	like English s	*seso* "brain"
l	like English *l*, but with the tip of the tongue against the front teeth	*lado* "side"
ll	like *lli* in English *million*, but a single sound beginning like *l* and ending like *y*; in Latín America, generally like English *y*	*llano* "plain"; *milla* "mile"
r	single flap of the tongue against the front teeth, somewhat like our American English *d*	*caro* "dear"
rr	several repeated flaps of the tongue against the front teeth, like the telephone operator's "th-r-r-ee"	*carro* "cart"
y	like English *y*	*reyes* "kings"
g (before *e, i*), j (elsewhere)	like English *h*	*gente* "people"; *junto* "together"

SPELLING	DESCRIPTION	EXAMPLES
h	stands for no sound at all, but is written in a number of words	*haba* "bean"; *hierba* "grass"

0.3 Syllables. A single consonant sound (and, in writing, two letters representing a single sound), or a consonant followed by *l* or *r*, belongs to the same syllable as the vowel following it: *ca-ro, ca-rro, mi-lla*. Other groups of two consonants are broken up, the first consonant belonging with the preceding vowel and the second with the following vowel: *juz-gar* "to judge"; *rec-tor* "rector".

0.4 Stress. Words ending in a vowel or in -*n* or -*s* are normally stressed on the next to the last syllable; words ending in any other consonant are stressed on the last syllable. Words having this type of stress bear no written accent mark: *cosa* "thing"; *cantan* "they sing"; *canias* "yon sing" (Fam); *cantar* "to sing". If a word does not conform to this pattern, an accent mark is written over the vowel letter of the syllable which is stressed: *vamonos* "let's go"; *jar-dín* "garden". In a few cases, a written accent serves only to mark the difference between one word and another written like it but having a different meaning: *¿cuándo?* "when?" (interrogative), but *cuando* "when" (relative).

II. Forms

1.1 Nouns and adjectives are inflected alike, and will be discussed together. A noun is an inflected form that may follow *el/la* and precede a verb; an adjective is a form that may follow *el/la* and' precede a noun. (For the definite article, cf §1.22.)

1.11 The plural of nouns and adjectives is formed in one of three ways:

1. By leaving the singular unchanged (words ending in -*s*, family names, and a few others): *jueves* "Thursday, Thursdays"; *López* "López, Lópezes"; *déficit* "déficit, déficits".

2. By adding -*s* to nouns ending in an unstressed vowel or stressed -*é*: *libro* "book", *libros* "books"; *cara* "face", *caras* "faces"; *café* "coffee", *cafés* "coffees".

3. By adding -*es* to most other nouns: *rubí* "ruby", pl *rubíes; buey* "ox", pl *bueyes; papel* "paper", pl *papeles*. The letter *c* is replaced by *qu,* and *z* by *c*, before -*es: frac* "frock coat", pl *fraques; lápiz* "pencil", pl *lápices*.

1.12 Gender. Nouns belong either to the masculino or the feminine gender; adjectives to both. The feminine of an adjective is formed on the masculine in one of the following three ways:

1. By substituting -a for -o of the masculine: *bueno* m, *buena* f "good".
2. By adding -a to the masculine: *inglés* m, *inglesa* f "English".
3. By leaving the masculine unchanged: *interesante* m, f "interesting"; *fácil* m, f "easy".

1.13 Reduced forms of adjectives. Certain adjectives are used in shortened or **reduced** forms when they stand before a noun they modify, e.g. *un buen libro* "a good book". The following adjectives have reduced forms in the masculine singular only: *buen(o)* "good": *mál(o)* "bad"; *primer(o)* "first"; *tercer(o)* "third", *un(o)* "one" and its compounds. *Santo* "Saint" has the form *San* before a masculina name in the singular: *San Francisco* "St. Francis". *Gran* takes the place of *grande* "great" (but *un gran hombre* is "an important man" while *un hombre grande* is "a large man"), and *cien* takes the place of *ciento* "100", before either masculine or feminine.

1.2 Pronouns are of five classes: personal, demonstrative, interrogative, relative, and indefinite.

1.21 Personal pronouns are of two main types: those which can be used apart from verbs, called **disjunctive** pronouns, and those which can be used only with verbs, called **conjunctive** pronouns.

1. Disjunctive pronouns are:

SINGULAR	PLURAL
NOMINATIVE	
1. *yo* "I"	1. *nosotros* (m), *nosotras* (f) "we"
2. *tú* "you" (Fam)	2. *vosotros* (m), *vosotras* (f) "you" (Fam)
3. *usted* "you"	3. *ustedes* "you"
él "he", *ella* "she"	*ellos* (m), *ellas* (f) "they"
PREPOSITIONAL	
1. *mí* "me"	1. *nosotros* (m), *nosotras* (f) "us"
2. *tí* "you" (Fam)	2. *vosotros* (m), *vosotras* (f) "you" (Fam)
3. *usted* "you"	3. *ustedes* "you"
él "him", *ella* "her"	*ellos* (m), *ellas* (f) "they"
REFLEXIVE PREPOSITIONAL	
sí "himself, herself, itself"	*sí* "themselves"

When the pronouns *mí, ti,* and *sí* (sg) are used as objects of the preposition *con* "with", the following forms result: *conmigo, contigo,* and *consigo.*

The word *usted* (abbreviated *Ud.* or *Vd.*) is used when speaking to persons with whom one is not well acquainted, and takes a verb in the third person singular; the plural *ustedes* (abbreviated *Uds.* or *Vds.*) is used in the same way. In Spanish America, *ustedes* is often used instead of *vosotros,* as the plural corresponding to *tú. Tú* is used only between relatives, young people, intimate friends, and in addressing children, servante, and pets. In South America, especially Argentina, *vos* is generally used for *tú.*

2. Conjunctive pronouns are:

SINGULAR	PLURAL
DIRECT OBJECT	
1. *me* "me"	1. *nos* "us"
2. *te* "you" (Fam)	2. *os* "you" (Fam)
3. *le* "you" (m), "him"	3. *los* "you, them" (m)
la "you." (f), "her", "it" (f)	*las* "you, them" (f)
lo "it"	

REFLEXIVE

se "yourself, himself, herself, itself"   se "yourselves, themselves"

INDIRECT OBJECT

1. *me* "tome"
2. *te* "to you" (Fam)
3. *le* "to you, to him, to her, to it"

1. *nos* "to us"
2. *os* "to you" (Fam)
3. *les* "to you, to them"

These conjunctive pronouns may occur either singly or in groups of two. The occurrence oí groups of two conjunctive pronouns is determined by the following rules:

a¹) If the pronoun *se* is present in the group, it always comes before the other conjunctive pronoun. When se is used in this way, it may have the meaning of:

aa) An unspecified actor: se *dice* "it is said"; se *ía trató bien* "she was treated well".

bb) A third person object, either reflexive or not: *se lo dice* "he says it to ≥iim (her)", or "he (she) says it to himself (herself)".

b¹) If the pronoun *se* is not present, the first pronoun of the group has the meaning of an indirect object, and the second that of a direct object: *me lo da* "he gives it to me". *Le, les* may not occur as the first member of a group of conjunctive pronouns, their place being taken by *se* (see a¹, bb, above). The conjunctive pronouns are placed after the verb they modify, and written together with it, in the following circumstances:

a²) After an infinitive or gerund: *dárselo* "to give it to him"; *diciéndolo* "sayingit".

b²) After other verb fonns, only in literary style or (to save money) in telegrams:/Mtmc "I went away".

With other verb fonns than the infinitive and gerund, the conjunctive pronouns are usually placed before the verb and written as sepárate words: *se lo da* "he gives it to him"; *me fui* "I went away".

1.22 Demonstrative pronouns have three genders: masculine, feminine, and neuter. The neuter occurs only in the singular and is used only to refer to something abstract or already spoken of. The demonstrative pronouns are ésíe "this", *ése* "that" (near you), *aquél* "that" (over there), and the definite article *(el, la, los, las, lo)* with *de* and *que,* meaning respectively "that (those) of", "the one (ones) with (in, on)", "that (those) which", and "the one (ones) which".

The forms of these pronouns are:

sg	m	éste	ése	aquél	el de, el que
	f	ésta	ésa	aquélla	la de, la que
	neu	esto	eso	aquello	lo de, lo que
pl	m	éstos	ésos	aquéllos	los de, los que
	f	éstas	ésas	aquéllas	las de, las que

6

The demonstrative adjectives are the same as the demonstrative pronouns but do not bear a written accent and they usually precede the noun.

Yo escribo con esta pluma.   "I'm writing with this pen."
Esta pluma y ésa.   "This pen and that one."

There is no neuter adjective in Spanish and the neuter demonstrative pronouns *esto, eso, aquello,* and *lo* bear no written accent. They are used to refer to a general idea or obj'ect without a determined gender.

Eso es verdad.   "That (what has been said) is true."
Esto me alarma.   "This (situation, outlook) alarma me."

When used before a noun or noun phrase (cf §2.14.1), *el, la,* etc, have about the meaning of English "the", and in this use are termed the **definite article.** The form *el* is used before a masculine singular noun or noun phrase: *el hombre* "the man", *el gran diccionario* "the great dictionary"; and also directly before a feminine noun beginning with the stressed sound *a: el alma* "the soul", *el hambre* "the hunger". Before other feminines, *la* is used: *la persona* "the person", *la otra persona* "the other person". In the plural, *los* is used before masculine and Zas before feminine nouns or noun phrases: ios *hombres* "the men", ios *grandes diccionarios* "the great dictionaries", Zas aZmas "the souls", Zas oirás *personas* "the other persons".

1.23 Interrogative pronouns are: ¿quét "what?", ¿quién? "who?", ¿quiénes? (pl), ¿de quién? "whose?", ¿de quiénes? (pl), ¿cuál? "which one?", ¿cuáles? "which ones?", ¿cuánto? "how much?", ¿cuántos? "how many?".

All interrogative adjectives and pronouns bear a written accent mark to distinguish them from the corresponding relative.

qué is not inflected. ¿de quién? is always followed immediately by *ser:* ¿De quién es este libro? "Whose book is this?"

When translating from English into Spanish, the interrogative ¿de quién? should not be confused with the possessive relative *cuyo* "whose, of which". "This book, whose influence has been so beneficial." *Ese libro, cuya influencia ha sido tan beneficiosa.* But "Whose book is this?" ¿De quién es este libro?

1.24 Relative pronouns are: *que* "that, which, who", *quien, quienes* "who, whom", *el que* "he who, the one who, the one which, that which", Za *que* "she who, the one who, the one which, that which", Zo *que* "that which, what", ios *que* "those who, those which", Zas *que* "those who, those which", *el cual, la cual* "he who (she who), the one who, that which", Zos *cuales, las cuales* "they who, the ones who, those which", lo cual "that, which, what", *cuanto* "all that, as. much as", *cuantos* "all that, as many as".

A simple relative (1, below) has an antecedent in the main clause and the compound relative (2, below) contains its own antecedent. This distinction concerns the use and not the form.

(1)   *El libro que está sobre la mesa es suyo.*   "The book which is on the table is yours."

(2)   *Quien trabaja mejor es María.*   "The one who works best is Mary."

lo que is used when reference is made to a phrase, a sentence, or to a specific thing without & specific gender: *Lo que Ud. pide es imposible.* "What (That which) you ask is impossible."
lo cual is used in supplementary clauses when the antecedent is a clause, a phrase, or an idea: *Se negó a recibirme, lo cual lamento mucho.* "He refused to receive me, which I regret very much."

1.25 Indefinite pronouns are: *alguien* "someone", *alguno, -a, -os, -as* "some-body, some", *algo* "something", *nadie* "no one", *ninguno, -a, -os, -as* "nobody, none", *nada* "nothing", *cualquiera* "whichever", and *quienquiera* "whoever"'

1.26 Possessive adjectives are:

	SINGULAR		PLURAL
1.	*mi, mis* "my"	1.	*nuestro, -a(s)* "our"
2.	*tu, tus* "your" (Fam)	2.	*vuestro, -a(s)* "your" (Fam)
3.	*su, sus* "his, her, its, your"	3.	*su, sus* "their"
1.	*mío, -ía, - íos, -ías* "mine"	1.	*nuestro, -a, -os, -as* "ours"
2.	*tuyo, -a, -os, -as* "yours" (Fam)	2.	*vuestro, -a, -os, -as* "yours". (Fam)
3.	*suyo, -a, -os, -as* "yours, his, hers, its"	3.	*suyo, -a, -os, -as* "theire"

Possessives agree in gender and number with the thing possessed. Possessive pronouns are formed by adding *el* to *mío, tuyo, suyo, nuestro,* and *vuestro*. *El suyo* is usually replaced (to avoid ambiguity) by *el de él, el de ella, el de ustedes, el de ellos: Mi libro, el suyo y el de él.* "My book, yours, and his." *El* is omitted after the verb *ser: El libro es mío.* "The book's mine."

The English possessive case ("-'s") is rendered by *de* and possessor noun or pronoun: *Ese es el libro de mi amigo.* "This is my friend's book."

1.3 Prepositions and conjunctiona: a, *de, en, por,* and *para* are the most frequently used prepositions in Spanish.

1. a "to" implies motion, in contrast with *en,* which corresponds to English "in" or "at" (place where or statel. Bear this distinction in mind in translating English "at"

> *Voy a Valencia.* "I'm going to Valencia."
> *Estoy en casa.* "I'm at home."

a) *a* is used as a sign of personal object, and as such is not translated into English:

Yo amo a María. "I love Mary."
María enseña a su hija. "Mary teaches her daughter."

It is also used with the infinitive after verbs of motion (see §2.44.3)
  b) *al (a+el)* followed by the infinitive corresponds to English "on" and "when": *al partir* "on leaving"

2. *de "of,* from" is replaced by *que* "that" and *estar* "be" when the position of a noun is purely accidental and not permanent or customary: *la casa de enfrente* "the house across the street", *el hombre que está delante de la casa* "the man who is in front of the house".

3. *por* points to the cause, motive, or reason for an action and corresponds to the English "through" (along, around), "by" (expressing agency, means, manner, unit of measure) and "for" (meaning "on account of", "because of", "in exchange for", "during", "as").

4. *para* points to the end or objective of an action and corresponds to the English "for" denoting purpose or destination.

5. *por* and *para* are frequently misused by foreign students of Spanish. English "for" is transldted in each case into Spanish according to its specific meaning:

"This.present's for you."   *Este regalo es PARA Ud.*
"Do it for me."   *Hágalo POR mi.*

1.31 Coordínate conjunctions are: *y* "and", *o* "or", *ni* "nor", *pero* "but" (nevertheless), and *sino* "but" (on the contrary).

1. *y* "and" is replaced by *e* when the word immediately following begins with *i* or *hi*: *franceses e italianos* "Frenchmen and Italiana"; *padre e hijo* "father and son".

2. *o* "or" is replaced by *u* before *o* or *ho*: *siete u ocho* "seven or eight"; *mujer u hombre* "woman or man".

1.32 Subordínate conjunctions are: *que* "that", *como* "as, since" (causal), *cuando* "when", *mientras* "while", *pues(que)* "for, since", *porque* "because", and *sí* "if, whether",

1. *que,* the most widely used subordinate conjunction, introduces noun clauses. In addition to its conjunctive uses, *que* is also a relative pronoun. (§1.24) or a comparative adverb ("than"). Unlike Spaniah, "that" is very often omitted in English:

Quiero que venga.   "I want him to come."
Creo que se ha ido.   "I think he's gone."
Me parece que sí.   "I think so."

2. *si* "if, whether" is used to introduce adverb clauses of condition.

3. *sí* "yes" bears a written accent to differentiate it from the conjunction *si,* and is an adverb of affirrnation: *Le pregunté si iba y me dijo que sí.* "I asked him if he was going and he said yes."

1.4 Adverbs of manner may be formed by adding *-mente* (which is the equiva-lent of English "-ly") to the feminine singular of the adjective: *lento, -a* "slow"; *lentamente* "slow, slowly".

Prepositional phrases are preferable in Spanish to the adverbs ending in *-mente*: *con lentitud* or *de una manera lenta* instead of *lentamente.*

1.41 Adverbs are placed as near as possible to the verb they modify: *Habla "bien él español.* "He speaks Spanish well."

1.42 *aquí* "here", *ahí, allí* "there", *allá* "over there" correspond respectively to the demonstratives *este, ese,* and *aquel.*

1.43 *no* "not" corresponds to English "do not", "is not", etc, and the adjective "no".

1. *no* is placed before the verb: *No oigo.* "I don't hear."

2. If another negative is used after the verb, *no* must always precede: *No oigo nada.* "I hear nothing."

3. When another negative word precedes the verb, *no* is omitted: *Nada oigo.* "I hear nothing."

1.44 When no verb is present, *no* usually follows pronouns and adverbs: *todos no* "not all of them"; *todavía no* "not yet". *sí* is similarly used.

1.45 In a negative sentence all forms are negative (§1.43).

1.5 Diminutives and augmentad ves: The suffixes *-ito, -illo, -cito, -cilio* added to nouns, adjectives, or adverbs imply small size or affectionate interest: *Pedrito* "little Peter", *chiquillo* "kid", *mujercita* "little woman, dear little wife", *pequeñito* "very small, tiny", *piececito* "tiny little foot".

1.51 The more frequent augmentative suffixes are *-ón, -ote, -azo, -acho,* which give the idea of large size or cornic effect: *mujerona* "large woman, awkward woman", *grandote* "very large", *manazo,* "huge hand", *ricacho* "rich person".

1.6 The absolute superlative cnding is regularly -istmo, corresponding to English "most, very, highly, exceedingly": *Es un hombre rarísimo.* "He's a most peculiar man." *Una mujer simpatiquísima.* "A most charming woman."

1.61 There are a number of other ways of expressing a high degree of quality in Spanish (see §§2.21, 2.5). The same idea expressed by the suffix *-ísimo* may be conveyed by *muy* "very" or *sumamente* "exceedingly, a most", with the exception of *muchísimo* (never *muy mucho*), regular form for "very much."

1.62 When *-ísimo* is added, adjectives and adverbs ending in *-co* or *-ca, -z, -go,* and *-oble* change their ending to *-qui, -c, -gui,* and *-bil* respectively: *cerca, cerquísimo; feroz, ferocísimo; largo, larguísimo; amable, amabilísimo.*

1.7 Verbs have ten tenses, or sets of **finite forms** which show the person and number of the actor; and three **non-finite forms,** or forms which do not show person and number. The non-finite forms are: infinitive, gerund, and past participle. The ten tenses are formed on three stems, the "present" stem, the "future" stem, and the "preterite" stem, as follows:

PRESENT STEM	FUTURE STEM	PRETERITE STEM
Present Indicative	Future	Preterite
Imperfect	Conditional	Past Subjunctive, *-se* form
Present Subjunctive		Past Subjunctive, *-ra* form
Imperative		

1.71. There are four classesof verbs, according to the ending of the infinitive:,.

    I. *-ar: cantar* "sing"   III. *-ir: vivir* "live"
    II. *-er: aprender* "learn"   IV. *-r: ver* "see""

In the following paragraphs, we shall give examples of the normal forms of these four conjugations, as shown in the four model verbs listed above.

---

* This manual lists as "Class IV verbs" certain verbs usually designated elsewhere as simply "irregular verbs." For irregular verbs of all classes see page 12.

1. Present tense. The present tense is generally used to refer to the present but it is often used as a graphic substitute for other tenses, as: a) emphatic future: *Mañana le escribo.* "I'll write him tomorrow." b) when immediate future time is involved: *¿Vamos ahora?* "Shall we go now?" c) for the perfect conditional in contrary-to-fact conditions: *Si dice algo en aquel . momento, le pego.* "I'd have hit him if he'd said something at that moment." d) for the simple past in historical narrative: *Por poco le cojo.* "I almost caught him." The forms of the present are:

1. sg	"I"	canto	aprendo	vivo	veo
2. sg	"you" (Fam)	cantas	aprendes	vives	ves
3. sg	"you, he, she, it"	canta	aprende	vive	ve
1. pl	"We"	cantamos	aprendemos	vivimos	vemos
2. pl	"you" (Fam)	cantáis	aprendéis	vivís	veis
3. pl	"you, they"	cantan	aprenden	viven	ven

2. Imperfect tense. This tense refers to past action that was going on at the same time as some other action ("I was singing") or that was habitual ("I used to sing")

1. sg	cantaba	aprendía	vivía	veía
2. sg	cantabas	aprendías	vivías	veías
3. sg	cantaba	aprendía	vivía	veía
1. pl	cantábamos	aprendíamos	vivíamos	veíamos
2. pl	cantabais	aprendíais	vivíais	veíais
3. pl	cantaban	aprendían	vivían	veían

3. Present subjunctive. This tense is used either to express a command (in the first person plural, or third person singular or plural) or in certain types of dependent clauses (see §§3.5-3.52).

1. sg	cante	aprenda	viva	vea
2. sg	cantes	aprendas	vivas	veas
3. sg	cante	aprenda	viva	vea
1. pl	cantemos	aprendamos.	vivamos	veamos
2. pl	cantéis	aprendáis	viváis	veáis
3. pl	canten	aprendan	vivan	vean

4. Imperative. This tense is used to give commands; it has only the second person singular and plural forms.

| 2. sg | canta | aprende | vive | ve |
| 2. pl- | cantad | aprended | vivid | ved |

5. Future. This tense refers to action in future time ("I'll sing") or probability.

1. sg	cantaré	aprenderé	viviré	veré
2. sg	cantarás	aprenderás	vivirás	verás
3. sg	cantará	aprenderá	vivirá	verá
1. pl	cantaremos	aprenderemos	viviremos	veremos
2. pl	cantaréis	aprenderéis	viviréis	veréis
3. pl	cantarán	aprenderán	vivirán	verán

6. Conditional. This tense refers to hypothetical action or to future action viewed from past time ("I'd sing").

1. sg	*cantaría*	*aprendería*	*viviría*	*vería*
2. sg	*cantarías*	*aprenderías*	*vivirías*	*verías*
3. sg	*cantaría*	*aprendería*	*viviría*	*vería*
1. pl	*cantaríamos*	*aprenderíamos*	*viviríamos*	*veríamos*
2. pl	*cantaríais*	*aprenderíais*	*viviríais*	*veríais*
3. pl	*cantarían*	*aprenderían*	*vivirían*	*verían*

7. Past absolute. This tense refers to action at a specific point in past time ("I sang"). The past absolute of most verbs is as follows:

1. sg	*canté*	*aprendí*	*viví*	*vi*
2. sg	*cantaste*	*aprendiste*	*viviste*	*viste*
3. sg	*cantó*	*apprendió*	*vivió*	*vio*
1. pl	*cantamos*	*aprendimos*	*vivimos*	*vimos*
2. pl	*cantasteis*	*aprendisteis*	*vivisteis*	*visteis*
3. pl	*cantaron*	*aprendieron*	*vivieron*	*vieron*

Certain irregular verbs, called "strong" verbs, have special changes in the stem for the past absolute and the two past subjunctive tenses, e.g.: *venir* "to come"; *vine* "I came"; and *viniera, viniese* "(that) I might come". The past absolute of these strong verbs is inflected as follows:

	SINGULAR	PLURAL
1.	*vine*	*vinimos*
2.	*viniste*	*vinisteis*
3.	*vino*	*vinieron*

8. Past subjunctive. Each Spanish verb has two forms of the past subjunctive, one ending in the singular in *-se* and the other in *-ra*. The forms of these tenses are always built on the same stem as the past absolute or preterite tense:

a) Past subjunctive in *-se:*

1. sg	*cantase*	*aprendiese*	*viviese*	*viese*
2. sg	*cantases*	*aprendieses*	*vivieses*	*vieses*
3. sg	*cantase*	*aprendiese*	*viviese*	*viese*
1. pl	*cantásemos*	*aprendiésemos*	*viviésemos*	*viésemos*
2. pl	*cantaseis*	*aprendieseis*	*vivieseis*	*vieseis*
3. pl	*cantasen*	*aprendiesen*	*viviesen*	*viesen*

b) Past subjunctive in *-ra:*

1. sg	*cantara*	*aprendiera*	*viviera*	*viera*
2. sg	*cantaras*	*aprendieras*	*vivieras*	*vieras*
3. sg	*cantara*	*aprendiera*	*viviera*	*viera*

1. pl	cantáramos	aprendiéramos	viviéramos	viéramos
2. pl	cantarais	aprendierais	vivierais	vierais
3. pl	cantaran	aprendieran	vivieran	vieran

1.72 Non-finite forms are such as are based on verbs, but do not show distinction of person and number and belong to other than verbal word classes. Verbs normally have:

1. Gerund—an adverb formed by adding *-ando* to the root of I-conju-gation verbs; *-endo* to roots ending in *-y, -U, -ñ;* and *-iendo* to others: *cantando, aprendiendo, viviendo, viendo; oyendo* "hearing" *(oír* "hear"), *bullendo* "boiling" *(bullir* "boil"), *riñendo* "wrangling" *(reñir* "wrangle").

2. Past participle—an adjective formed by adding *-ado* to the root of I-conjugation verbs, *-ido* to the root of II- and III-conjugation verbs, and *-do* to the root of IV-conjugation verbs. Irregular past participles are all those that have other ~endings than these, as: *abierto* "opened", *cubierto* "covered", *dicho* "said", *escrito* "written", *hecho* "done", *impreso* "printed", *muerto* "dead", *provisto* "provided", *resuelto* "resolved", *roto* "broken", *visto* "seen", *vuelto* "returned".

3. Infinitive—a masculine singular noun ending in *-r.* Occasionally an infinitivo is used in the plural, which then ends in *-es.*

1.73 Irregular, verbs. A number of verbs vary in one way or another from the patterns set forth abo ve. Some of them fall into regular patterns of irregularities:

1. Radical-changing verbs are such as have the regular endings of the conjugation to which they belong, but have certain changes in the vowel of the last syllable of the root, depending on the form involved. There are three main types of radical-changing verbs:

a) Type I, in which a diphthong is substituted for a vowel *(ie* for *e* or *t; ue* for *o* pr *u)* when it is stressed. (At the beginning of a verb, the sounds *ie* are spelled *ye,* and the sounds *ue* are spelled *hue.)* These forms are (with *contar* "count" and *pensar* "think" as examples):

PRESENT	1- sg	cuento	pienso
	2. sg	cuentas	piensas
	3. sg	cuenta	piensa
	3. pl	cuentan	piensan
PRESENT SUBJUNCTIVE	1. sg	cuente	piense
	2. sg	cuentes	pienses
	3. sg	cuente	piense
	3. pl	cuenten	piensen
IMPERATIVE	2. sg	cuenta	piensa

b) Type II, in which *ie* is substituted for *e,* and *ue* for *o,* in all forms where stress falls on this vowel, and *i* is substituted for *e,* and *u* for *o,* wherever the root is unstressed but followed by *a, ie,* or *ió,*

c) Type III, in which *i* is substituted for *e* both in forms where the last syllable of the root is stressed and where the root is unstressed but followed by *a, ie,* or *ió.*

Examples of types II and III are *sentir* "feel", *dormir* "sleep", *pedir* "ask":

PRESENT			
	1. sg *siento*	*duermo*	*pido*
	2. sg *sientes*	*duermes*	*pides*
	3. sg *siente*	*duerme*	*pide*
	3. pl *sienten*	*duermen*	*piden*
PRESENT SUBJUNCTIVE			
	1. sg *sienta*	*duerma*	*pida*
	2. sg *sientas*	*duermas*	*pidas*
	3. sg *sienta*	*duerma*	*pida*
	1. pl *sintamos*	*durmamos*	*pidamos*
	2. pl *sintáis*	*durmáis*	*pidáis*
	3. pl *sientan*	*duerman*	*pidan*
IMPERATIVE	2. sg *siente*	*duerme*	*pide*
PRETERITE			
	3. sg *sintió*	*durmió*	*pidió*
	3. pl *sintieron*	*durmieron*	*pidieron*
PAST SUBJUNCTIVE			
	1, 3. sg *sintiese*	*durmiese*	*pidiese*
	1, 3. sg *sintiera*	*durmiera*	*pidiera*
PRBSENT PARTI CIPLE	*sintiendo*	*durmiendo*	*pidiendo*

2. Roots ending in *-y* lose this *y* wherever it would come before stressed *i*, and unstressed *i* oí an ending is lost after this *y*. Thus, from the root *dis-tribuy-* (III) "distribute" we have: infinitive *distribuir*; present 1. pl *distribuimos*, 2. pl *distribuís*; imperfect *distribuía*, etc; imperative 2. pl *distribuid*; future *distribuiré*, etc; conditional *distribuiría*, etc; pretérite 1. sg *distribuí*, 2. sg *distribuiste*, 3. sg *distribuyó*, 1. pl *distribuimos*, 2. pl *distribuísteis*, 3. pl *distribuyeron*; past participle *distribuido*; present participle *distribuyendo*. All verbs with infinitive in *-uir* are of this type.

3. Certain verbs, which \ve shall term the *-zc-* verbs, substituto *-zc-* for *-c-* wherever *-o* or *-a* follows. Thus *conocer* (II) "know" has:

PRESENT INDICATIVE	1. sg	*conozco*		
PRESENT SUBJUNCTIVE	1. sg	*conozca*	1. pl	*conozcamos*
	2. sg	*conozcas*	2. pl	*conozcáis*
	3. sg	*conozca*	3. pl	*conozcan*

4. Other irregular verbs, which do not fall into regular sub-patterns, are the following, here Usted with inclication of the class of verb to which they belong and with the individual forms which are irregular:

abrir III "open": past part. *abierto.*
andar I "walk": pretérito *anduve* etc; past subj. *anduviese, anduviera.*
atenerse II "depend": like *tener.*
atraer II "attract": like *traer.*
avenirse III "agree": like *venir.*
bendecir III "bless": like *decir*, but past part. *bendito.*
caber II "be contained, fit": pres. 1. sg *quepo;* pres. subj. *quepa* etc; fut. *cabré;* condit. *cabría;* pret. *cupe* etc; past subj. *cupiese, cupiera,*
caer II "fall": pres. I.sg *caigo;* pres. subj. *caiga* etc; pret. 3. sg *cayó*, 3. pl *cayeron;* past subj. *cayese, cayera;* pres. part. *cayendo,*
componer II "compose": like *poner,*
contener II "contain": like *tener,*
contradecir III "contradict": like *decir,*
contraer II "contract": like *traer,*
convenir III "agree": like *venir,*
cubrir III "eover": past part. *cubierto,*
dar IV "give": pres. I.sg *doy;* impérf. *daba* etc; pres. subj. I.sg *dé*, 3.sg *dé;* pret. *di, diste, dio, dimos, disteis, dieron;* past subj. *diese, diera.*
decaer II "decay": like *caer,*
decir III "say": radical-changing type III and: pres. I.sg *digo;* pres. subj. *diga* etc; imperative 2.sg *di;* fut. 1 .sg *diré* etc; condit. *diría* etc; pret. *dije* etc; past subj. *dijese, dijera;* past part. *dicho,*
descubrir III "discover": like *cubrir,*
desenvolver II "unroll, unwrap": like *volver,*
detener II "hold back, detain": like *tener,*
disolver II "dissolve": rad-ch I and past part. *disuelto.*
disponer II "dispose": like *poner,*
distraer II "distract": like *traer,*
entretener II "entertain": like *tener,*
escribir III "write"; past part. *escrito,*
estar IV "be": pres. I.sg *estoy*, 2.sg *estás*, 3.sg *está*, 3.pl *están;* impérf. *estaba* etc; pres. subj. *esté, estés, esté, estemos, estéis, estén;* pret. *estuve* etc; past subj. *estuviese, estuviera,*
exponer II "expose": like *poner,*
haber II "have, for there to be" (normally used in verbal phrases to form perfect tenses or in 3.sg meaning "there is, there was" etc): pres. *he, has, ha, hemos, habéis, han;* pres. subj. *haya* etc; fut. *habré;* condit. *habría;* pret. *hube* etc; past subj. *hubiese, hubiera.* The special form *hay* is used in pres. 3.sg in the meaning "there is, there are".
hacer II "do, make": pres. I.sg *hago;* pres/subj. *haga* etc; fut. *haré;* condit. *haría;* pret. *hice* etc; past subj. *hiciese, hiciera;* past part. *hecho.*
imponer II "impose": like *poner,*
indisponer II "indispose": like *poner,*
interponer II "interpose": like *poner,*
intervenir III "intervene": like *venir,*
ir IV "go": pres. *voy, vas, va, vamos, vais, van;* impérf. *iba* etc; pres. subj. *vaya* etc; fut. *iré;* condit. *iría;* pret. and past subj. same as those of *ser.*
maldecir III "curse'.': like *decir*, but past part. *maldito,*
mantener II "maintain": like *tener.*

morir III "die": rad-ch I and past part. *muerto.*
obtener II "obtain": like *tener.*
oponer II "oppose": like *poner.*
poder II "be able": rad-ch I and: fut. *podré;* condit. *podría;* pret. *pude* etc; past subj. *pudiese, pudiera,*
poner II "place": pres. l.sg *pongo;* pres. subj. *ponga* etc; fut. *pondré;* condit. *pondría;* pret. *puse* etc; past subj. *pusiese, pusiera;* past part. *puesto.*
prevenir III "prepare, warn": like *venir,*
proponer II "propose": like *poner,*
retener II "retain":¡ like Jener.,
saber II "know": pres. l.sg *sé;* pres. subj. *sepa* etc; fut. *sabré;* condit. *sabría;* pret. *supe* etc; past subj. *supiese, supiera,*
salir III "go out": pres. l.sg *salgo;* pres. subj. *salga* etc; fut. *saldré;* condit. *saldría.*
satisfacer II "satisfy": like *hacer,*
ser IV "be": pres. *soy, eres, es, somos, sois, son;* imperf. *era* etc; pres. subj. *sea* etc; pret. *fui, fuiste, fue, fuimos, fuisteis, fueron;* past subj. *fuese, fuera;* pres. part. *siendo;* past part. *sido,*
sostener II "uphold, sustain": like *tener,*
suponer II "suppose": like *poner,*
tener II "have, hold": rad-ch I and: pres. l.sg *tengo;* pres. subj. *tenga* etc; fut. *tendré;* condit. *tendría;* pret. *tuve* etc; past subj. *tuviese,* tuviera,
traer II "bring": pres. l.sg *traigo;* pres. subj. *traiga* etc; pret. *traje* etc; past subj. *trajese, trajera,*
valer II "be worth": pres. l.sg *valgo;* pres. subj. *valga* etc; fut. *valdré;* condit. *valdría,*
venir III "come": rad-chl and: pres. 1. sg *vengo;* pres. subj. *venga* etc; fut. *vendré;* condit. *vendría;* pret. *vine* etc; past subj. *viniese, viniera,*
ver IV "see": pret. *vi, viste, vio, vimos, visteis, vieron;* past subj. *viese, viera;* past part. *visto.*
volver II "turn": rad-ch I and past part. *vuelto.*

1.8 Special uses of some important verbs:

1. *ser* "be" is used with a noun or adjective denoting pennanent condition, inherent characteristic or quality, origin, material, or ownership, and also in impersonal expressions and expressions of time:

¿Quiénes?	"Who is it?"
Soy yo.	"It's me."
¿De dónde esf	"Where's he from?"
Es de Cuba.	"He's from Cuba."
Yo soy español.	"I'm a Spaniard."
Ella es pintora.	"She's a painter."
Esa mesa es de madera.	"That table's made of wood."
¿De quién esf	"Whose is it?"
Es de ella.	"It's hers."
Es para tí.	"It's for you."
¿Qué hora es?	"What time is it?"
Son las cinco.	"It's five o'clock."
Es tarde.	"It's late."

Pero es necesario ir.	"But it's necessary to go."
Es evidente.	"It's evident."

2. *estar* "be" is used to express a temporary condition, location, and also as the auxiliary of the progressive tense:

¿Cómo está Ud.?	"Hdw are you?"
¿Dónde está el libro?	"Where's the book?"
Está sobre la mesa.	"It's on the table."
Ellos están en Chile.	"They're in Chile."
¿Quién está hablando?	"Who's speaking?"
El niño está jugando.	"The child's playing."
Ella está enferma.	"She's sick."

a) In order to determine whether to use *ser* or *estar* when the predicate is an adjective, the following rule should be kept in mind: *ser* is used when the predicate adjective indicates the nature of an object or an inherent charac-teristic (1, below); *estar* js used when the predicate adjective indicates a temporary condition (2, below):

(1) *La lechuga es verde.*	"Lettuce is green." (by nature)
(2) *La fruta está verde.*	"The fruit's green." (a state of the fruit)
(1) *María es pálida.*	"Mary's palé." (by nature)
(2) *María está pálida.*	"Mary looks pale."
(1) *Es un hombre raro.*	"He's a queer man."
(2) *Está muy raro hoy.*	"He acts very queer today."

b) *estar* should never be used with a predicate noun.

c) *ser* should never be used with the past participle except to form an unequivocal passive voice:

La ventana está abierta.	"The window's open."
La ventana fue abierta por María.	"The window was opened by Mary."
La casa está bien construida.	"The house is well built."
La casa fue construida en 1945.	"The house was built in 1945."

3. *haber* never means "have" in the sense of "possess". This meaning is rendered by *tener: el tiene el libro* "he has the book".

a) When *haber* is not used as an auxiliary verb to form the compound tenses, it is an impersonal verb corresponding to English "there is, there are, there was, there were", etc, and as such has the form *hay* in the present tense:

Hay tres libros sobre la mesa.	"There are three books on the table."
Hay un hombre en la habitación.	"There's a man in the room."

b) In all other tenses the impersonal form is identical with the third person singular of the auxiliary:

había	"there was, there were"
hubo	"there was, there were"
habrá	"there'll be"
habría	"there'd be"

4. *tener,* which njeans "have" in the sense of "possess", used with *que* + in-finitive expresses a strong obligation equivalent to English "have to, must":

Tenemos que hacerlo hoy. "We must do it today."

a) *hay que* isísubstitutéd for *tener que* inimpersonal-constructions and is translated into English as "must, it's necessary":
Hay que decir la verdad. "It's necessary to (One must) tell the truth.'

b) *tener* as used in many idioms is translated "be" in English. In such cases the Spanish adjective *mucho* is rendered in English by the adverb "very"

Tengo hambre.	"I'm hungry."
Tengo mucha hambre.	"I'm very hungry."
Tengo sed.	"I'm thirsty."
Tengo frío.	"I'm cold."
Tengo miedo.	"I'm afraid."
Tengo prisa.	"I'm in a hurry."

5. The pronoun "it", which is used in the impersonal construction in English, is never required in Spanish:

Llueve. "It's raining."	*Escampa.* "It's clearing off."
Truena. "It's thundering."	*Hace fresco.* "It's cool."

6. *hacer* is used impersonally in expressions of weather:

Hace calor. "It's warm."	*Hace frío.* "It's cold."

a) *hace . . . que, hacía . quc,* and *hace (hacía)* preceded by *desde* may be used to indícate time elapsed:

Hace dos días que llegó.	"It's two days since he arrived."
Está aquí desde hace dos días.	"He's been here two days."
No la había visto desde hacía dos años.	"I hadn't seen her for two years."

III. Phrase Structure

Two or more words may be combined into groups of words, or phrases, which are used in sentences to take the place of, and fulfill the functions of, the various parts of speech. In this section we shall list the main types of phrases which occur in Spanish, according to the parts of speech whose place they take. We shall use the term head to refer to the central word of the phrase, and modifier to refer to a word modifying the head: thus, in English "good boy", the noun "boy" is the head of the phrase and "good" is a modifier.

2.0 Universal phrase types are such as occur with all parts of speech. In them two or more heads, usually belonging to the same part of speech, are placed next to each other, either not connected at all or connected by con-junctions.

1. No conjunction is present in some phrases which serve to enumérate things, actions, etc:

Se lo dije una, dos, tres veces. "I told him once, twice, three times."
Museos, escuelas, templos, iodo lo saquearon. "Museums, schools, and churches— they pillaged everything."

2. A conjunction is used in other phrases:

 a) Before the last head: *el hambre, el frío, la fatiga, y demás dolores* "hunger, cold, fatigue, and other sorrows".

 b) Before each head: *ni esto ni aquello* "neither this nor that".

2.1 Noun phrases normally contain a noun as their head, and an adjective or other element as modifier. This modifier may occur either before or after the head of the phrase, giving two main types of noun phrases:

2.11 Modifier + head. This order occurs primarily when the modifier is:

1. One of the adjectives mentioned in §1.13: *buen(o)* "good", *gran(de)* "great", *den(to)* "100", *mal(o)* "bad", *posírer(o)* "last", *primer(o)* "first", *San(to)* "Saint", *tercer(o)* "third", and *un(o)** "one"; or one of certain others: *pequeño* "little", *viejo* "oíd", *bonito* "pretty".

2. A numeral: *diez hombres* "ten men".

3. An interrogativo or indefinite adjective: *¿cuáles libros?* "which books?"; otros *personas* "other persons"; *los demás libros* "the other books".

2.12 Head+modifier. This order is the normal one when the modifier is:

1. An adjective other than the types mentioned in §2.11: *un hombre fuerte* "a strong man"; *una puerta abierta* "an open door".

2. An adjective phrase (adverb+adjective), or a phrase consisting of preposition+noun, pronoun, or verb: *un hombre muy fuerte* "a very strong man"; *un vaso de agua* "a glass of water"; *su libro de él* "his book"; *la casualidad de haberse encontrado con ella* "the'chance of having met her". .

3. A clause, normally mtroduced by a relative pronoun or adjective: *un caballero que desea hablarle* "a gentleman who wants to talk to you".

2.13 Reversal of normal order of adjective and head in a noun phrase (placing the adjective before the noun when it would normally follow, or vice versa) gives to the adjective an added meaning of emphasis, rhetorical orna-ment, or figurative speech: *la blanca nieve* "the white, white anow"; *cierta ciudad* "a certain city"; *un hombre malo* "a very bad man".

2.14 Phrase markers are certain types of words which may precede any noun or noun phrase and mark it as such. They are:

1. The definite article (§1.22): *la infeliz madre* "the unhappy mother"; *loa libros escritos en español* "the books written in Spanish".

---

* *Uno* used as a pronoun does not drop the o.

2. The indefinite article *un, una,* which in the singular has the meaning "a, an" and in the plural "some": *un libro interesante* "an interesting book"; *unos libros interesantes* "some interesting books".

3. A possessive adjective: *mi viejo amigo* "my oíd friend".

4. A demonstrative adjective: *estos cinco libros* "these five books".

2.2 Adjective phrases are of the following types:

2.21 Modifier+head. The modifier in this type of phrase is normally an adverb- *muy bonito* "very pretty". A speeial formation of this type is the comparativo and superlative of adjectives: *más* "more" or *menos* "less" placed before an adjective makes a phrase with comparative meaning: *más interesante* "more interesting"; *menos útil* "less useful". The definite article placed before a phrase containing a comparative adjective gives it the meaning of a superla-tive: *el más interesante* "the most interesting"; *el menos útil* "the least useful".

2.22 Head+modifier. The medifier may be one of the following:

1. A phrase introduced by a preposition: *esta agua es buena para beber* "this water's good to drink".

2. A clause introduced by *que* or *de* "than" or *como* "as" (often elliptical) after a comparative phrase (§2.21): *más habladora que su madre* "more talkative than her mother"; *tiene tantas tarjetas como ella* "he has as many cards as she".

2.3 Pronoun phrases have the structure head+modifier. The modifier may be:

1. An adjective: *yo solo* "I alone".

2. A phrase introduced by a preposition: *el de mi padre* "the one of my ather, my father's".

3. A clause: *lo que me gusta* "that which pleases me, what I like".

2.4 Verb phrases are of the following types:

2.41 Yerb+verb. These may be classified according to the form of the second verb in the phrase:

1. Past participle. The first verb may be:

a) *haber* "have", which forms perfect tenses with the past participle of other verbs. In such phrases, the past participle is always in the masculino singular: *ha enviado los libros* "he's sent,the books"; *ios libros que ha enviado* "the books he's sent"; *los ha enviado* "he's sent them".

b) *ser* "be", which forms passive tenses with the past participle of other verbs. This type of phrase is chiefly literary in use; the past participle agrees in gender and number with the subject: *este libro fue escrito por Pérez Galdós* "this book was written by Pérez Galdós".

c) *estar* "be", *tener* "have", *quedarse* "remain", and similar verbs. The past participle agrees in gender and number with the noun to, which it refers: *la puerta está abierta* "the door's open"; *ios niños estaban sentados en el suelo* "the children were sitting on the floor"; *tengo escrita la carta* "1 have:the letter written".

2. Gerund, with *estar* "be", *seguir* "keep on", etc, as.the first verb. This construction is equivalent to the English present progressive, which consists of a form of "be"+a verb form in "-ing": *está hablando* "he's talking".

3. Infinitivo. The first verb is one which indicates desire, ability, obliga-tion, cause, intention, or emotion: *debo irme* "I have to go away"; *creía haberlo visto* "he thought he'd seen it". Among the many verbs which occur in this construction are-

acostumbrar "be accustomed to"
bastar "be enough to"
conseguir "succeed in"
creer "believe, think"
deber "ought, should"
decidir "decide to"
dejar "let, allow to"
desear "wish to, desire to"
gustar "like, be pleasing to"
hacer "cause to, have done"
intentar "attempt to, try to"
lograr "succeed in"
mandar "order to, command to"
necesitar "need to"
parecer "seem to, appear to"
pensar "intend to"
poder "be able to"
procurar "try to"
querer "wish to"
resolver "decide to"
saber "know how to"
servirse "be so kind as to"
temer "fear, be afraid"
ver "see"

2.42 Verb+direct object, which is normally a noun, pronoun, or clause: *no tenemos libros* "we haven't any books"; *no me tratan bien* "they don't treat me well"; *quiero que estén contentos* "I want them to be happy". But this construction is normally replaced by that of verb+indirect object (cf §2.44.3) with proper nouns or nouns referring to specific persons (or personified objects or animáis), and with clisjunctive personal pronouns, relative, demonstrative, and indefinite pronouns referring to persons (except *que*).

2.43 Verb+predícate complement, which is normally a noun or pronoun used after *ser* or *estar* "be" and certain other verbs indicating identity or development, and agreeing with the subject in gender and number: *mi amigo es abogado* "my friend's a lawyer"; *estamos cansados* "we're tired".

2.44 Verb+adverbial complement. This latter may be:

1. An adverb: *habla muy bien* "he speaks very well".

2. An adjective or noun used as an adverb: *el enemigo atacó duro* "the enemy attacked hard".

3. A phrase introduced by a preposition: *sigue viviendo a la antigua* "he continúes to live in the oíd way"; *nos entendimos por fin* "we understood each other at last". This type of adverbial complement, with the preposition *a,* is normal instead of a direct object, in referring to a person (cf 2.42, above). Furthermore, the preposition a is normally used to introduce an infinitive after most verbs indicating motion, beginning, teaching, and learning, among others the following:

acostumbrarse "become accustomed"
acudir "come up, run"
aprender "learn"
atreverse "daré"
ayudar "help"
comenzar "begin"
correr "run"
decidirse "decide"
disponerse "get ready"
resistirse "resist"
subir "go up, come up"
tornar "return, do again"
empezar "begin"
enseñar "teach"
invitar "invite"
ir "go"
llegar "come, succeed"
negarse "refuse"
obligar "obligo"
ponerse "start, begin"
probar "try"
venir "come"
volver "return, come back"

The preposition *de* is normally used to introduce an infinitive after the following verbs:

> *acabar* "finish, have just . . ."
> *acordarse* "remember (to)"
> *cansarse* "get tired (of)"
> *cesar* "stop"
> *dejar* "stop, fail (to)"
> *guardarse* "take care not (to)"
> *haber* "have (to), be going (to)"
> *olvidarse* "forget (to)"
> *quejarse* "complain (of)"
> *tratar* "try (to)"; (reflexivo) "be a question (of)"

The preposition *en* is used after the following (and other) verbs:

complacerse "take pleasure (in)"   *insistir* "insist (on)"
consentir "consent (to)"   *pensar* "think (of, about)"
consistir "consist (of)"   *persistir* "persist (in)"
convenir "agree (to)'   *tardar* "delay (in)"
empeñarse "insist (on)"

    4. A clause: *Antes venía porque me obligaban.* "I used to come because they forced me to."

    2.5 Adverb phrases are normally of the structure modifier+head, with the modifier another adverb: *muy bien* "very well". An adverb phrase with *más* "more" or *menos* "less" as modifier has the meaning of the English comparative or superlative of an adverb: *más tarde* "later"; *menos bien* "less well".

    Phrases consisting of preposition+noun, pronoun, or verb may also be used adverbially: *en el zaguán saludó a la portera* "he greeted the janitress in the main entrance".

    2.6 Preposition phrases normally consist of an adverb (or equivalent phrase) followed by a preposition: *junto a* "together with"; *a pesar de* "in spite of".

    2.61 Prepositional phrases are used in Spanish where in English two or more nouns can be combined to form compound nouns*: *máquina de coser* "sewing machine"; *ropa para caballeros* "men's wear"; *neumático de repuesto* "spare tire".

    2.7 Conjunction phrases usually consist of an adverb or preposition or equivalent phrase followed by a subordinate conjunction (normally *que* "that"): *para que* "in order that"; *sin que* "without".

---

* In Spanish there are only a few genuine compounds of the type *oí ferrocarril* "railroad", *radiodifusión* "broadcasting", which generally have an initial member ending in *-o*.

IV. Clause Structure

3.0 The clause is the basic unit of the sentence in Spanish as in English. Clauses are either major or minor; major clauses are the customary normal type, and minor clauses are all others. The structure of major clauses and their combinations will be discussed in §§3.1-3.53; of minor clauses, in §§3.6-3.62. A major clause always contains a predicate and may or may not contain a subject as well.

3.1 The **predicate** always has as its main element a verb or verb phrase: nos *inclinamos para ver mejor* "we bent over to see better"; *estoy cansado* "I'm tired"; *han matadora la señora* "they've killed the lady". Since the verb indicates by its endings the person and number of the agent, a predicate often occurs alone (as in the above examples), where English would have a pronoun subject.

3.2 The **subject** may be one of the following:

1. A noun or noun phrase: *Inglaterra es grande y bella* "England is great and beautiful"; *las antiguas explotaciones petrolíferas han sido abandonadas* "the old oil drillings have been abandoned".

2. An adjective or other part of speech serving as noun: *todo le ayudaba* "everything helped him"; *lo mejor y más granado* "the finest and most select type".

3. A pronoun: *él iba delante* "he went first"; *me gusta éste* "I like this one".

3.21 Agreement in number. The subject normally agrees in number with the verb of the predicate: *lo hago yo* "I'll do it"; *lo hacemos nosotros* "we'll do it".

3.22 Agreement in person. The verb of the predicate is normally in the grammatical person of the lowest-numbered person represented in the subject. *(usted, ustedes* "you" naturally count as third person in this respect.) If the subject contains heads belonging to two different grammatical persons, the verb is in the first person if the first person element is present, otherwise in the second: *nos casaremos, tú y yo* "we'll get married, you and I".

3.23 Agreement in gender. A predicate complement (§2.43) agrees in number and gender with the subject: *él estaba cansado* "he was tired"; Zas *señoritas estaban cansadas* "the young ladies were tired".

3.3 Order of subject and predicate is much freer in Spanish than in English. In general, the normal order is subject+predicate; inversión of this order implica emphasis or rhetorical forcé, but is very frequent: *eso lo hago yo* "I'll do that"; *así continuaba el joven* "the young man continued thus". Inverted order is normal in a clause containing a subjunctive used as an imperative: *quítese usted el sombrero* "take off your hat".

Likewise the direct object, predicate complement, or adverbial complement is often placed before the verb and subject, giving a meaning of greater emphasis than does the normal order: eso *es* "that's it" (literally, "it is that"); *el que no se entera de nada soy yo* "I'm the one who doesn't understand"; *mejor será avisar a la -policía* "it'll be better to notify the police"; *mucho lo siento* "I'm very sorry". In a sentence containing a specifically interrogative word, the phrase containing this word comes first: *¿qué quiere usted?* "what do you want?"; *¿desde cuándo le conoces?* "since when have you known him?"

3.4 Coordination is the relation to each other of two or more clauses of equal rank in a sentence. Of two coordinate clauses, the second is usually joined to the first by a coordinating conjunction, such as *pero* "but", *y* "and". The conjunction *que* may introduce an independent or coordinate clause when followed by a verb in the subjunctive indicating a command: *que lo haga él* "let him do it".

3.5 Subordination. If a clause has, in another clause, the function of one of the parts of speech, and modifies some element of that clause, it is said to be **subordinate** to or **dependent** on the element it modifies. Subordinate clauses are normally introduced by a subordinating conjunction, often one formed with *que* "that". The use of a clause in a subordinate position often requires the use of a subjunctive form in the main verb of the subordinate clause. The use of the subjunctive may be automatic, i.e. obligatory in certain constructions. In others, the use of the subjunctive is not obligatory, and its use is significant, i.e. it gives the clause a different meaning than the use of the indicative would .

3.51 Automatic use of the subjunctive is found in the following types of subordinate clauses:

1. Those containing certain verbs:

a) Verbs whose general meaning is that of desire, command, judgment or opinión, emotion, or doubt. The chief of these verbs are:

agradecer "be grateful"
alegrarse "be glad"
dejar "let, allow"
deplorar "regret"
desear "desire"-
estar "be" + certain adjectives (e.g. *contento (de)* "glad", *enojado* "annoyed")
gustar "like"
impedir "hinder"
insistir (en) "insist (on)"

mandar "command"
pedir "ask"
perdonar "forgive"
permitir "permit, allow"
preferir "prefer"
prohibir "forbid"
querer "want, wish"
sentir "be sorry"
sorprenderse "be surprised"
sugerir "suggest"
tener miedo (de) "be afraid"

b) Impersonal expressions (used only in the third person singular) in which *ser* "be" is followed by any of a number of adjectives, among them:

bueno "good"
difícil "difficult"
extraño "strange"
fácil "easy"
importante "important"
justo "right"

malo "bad"
mejor "better"
necesario "necessary"
peor "worse"
posible "possible"
probable "probable"

c) Verbs, usually when they are in the negative or interroga ti ve, whose general meaning is that of perceiving, thinking, knowing, declaring; the meaning given by use of the subjunctive is that of uncertainty or doubt. The most important of the determining verbs are:

concebir "conceive, imagine"
creer "believe"
decir "say"
estimar "consider"

juzgar "judge"
pensar "think"
saber "know"
suponer "suppose"

But after such verbs as *dudar* "doubt" and *negar* "deny", with essentially negative meaning, the subjunctive is used when the rnain verb is in the positive, and the índicative when it is in the negative: *dudo que sea -posible* "I doubt that it's possible".

    2. Clauses serving as adverbs: after a number of conjunctions, such as:

a condición que "on condition that"	*aun cuando* "even if"
a fin (de) que "in order that"	*para que* "so that"
a menos que "unless"	*supuesto que* "supposing that"

3.52 Significant use of the subjunctive is found in the following types of clauses:
1. Clauses used as adjectives, giving the clauses the meaning of:

a) A desired characteristic or purpose: *busco un libro que sea interesante* "I'm looking for a book that'll be interesting".

b) Uncertainty or doubt: *las expresiones que Uds. hayan olvidado* "the expressions you may ha ve forgotten". This type of clause is especially frequent after indefinite and concessive expressions: *cualquier libro que escriba* "whatever book he may write"; *por rico que sea* "no matter how rich he may be". It is also found after superlativos or equivalen! expressions: *el libro más interesante que haya* "the most interesting book there is".

2. Clauses used as adverbs, giving the meaning of:

a) Intent, purpose, or anticipation: *hable Ud. de manera que todos le oigan* "talk in such a way that all can hear you"; *aunque venga, no nos lo enseñará* "even though he may come, he won't show it to us".

b) Futurity: *cuando venga, dígaselo* "when he comes, tell it to him".

3.53 Conditional sentences. If a sentence contains a clause beginning with *si* "if", the tense of the verb in this clause is determined by the tense of the verb in the main clause, normally as follows:

IF THE MAIN CLAUSE HAS A VERB IN THE:	THE "IF"-CLATJSE HAS A VERB IN THE:
Present } Imperative } Future	Present
Imperfect	Imperfect
Preterite	Preterite
Conditional	Past Subjunctive (-ra or -se)

Thus: *si está aquí, trabaja* "if he's here, he's working"; *si estaba aquí, trabajaba* "if he was here, he was working"; *si está aquí mañana, trabajará* "if he's here tomorrow, he'll be working"; *si estuviera aquí, trabajaría* "if he were here, he'd be working". A main verb indicating a condition contrary to fact may also be in the *-ra* form of the subjunctive: *si estuviera aquí, trabajara* "if he were here, he'd be working".

    3.6 Minor clauses, which do not conform to the customary structure of clauses, are chiefly of the following two types:

3.61 Fragmentary or elliptical clauses: a phrase or single word, such as could enter into the structure of a full olause if the rest of a full clause were uttered. Under this type come most cases of incomplete sentences in normal conversation, answers to questions, etc: ¿Qué le dijo?—Nada. "What did he say to him?—Nothing."; Buenos días. ¿Cómo está Úd.f—Muy bien, gracias. ¿Y Ud.? "Hello. How are you?—Very well, thanks. And you?" *

3.62 Interjectional clauses, consisting of words which do not have the inflection or function of any of the parts of speech, and may be used as sepárate utterances or joined with other clauses: ¡Ahí "Ah!"; ¡Ay! "Ouchl"; ¡Hola! "Helio!"; ¡Oh! "Oh!";,etc.

Dictionary of Idioms (English/Spanish)

	PAGE
ABC ...... BECOME OF	1
BEELINE ...... BURN UP	2
BURNING HOT...... COCK AND BULL STORY	3
COIN MONEY ...... DOWN IN THE MOUTH	4
DOWN TO EARTH ...... FIND OUT	5
FIRSTHAND ...... GIVE A BUZZ (GIVE A CALL)	6
GIVE A GOOD ACCOUNT OF ...... HAVE A LOT ON THE BALL	7
HAVE A SCREW LOÓSE......IN THE DARK	8
IN THE DOGHOUSE ...... LAND-OFFICE BUSINESS	9
LAST STRAW...... MAKE A FACE	10
MAKE A GOOD LIVING ...... ODDS AND ENDS	11
OF AGE ......PLAY HOOKY	12
PLAY INTO THE HANDS OF ...... RIGHT AWAY	13
RIGHT-HAND MAN ...... SLEEP LIKE A TOP	14
SLEEP ON ...... TAKE CARE	15
TAKE CHARGE OF ......TIP OFF	16
TIRED (TUCKERED) OUT.........WRAP UP	17

Dictionary of Idioms (English/Spanish)

ABC	los fundamentos
A-I	de primera
ABOUT TO	a punto
ABOVEBOARD	honestas
ACCORDING TO HOYLE OF AGE	apropiado
ALL ALONG	mayor de edad
ALL AT ONCE	desde el principio
ALL EARS	de repente
ALL IN	todo oídos
ALL IN ALL	se rindió de cansancio
ALL IS UP	en general
ALL OVER	se le terminó
ALL RIGHT	había terminado; por todas partes
ALL SET	es correcto
ALL THE SAME	están listos
ALL THERE	a pesar de ello
ALLOW FOR	está muy bien
APPLE OF ONE'S EYE	tener en cuenta
APPLE-PIE ORDER	la preferida de sus padres
AS A MATTER OF FACT	en orden
AS YET	de seguro
AT FAULT	hasta ahora
AT FIRST BLUSH	se equivocó
AT LEAST	de primer momento
AT ONCE	como mínimo
AT ONE'S FINGERTIPS	immediatamente
AT ONE'S WIT'S END	en la punta de los dedos
AT THE TOP	está para volverse loca
AT TIMES	con todos sus pulmones a veces
AX TO GRIND	se está quej ando de algo
BACK NUMBER	atrasados
BACK OUT	se volvió atrás
BACK UP	dio marcha atrás; respaldado
BAD BLOOD	enemistad
BAD EGG	calavera
BAG AND BAGGAGE	con todas sus pertenencias
BARGE IN	llegó inesperadamente
BAWL OUT	regañó
BEAR OUT	confirmará
BEAR UP	resignarse
BEAR WITH	tener paciencia
BEARD THE LION	hacerle frente al león
BEAT ABOUT THE BUSH	andes por las ramas
BEAT IT	pon los pies en polvorosa
BEAT ONE TO IT	se me adelantó
BECOME OF	será de

BEELINE	derechito
BEHIND BARS	en la cárcel
BEHIND ONE'S BACK	en su ausencia
BELOW THE BELT	bajo la faja
BESIDE ONESELF	perdió el control
BESIDE THE POINT	no viene al caso
BEST MAN	padrino de boda
BETTER HALF	esposa
BETTER OFF	en mejores condiciones
BETWEEN THE DEVIL AND THE DEEP SEA	estar entre la espada y la pared ovación
BIG HAND	persona de influencia
BIG SHOT (BIG WHEEL; BIGWIG)	alas de una mismo pájaro
BIRDS OF A FEATHER	bravísima
BITE ONE'S HEAD OFF	todos sus detalles
BLACK AND WHITE	un comprimiso con un desconocido
BLIND DATE	desahogarse
BLOW OFF STEAM	estalló
BLOW ONE'S TOP	pase
BLOW OVER BLOW UP	la volaron
BOBBY-SOXER	jovencitas chillonas
BONE TO PICK	vérmelas contigo
BOSOM FRIENDS	amigos íntimos
BOUNCE OUT	echaron
BOUND FOR	va para
BOUND TO BREAK AWAY	probablemente
BREAKDOWN	librarse
BREAK DOWN	colapso
BREAK IN	echó abajo; se descompuso
BREAK OUT	enseñar; se entrometía
BREAK THE ICE	rompieron
BREAK THE NEWS	rompió la seriedad
BREAK THROUGH	dio la noticia
BREAK UP	abrirse paso a través del
BREAK WITH	destruir; terminó; se pondrá muy triste
BRING ABOUT (BRING ON)	
BRING DOWN	rompió con
BRING HOME	fue causado
BRING HOME THE BACON	disminuyan demostró
BRING TO LIGHT	sufragaba los gastos reveló
BRING TO MIND	nos recordó
BRING UP	educar
BROKE	sin un centavo no hizo caso de
BRUSH ASIDE	rechazo
BRUSH-OFF	propaganda
BUILD-UP	se consumió
BURN OUT	te agotas
BURN THE CANDLE AT BOTH ENDS	no quedarse tarde estudiando
BURN THE MIDNIGHT OIL	destruido totalmente; enfurece
BURN UP	abrasadores

BURNING HOT	se echó a llorar
BURST INTO TEARS	se echó a reír
BURST OUT LAUGHING	
BURY THE HATCHET	dejaron de pelear
BUTT IN	interrumpe
BUY OUT	comprar a
BUY UP	comprar todos
BY ACCIDENT	inesperadamente
BY ALL MEANS	sin falta
BY AND LARGE	en general
BY ONESELF	sin ayuda; solo
BY THE SKIN OF ONE'S TEETH	por un pelo de milagro
BY THE WAY	a propósito
CALL DOWN	reprendieron
CALL FOR	viene a buscar; pidió
CALL IN	consulta
CALL OFF	cancela
CALL ON	fuimos a visitar
CALL OUT	llamaron; requirieron
CALL UP	llámanos por telefono
CARRY ON	sigue con; sigas comportándote; amores
CARRY OUT	ilícitos llevó a cabo
CARRY THE BALL	se encarga
CATCH FIRE	coger fuego
CATCH HOLD OF	se agarró
CATCH ON	lo entiendan
CATCH ONE'S EYE	le llamó la atención
CATCH RED-HANDED	cogieron en flagrante
CATCH UP WITH	alcanzó
CHAIN SMOKER	fumador empedernido
CHALK UP	atribuyó
CHANCE HANDS	cambió de dueño
CHANCE ONE'S MINO	cambió de parecer
CHECK IN	llegó al
CHECK OUT	te vayas
CHECKUP	un examen médico
CHECK UP ON	investigó
CHECK WITH	consultó con
CHEW THE FAT	chismear
CHICKEN FEED	migaja
CHICKEN-HEARTED	tímido
CHICKEN OUT	se acobardó
CHILD'S PLAY	muy fácil
CHIP IN	contribuyeron
CHIP OFF THE OLD BLOCK	de tal palo tal astilla
CHIPS ARE DOWN	situación es crítica
GLOSE CALL	por poco
COCK AND BULL STORY	cuentos increíbles

COIN MONEY	se enriquecen con rapidez
COME ALONG	acompañes; progresa
COME BY	ganó
COME DOWN WITH	estuvo enfermo
COME IN HANDY	es útil
COME ON	saldrán; le va a caer
COME OUT	aparecerá; sale
COME OUT FOR	apoyaron
COME TO	fué
COME TO ONE'S SENSES	recobraras el sent ido común
COME TO TERMS	llegaron a un acuerdo
COME TO THE POINT	presentar el problema
COME TRUE	se realizaron
COME UPON	llegues a
COOK ONE'S GOOSE	arruinó su oportunidad
COOL AS A CUCUMBER	serena
COOL ONE'S HEELS	esperar
COUNT ONE'S CHICKENS BEFORE THEY ARE HATCHED	no cantes victoria
CRACK A JOKE	dijo chistes
CRACK-UP	trastornó
CREAM OF THE CROP	la esperanza
CRY WOLF	pidas auxilio
CUT	porción
CUT DOWN	reducir
CUT IT OUT	no siguiera
CUT OFF	desconectaron; cortó
CUT OUT	eliminar
CUT OUT FOR	perfecta
CUT SHORT	terminó de repente
DARK HORSE	candidato desconocido
DASH OFF	escribió rápidamente
DATE	invitarla
DAY IN AND DAY OUT	día tras día
DEAD AS A DOORNAIL	paralizados
DIE DOWN	se acabó gradualmente
DIE OUT	desapareciendo gradualmente
DIRTY LOOK	miró con desagrado
DO AWAY WITH	suicidarse
DO IN	arruinó
DO OVER	hacer de nuevo
DO WITHOUT	no necesitamos
DOG-TIRED	cansado que un perro
DOLL UP	engalanado
DONE	cocinado; no se hace
DOUBLE-CROSS	engañó
DOWN AND OUT	sin dinero
DOWN IN THE MOUTH	muy triste
	práctica

DOWN TO EARTH	paro de beber
DRAW THE LINE	escribirá
DRAW UP	se puso muy elegante
DRESS UP	volverás loco
DRIVE SOMEONE MAD	qué se propone
DRIVING AT	me visiten
DROP BY (DROP IN)	gota de agua
DROP IN THE BUCKET	se desprendían
DROP OFF	se retiró
DROP OUT OF	me escriben
DROP SOMEONE A LINE	no se venden
DRUG ON THE MARKET	callar
DRY UP	cada cual se pagaba lo suyo
DUTCH TREAT	
EAT ONE'S CAKE AND HAVE IT	cosas no siempre suceden a pedir de boca
EAT ONE'S HEART OUT	sufre callada
EAT ONE'S WORDS	retractarse
EVERY SO OFTEN	de vez en cuando
FACE THE MUSIC	hazle frente a las consecuencias
FACE UP TO	enfrentarte con
FAIR AND SQUARE	sincero y honesto
FALL FOUL OF	perder la simpatía de
FALL OFF	disminuyó
FALL OUT	nos desconcertemos
FALL THROUGH	fracasará
FAR AND WIDE	de todas partes
FAR CRY	como del día a la noche
FARFETCHED	exagerado
FEATHER IN ONE'S CAP	triunfo para él
FEATHER ONE'S NEST	prepararte
FED UP	harto
FEEL BLUE	siento triste
FEEL FOR	se condolió de
FEEL IT IN ONE'S BONES	se lo dijo su corazón
FEEL LIKE	tengo ganas
FEEL ONE'S WAY	procedí con cautela
FELLOW TRAVELERS	simpatizantes
FENCE SITTER	es un cambiacasaca
FEW AND FAR BETWEEN	escasos
FIFTY-FIFTY	a la mitad
FIGURE ON	contamos con
FIGURE OUT	resolver; comprender
FIGURE UP	calculó
FILL IN	llene; informó
FILL OUT	complete
FIND FAULT WITH	criticándose
FIND OUT	averigua

FIRSTHAND	directamente
FIT AS A FIDDLE	en buena salud
FLASH IN THE PAN	fue un éxito
FLY IN THE OINTMENT	el problema
FOOL AROUND	pierdas el tiempo
FOOT THE BILL	pagará los gastos
FOR A SONG	por casi nada
FOR GOOD	para siempre
FOR THE TIME BEING	por ahora
FORTY WINKS	siestecita
FREE-LANCE	independiente
FROM A TO Z	del principio al fin
GAME LEG	cojea
GET ABOUT	se levanta y anda
GET ACROSS	hacer comprender
GET ALONG	no las arreglamos; marcharse; se llevan
GET AT	tocar; quieres conseguir
GET AWAY	se escapo
GET BACK	regresar; recuperar
GET BY	pasar sin ser visto
GET EVEN WITH	se vengará de
GET GOING	ponte en marcha
GET IN	llegará; entraremos en él; reciben
GET IN ONE'S HAIR	incomodar
GET IN TOUCH WITH	comunicaré con
GET IN WITH	asociarse con
GET IN	recibirás un castigo; lo compré
GET OFF	bajaron del; mandaremos
GET ON	subieron al; continuar; ponte
GET ON ONE'S NERVES	me desesperan
GET ON THE BANDWAGON	unámonos a la fiesta
GET OUT	publicar; se publique
GET OUT OF HAND	se descontroló
GET OVER	olividará; llegarás
GET OVER WITH	termino
GET READY	se prepare
GET RID OF	disponer de
GET THE BETTER OF	sale ganando
GET THE UPPER HAND	adueñó
GET THROUGH	terminar
GET TO	volveremos
GET TOGETHER	nos reuniremos; se pusieron; de acuerdo
GET UNDER ONE'S SKIN	conquistarle
GET WIND OF	se enteraron de
GHOST OF A CHANCE	la menor probabilidad
GIFT OF GAB	la labia que tiene
GIMMICK	clave
GIVE A BUZZ (GIVE A CALL)	

GIVE A GOOD ACCOUNT OF	te llamaré por teléfono
GIVE A PIECE OF ONE'S MIND	salió muy bien
GIVE A RAP	dijo las verdades
GIVE-AND-TAKE	no te importe un bledo
GIVE IN	toma y dada
GIVE OFF	se rindió
GIVE OUT	dio
GIVE RISE TO	repartiré; se agotaron
GIVE THE COLD SHOULDER	produce
GIVE UP	viró la espalda
GIVE WAY	perdieron
GO-AHEAD	se rompió
GO AROUND	le avisó
GO BACK ON ONE'S WORD	alcanzaron para todos
GO FOR	faltaba a su palabra
GO-GETTER	buscar; se enamoró de
GO IN FOR	ambicioso en su trabajo
GO INTO	se interesa en
GO OFF	discutirá
GO ON	se descargaron; irse; comenzó
GO OUT	sigue; iniciar el caso
GO OUT OF ONE'S WAY	se apagó; salió
	hago todo lo posible
GO OVER	examino; tenga éxito
GO STRAIGHT	viva honestamente
GO THROUGH	gasto
GO THROUGH WITH	completaron
GO TO BAT FOR	ayudó
GO TO POT	quebró
GO TO THE DOGS	arruinó
GO WITHOUT SAYING	no hay que decirlo
GO WRONG	salió mal; se descarriló
HALF-BAKED	poco juiciosas
HALFHEARTED	fríos
HAND IN	presentarán
HAND IN HAND (HAND IN GLOVE)	de acuerdo
HAND OVER	entregó
HAND TO MOUTH	de un día para otro
HANDLE WITH KID GLOVES	trata con sumo cuidado
HANG AROUND	reunirse en
HANG ON	agárrate
HANG UP	colgó el teléfono
HARD-BOILED	cruel
HAVE A BONE TO PICK	tiene algún asunto que aclarar
HAVE A CHIP ON ONE'S SHOULDER	es pendenciero
HAVE A CRUSH	está enamorado
HAVE A DAY OFF	tiene un día libre
HAVE A GOOD TIME	se divirtieron
HAVE A LOT ON THE BALL	tiene mucha habilidad

HAVE A SCREW LOOSE	tener un tornillo flojo
HAVE COLD FEET	tiene miedo
HAVE DRAG	tiene influencia
HAVE IRONS IN THE FIRE	un par de ellos entre manos
HAVE IT OUT	aclarar las cosas
HAVE ONE'S HANDS FULL	tiene mucho que hacer
HAVE ONE'S HEART IN ONE'S MOUTH	tenía el alma en un hilo
HAVE ONE'S HEART SET ON	estaba loca por
HAVE ONE'S OWN WAY	salirse con la suya
HAVE PULL	tenía influencia
HAVE SOMETHING ON ONE'S MIND	tiene muchos problemas
HAVE UNDER ONE'S THUMB	tiene en la mano
HEAD FOR	fue al
HEAD OR TAIL	entender nada
HEAD OVER HEELS	locamente
HIT	éxito
HIT IT OFF	simpatizaron
HIT THE CEILING	me enfado
HIT THE NAIL ON THE HEAD	tenías razón
HOLD BACK	se reservó
HOLD DOWN	mantuvo
HOLD FORTH	hablar
HOLD GOOD	duró
HOLD ON	esperara
HOLD ON TO	retener
HOLD ONE'S HORSES	cálmense
HOLD ONE'S TONGUE	callarse
HOLD OUT	pudo sobrevivir; pudo resistir
HOLDOVER	continúa
HOLD OVER	se exhibió
HOLD THE LINE	hacer frente
HOLD UP	asaltaron; fue demorado
HOLD WATER	ilógicas
HOLDING THE BAG	con el problema en las manos
HOT AIR HOW COME	muy falsa
HURRY UP	cómo es
	apurémonos
IN A BODY	a la vez
IN A JAM	compromiso serio
IN A JIFFY	en seguida
IN A NUTSHELL	en pocas palabras
IN A PERSON'S SHOES	en sus zapatos
IN A WAY	hasta cierto punto
IN ANY EVENT	de todos modos
IN CLOVER	como un rey
IN DUTCH	tiene liós
IN ONE'S RIGHT MIND	estar tranquilo y no estar loco
IN ORDER	arreglado
IN PLAIN ENGLISH	sin miramientos
IN THE DARK	en ayuno

IN THE DOGHOUSE	emperrado
IN THE DUMPS	desconsalado
IN THE LONG RUN	a la larga
IN THE NICK OF TIME	en el último minuto
IN THE SAME BOAT	en las mismas circunstancias
IN THE WIND	se dice
INS AND OUTS	detalles
IRON OUT	allanar
JACK UP	han subido
JOT DOWN	anotaré
JUMP AT	se apresuró a aceptar
JUMP THE GUN	nos adelantamos
JUMP TO A CONCLUSION	no creas que
KEEP A STIFF UPPER LIP	fue valiente
KEEP A STRAIGHT FACE	permanecer serio (quedarse serio)
KEEP ABREAST OF	estar al corriente de
KEEP AN EYE ON	cuida
KEEP COMPANY	cortejó
KEEP HOUSE	se ocupó de la casa
KEEP IN HAND	controlada
KEEP IN MIND	ten presente
KEEP IN TOUCH WITH	comunícate con
KEEP ON	sigue
KEEP ONE'S CHIN UP	no se dejó vencer
KEEP ONE'S HEAD	no perdió el control
KEEP ONE'S SHIRT ON	no te excites
KEEP ONE'S TEMPER	perdió la calma
KEEP OUT	no se meta
KEEP THE BALL ROLLING	animarlo
KEEP THE WOLF FROM THE DOOR	no pasar hambre
KEEP TRACK OF	lleva la cuenta de
KEEP UP	sigues
KEEP UP WITH	se mantuv9 al corriente de
KICK IN	contribuyo
KICK OUT	expulsaron
KICK THE BUCKET	muera
KILL TIME	matar el tiempo
KILL TWO BIRDS WITH ONE STONE	matar dos pájaros de un tiro
KNOCK OFF	suspendes el trabajo
KNOW-HOW	habilidad
KNOW ON WHICH SIDE ONE'S BREAD IS BUTTERED	sabe lo que le conviene
KNOW ONE'S STUFF	sabe lo que está haciendo estar al tanto de
KNOW THE ROPES	los detalles
LADIES' MAN	gran galante
LAID UP	recluida
LAND-OFFICE BUSINESS	gran negocio

LAST STRAW	el colmo
LAUGH UP ONE'S SLEEVE	me reí interiormente
LAY OFF	dejaron cesante; no toques
LEAD BY THE NOSE	domina
LEAK OUT	se supo
LEAVE FLAT	dejó plantado
LEAVE IN THE LURCH	abandonó
LEAVE NO STONE UNTURNED	no dejes una piedra por mover
LEAVE OUT	no omitas
LEAVE SOMEONE HIGH AND DRY	abandonó
LEAVE WORD	dejé dicho
LEAVE A PERSON FLAT	la dejó plantada
LEFTHANDED COMPLIMENT	elogio mal intencionado
LEG TO STAND ON	razones en que apoyarse
LEND A HAND	ayúdanos
LET ALONE	déjame en paz
LET BYGONES BE BYGONES	lo que pasó, pasó
LET DOWN	falles
LET GO	déjame ir; suéltame
LET IN ON	dijimos
LET ME OUT	déjeme salir
LET OFF	dejó en libertad
LET ON	reveles
LET ONE'S HAIR DOWN	se sintió en confianza
LET ONESELF GO	se descuidase
LET THE CAT OUT OF THE BAG	descubras el secreto
LET UP	dejas tranquilo
LIKE A FISH OUT OF WATER	como el pez fuera del agua
LIVE UP TO	vivir de acuerdo con
LONG FACE	una cara muy triste
LOOK AFTER	se ocupó de; siguió con la vista
LOOK DOWN ON	desprecie
LOOK FORWARD TO	esperamos con placer
LOOK HIGH AND LOW	buscó por todas partes
LOOK INTO	investigar
LOOK ON	mira
LOOK OUT	cuídate
LOOK OUT UPON	mira
LOOK OVER	observo
LOOK SOMEONE UP	ven a verme
LOOK UP	encontrar
LOOK UP TO	miran con respeto
LOSE ONE'S MIND	se vuelve loca
LOSE ONE'S TEMPER	perdió el control
MAIDEN NAME	nombre de soltera
MAKE A BEELINE FOR	fui en seguida a
MAKE A BREAK	descontinuar
MAKE A CLEAN BREAST	confesó
MAKE A FACE	hizo una mueca

MAKE A GOOD LIVING	gana bastante dinero
MAKE A KILLING	tuvo suerte
MAKE A MESS OUT OF	arruinar
MAKE A MOUNTAIN OUT OF A MOLEHILL	exagera cualquier cosa
MAKE A PLAY FOR	tratando de conquistar
MAKE A RACKET	hacen bulla
MAKE A TRAIN	salimos en el tren
MAKE ALLOWANCE FOR	tener en cuenta
MAKE ANYTHING OF IT	lo entiendo nada
MAKE BELIEVE	fingió
MAKE ENDS MEET	para vivir
MAKE EYES AT	miró amorosamente
MAKE FOR	vamos a
MAKE FUN OF	se burlaron
MAKE GOOD	tener éxito
MAKE GOOD MONEY	gana buen sueldo
MAKE GOOD TIME	ganamos tiempo
MAKE HAY WHILE THE SUN SHINES	aprovecho de la ocasión
MAKE IT SNAPPY	me apurara
MAKE NO BONES ABOUT	no se anduvo con rodeos
MAKE ONE'S BLOOD BOIL	me disgustó
MAKE ONESELF SCARCE	vayase con disimulo
MAKE OUT	escribió; se mantuve bien; identificar
MAKE OVER	convertir
MAKE SURE	esté seguro
MAKE THE GRADE	tendrás éxito
MAKE THE MOST OF	aprovecha todo lo posible
MAKE UP	hicieron; inventó; se hace el maquillaje; hicieron las paces
MAKE UP FOR	compensaremos
MAKE UP ONE'S MIND	decide
MAKE-UP	maquillaje
MAN IN THE STREET	ciudadano común
MEAN WELL	haber tenido buena intención
MEET HALFWAY	hacemosa la mitad
MISS THE POINT	no comprendió el objetivo
MIXED-UP	confusas
MONKEY AROUND WITH	pones a jugar con
NARROW ESCAPE	salvo por un pelo
NEAR MISS	poquito les cae
NECK AND NECK	lado a lado
NEVER MIND	no te ocupes de
NICK OF TIME	ultimo minuto
NIP IN THE BUD	atajado desde el principio
NO MATTER	cueste lo que cueste
NOW AND THEN	de vez en cuando
ODDS AND ENDS	piezas de todas clases

OF AGE	mayoría de edad
OF ONE'S OWN ACCORD	voluntariamente
OFF DAY	día malo
OLD GLORY	la bandera nacional
OLD HAND	mucha experiencia
ON A SHOESTRING	con poco dinero
ON EDGE	nervioso
ON ITS LAST LEGS	ya que no sirve
ON OCCASION	de vez en cuando
ON ONE'S TOES	mantienes alerta
ON PURPOSE	adrede
ON THE AIR	en el aire
ON THE BALL	muy eficiente
ON THE CARPET	le reprobaron
ON THE DOT	en punto
ON THE GO	siempre activo
ON THE HOUSE	por cuenta del dueño
ON THE LEVEL	sincera
ON THE SHELF	no sirvo para nada
ON THE SPOT	en aprietos; en seguida
ON THE SQUARE	honesto
ON THE WHOLE	en general
ON TIME	puntual
ONCE AND FOR ALL	definitivamente
ONCE IN A BLUE MOON	de tarde en tarde
ONCE IN A WHILE	de vez en cuando
ONCE-OVER	vistazo rápido
ONE-HORSE TOWN	pueblito sin importancia
OUT OF DATE	fuera de moda
OUT OF ORDER	descompuesto
OUT OF PRINT	agotado
OUT OF STEP	en desacuerdo
OUT OF THE QUESTION	imposible
OVER AND OVER AGAIN	muchas veces
OVER ONE'S DEAD BODY	sobre mi cadáver
PASS AWAY	falleció
PASS OUT	se desmayó
PAY THROUGH THE NOSE	pagaron; un precio exorbitante
PAY UP	si pagas lo que me debes
PICK A QUARREL	arman pendencias
PICK OFF	matará
PICK ON	seleccionamos; molesta
PICK UP	encontró; adquirió; aumenta la velocidad; recobró
PIPE DOWN	disminuye el ruido
PLAY AROUND	diviertes
PLAYBOY	niño de sociedad
PLAY DOWN	no dio importancia a
PLAY HOOKY	fueron a la escuela

PLAY INTO THE HANDS OF	se dejó engañar por
PLAY SAFE	fué cauteloso
PLAY SECOND FIDDLE	está subordinado
PLAY THE MARKET	especulan
PLAY THE PONIES	apostaba a los caballitos
PLAY UP	hicieron mucha propaganda por
PLAY UP TO	alabó a
PLAY WITH FIRE	jugar con candela
PLAYED OUT	estoy agotado
POLISH OFF	de un golpe se bebió
POP IN	me detuve
POP THE QUESTION	le propuso el matrimonio
PULL A BONER	cometiste un error estúpido
PULL A FAST ONE	engañó
PULL DOWN	desmontes; ganan
PULL IN	llegó; arrestados
PULL OFF	quítate; hagas
PULL ONE'S LEG	me tomando el pelo
PULL ONESELF TOGETHER	se controló
PULL OUT	salió
PULL OVER	arrima
PULL STRINGS (PULL WIRES)	usar influencias
PULL THE WOOL OVER SOMEONE'S EYES	engañas como un bobo
PULL THROUGH	saliste de la gravedad
PULL TOGETHER	cooperamos
PULL UP	arrancó; arrímate
PUT AWAY	comió; pongan
PUT DOWN	suelten; sofocar: atribuyó
PUT HEADS TOGETHER	consultándose
PUT OFF	posponiendo
PUT ON WEIGHT	aumentar de peso
PUT ONE'S CARDS ON THE TABLE	fué franca
PUT ONE'S FOOT DOWN	se opuso con energía
PUT ONE'S FOOT IN IT	cometiste un error
PUT OUT	apaga; sacaron; disgustado
PUT TWO AND TWO TOGETHER	atando cabos
PUT UP	instalaron; hospedaron; dio
PUT UP WITH	aguantarte
QUEER DUCK	muy raro
RAIN CATS AND DOGS	llovía a cántaros
RAIN OR SHINE	con buen o mal tiempo
RAISE CAIN	se pondrá bravísimo
RAW DEAL	fue injusto
RED TAPE	papeleo
REST ON ONE'S LAURELS	dormirse en sus laureles
RIDE HIGH	viven muy bien
RIGHT AWAY	en seguida

RIGHT-HAND MAN	brazo derecho
RIGHT NOW	ahora mismo
RING A BELL	me recuerda algo que olvidé
ROUGH IT	vivir con incomodidades
RULES THE ROOST	lleva los pantalones
RUB SOMEONE THE WRONG WAY	me cae antipática
RUN ACROSS	no encontramos con
RUN AROUND WITH	salió con
RUN DOWN	agotado; arrolles; deteriorado; abusa de; leyó
RUN INTO	encontré
RUN OFF	publicaremos
RUN OUT	se acabó
RUN UP	acumula
SAFE AND SOUND	sano y salvo
SAVE FACE	simular buena cara
SCARE THE DAYLIGHTS OUT OF	se pararon los pelos
SCRAPE TOGETHER	pudimos reunir
SECOND-HAND	de uso
SECOND-RATE	de segunda clase
SEE ABOUT	ponte a preparar
SEE EYE TO EYE	estamos de acuerdo
SEE OFF	despedimos
SEE RED	me enfurece
SEE STARS	vi estrellas
SELL DOWN THE RIVER	traicionaría
SELL OUT	ha vendido todas las entradas
SERVE A TERM	estuvo en la cárcel
SET IN	comienza
SET OUT	colocó; salimos
SET UP	establecida
SETTLE DOWN	se formalizará
SETUP	organización buena
SHELL OUT	contribuiremos dinero
SHIFT FOR ONESELF	me las arreglo solo
SHORT CUT	sin sudar la gota gorda
SHORTHANDED	pocos sirvientes
SHOW UP	asiste
SHOW-OFF	ostentadora
SHUT DOWN	cerrar
SHUT UP	se callase
SIDE WITH	se pusieron al lado del
SIT IN ON	estuvieron presentes en
SIT OUT	sentarnos durante
SIX OF ONE AND A HALF DOZEN OF THE OTHER	lo mismo es lo uno que lo otro
SKATE ON THIN ICE	juegas con candela
SLAP DOWN	rebajó
SLEEP LIKE A TOP	duerme como un lirón

SLEEP ON	consideraré
SLIP OF THE TONGUE	dije sin querer
SLIP THROUGH ONE'S FINGERS	se le fue
SLOUCH	principiante
SMALL FRY	niños; segundo lugar
SMELL A RAT	oler gato encerrado
SNEEZE AT	despreciarse
SO LONG	hasta luego
SOFT SOAP	lisonjees
SOW ONE'S WILD OATS	a los placeres
SPEAK UP	habla que to oigan
SPICK-AND-SPAN	limpia y ordenada
SPLIT HAIRS	nos disgustemos
SPLIT THE DIFFERENCE	dividamos la diferencia
SPONGE ON	abuses de^
SPREAD LIKE WILDFIRE	se propago immediatamente
SQUARE DEAL	tratos justos
STAND A CHANCE	tuvo chance alguno
STAND ASIDE	nos hicimos a un lado
STAND BY	auxiliaremos; quédate aquí
STAND FOR	permitirá; representa
STAND ONE'S GROUND	no cambia de opinión
STAND OUT	destacas notablemente
STAND PAT	defendió
STAND TO REASON	es lógico
STAND UP FOR	sale en defensa de
STAY IN	se quedan
STAY PUT	se queda quieta
STEAL A MARCH	se adelantó
STEP LIVELY	darnos prisa
STEP ON THE GAS	acelera
STEW IN HIS OWN JUICE	se quemara en su propia salsa
STICK OUT LIKE A SORE THUMB	sobresalía
STICK UP FOR	defiendo
STICK-UP	asalto
STRAIGHT FROM THE HORSE'S MOUTH	de buena fuente
STRAIGHT FROM THE SHOULDER	sin embages ni rodeos
STRETCH A POINT	hicieron una concesión
STRIKE OIL	éxito completo
STRIKE WHILE THE IRON IS HOT	si no aprovechamos de la oportunidad
STUCK-UP	presumido
STUFFED SHIRT	almidonado
SUIT TO A T	asienta perfectamente
SWITCH ON	pon
	final
TAIL END	tomar un descanso
TAKE A BREAK	se parece mucho a
TAKE AFTER	desarmar
TAKE APART	cuida
TAKE CARE	me encargaré de

TAKE CHARGE OF	toma nota de
TAKE DOWN	humillaron
TAKE DOWN A PEG	di por sentado
TAKE FOR GRANTED	contrólate
TAKE HOLD OF	fue engañado; fuiste; ganaron
TAKE IN	sin mucha preocupación
TAKE IN ONE'S STRIDE	descansa
TAKE IT EASY	levantó el vuelo; se quitó
TAKE OFF	
TAKE OFF ONE'S HAT	felicito
TAKE ON	emplean
TAKE ONE'S TIME	no te apures
TAKE OUT	lleva; extrajo
TAKE OVER	hacerte cargo del negocio
TAKE PAINS	cuídate
TAKE PLACE	tuvo lugar
TAKE SICK	se enfermó
TAKE SOMEONE'S PART (TAKE SOMEONE'S SIDE)	a tu favor
TAKE SOMETHING UP WITH SOMEONE	discutir este asunto contigo
TAKE THE BULL BY THE HORNS	se enfrentó al problema
TAKE THE FLOOR	tomó la palabra
TAKE THE RAP FOR	pagar las consecuencias por
TAKE THE WORDS OUT OF SOMEONE'S MOUTH	me quitaste las palabras de la boca
TAKE TIME OFF	se ausentó del trabajo
TAKE TIME OUT	suspendemos el trabajo
TAKE TO TASK	reprendió
TAKE TURNS	se alternaron
TAKE UP	aprender; ocupa
TALK OF THE TOWN	tema del pueblo
TALK SHOP	hablan de negocios
TALK THROUGH HIS HAT	habla disparates
TALK TURKEY	hablemos del negocio
TALL STORY	historia más fantástica
TELL IT TO THE MARINES	vete con el cuento a otra parte
TELL SOMEONE	a mi me lo vas a decir
TELL SOMEONE OFF	le reprendió
THANK ONE'S LUCKY STARS	gracias a mi estrella
THINK BETTER OF IT	cambió de opinión
THINK LITTLE (HIGHLY) OF	admiro poco (mucho)
THINK OUT	resolvemos
THINK OVER	pensarlo
THINK UP	buscar
THROUGH THE GRAPEVINE	oído decir
THROUGH THICK AND THIN	a través de buenas y malas situaciones
THROW (HAVE) A FIT	se encolerizaron
THROW A PARTY	dieron una fiesta
THROW IN THE SPONGE	se dio por vencido
TIP OFF	informado

TIRED (TUCKERED) OUT	agotado
TOM, DICK AND HARRY	Juan de los Palotes
TOOTH AND NAIL	fervorosamente
TRY ON	pruébatelo
TURN A DEAF EAR	se hizo la sorda
TURN A HAIR	se alteró
TURN DOWN	rehusó; baja
TURN IN	me acuesto; entregó
TURN OFF	apagué
TURN ON	puse
TURN OUT	resultó; fueron; produce
TURN OVER	
TURN OVER A NEW LEAF	
TURN UP	dejaré; se volcó
TWIDDLE ONE'S THUMBS	me enmendaré
TWO-FACED	apareció; pon más alto
	se puso a jugar
UNDER ONE'S BREATH	persona de dos caras
UNDER THE TABLE	
UNDER SOMEONE'S THUMB	en voz baja
UNDER THE WEATHER	secretamente
UP AND ABOUT	bajo el dominio de su esposa
UP TO	me siento mal
UP-TO-DATE	andaba de arriba para abajo
UP-TO-THE-MINUTE	tramando; depende de
UPSET THE APPLECART	completa hasta la fecha
	último minuto
WAIT UP	estropeó los planes
WATER WAGON	
WEAR OFF	se desvelaron esperando
WELL-HEELED	bebo bedidas alcohólicas
WELL-OFF	desaparecerán
WELL-TO-DO	bien de dinero
WET BLANKET	buena cantidad de dinero; no tienes
WHAT'S UP?	adinerada problemas
WHITE ELEPHANT	aguafiestas
WILD-GOOSE CHASE	qué pasa
WIN HANDS DOWN	mal negocio
WIND UP	búsqueda infructuosa
WITH FLYING COLORS	ganó fácilmente
WOLF	terminemos
WORK OUT	sale muy bien
WORK UP	comas de prisa
WORN OUT	resolverá; saldrán bien
WRAP UP	prepararemos
	rendida
	concluiremos

ENGLISH-SPANISH/SPANISH-ENGLISH VOCABULARY

CONTENTS

	Page
ENGLISH-SPANISH VOCABULARY	1
SPANISH-ENGLISH VOCABULARY	21
SUPPLEMENTAL VOCABULARY, LEGAL AND CRIMINAL	36

ENGLISH-SPANISH/SPANISH-ENGLISH VOCABULARY

ENGLISH-SPANISH VOCABULARY

a—un, una
abode—domicilio, m; residencia, f
about—acerca de, tocante a, de, como
above—arriba
absence—ausencia, f
absent—ausenta
accent—acento, m
accord—acuerdo, m
according to—según
ache—dolor, m
acquaintance—conocido, -a
acre—acre, m
addict—adicto, -a
address—dirección, f
admission—admisión, f
advice—aviso, m; consejo, m
a few—unos, unos cuantos, unos pocos
affair—asunto, m; negocio, m
affidavit—declaración, f
afoot—a pie
after—después (de), después (de) que, detrás (de)
afternoon—tarde, f
af terwards—des pues
again—otra vez, de nuevo
against—en contra de, contra
age—edad, f
agent—agente, m
ago—hace
a great deal of—mucho, -a
agreement—acuerdo, m; pacto, m
ahead—adelante, delante
air—aire, m
airplane—avión, m
airport—aeropuerto, m
alien—extranjero, -a
all—todo alley—callejón, m
all right—está bien, bueno
almost—ya mero, casi
alone—solo, -a
along—a lo largo de
a lot of—mucho, -a

already—ya
also—también
although—aunque
always—siempre
America—América, f
American—americano, -a
ammunition—munición(es), f; parque, m
among—entre
an—un, una
and—y
angry—enojado, -a
animal—animal, m
announcement—anuncio, m
another—otro, -a
ánswer—contestación, f; respuesta, f
any—algún(o), -a; cualquier(a)
anybody—alguien, cualquiera, nadie
anyhow—de cualquier modo, de todos modos
anyone—nadie, alguien, cualquier(a)
any place—cualquier lugar, algún lugar, ningún lugar
anything—algo, nada
anyway—de cualquier modo, de todos modos
anywhere—cualquier lugar, algún lugar, ningún lugar
apartment—apartamiento, m
apple—manzana, f
application—aplicación, f; solicitud, f
appointment—cita, f; compromiso, m
April—abril
archive—archivo, m
are there?—¿hay?
argument—disgusto, m
arm—brazo, m
army—ejército, m
around—alrededor
arrangement—arreglo, m
arrival—llegada, f
artist—artista, m-f
as—como, de, tan
as far as—en cuanto, hasta

as many—tantos, -as
as much—tanto, -a
assistant—ayudante, m
as soon as—luego que, tan pronto como
as soon as possible—lo más pronto posible
at—en, a
at dawn—al amanecer, a la madrugada
at dusk—al anochecer
at first—al principio
at home—en casa
at last—al fin
at least—a lo menos, por lo menos, al menos
at once—en seguida, al instante
at present—actualmente
at sun down—a la caída del sol, a la caída de la tarde
at the beginning---al principio
at the end oí—al fin de
at times—a veces
August—agosto
aunt—tía, f
authority—autoridad, f
automobile—automóvil, m; carro, m; coche, m
autumn—otoño, m
avenue—avenida, f
axe—hacha, f (el)
Aztec—azteca

B

baby—niño (a); bebí; nene, m; nena, f; infante, m
bachelor—soltero, m
back—detrás (de), atrás (de), espalda, f
back door—puerta de atrás, f; puerta trasera, f
back seat—asiento de atrás, m; asiento trasero, m
bacon—tocino, m
bad—mal(o), -a
badge—placa, f
badly—mal
bag—bolsa, f
baggage—equipaje, m
baggage check—contraseña, f
bail—fianza, f

baker—panadero, m
bakery—panadería, f
bald—pelón, -a (slang); calvo, -a
banana—banana, f; plátano, m
bandit—bandido, m
bank—banco, m; orilla, f
banker—banquero, m
banner—bandera, f
banquet—banquete, m
baptismal certifícate—fe de bautismo, f
baptismal ñame—nombre de pila, m
bar—cantina, f
barbecue—barbacoa, f
barber—peluquero, m; barbero, m
barber shop—peluquería, f; barbería, f
barely—apenas
barge—barco, m; lancha, f
barmaid—cantinera, f
barrack—barraca, f
barrel—barril, m
bartender—cantinero, m
base—base, f
bastard—bastardo
bath—baño, m
bathroom—cuarto de baño, m
battery—batería f; pila, f; acumulador, m
beach—playa, f
bean—frijol, m
bear—oso, -a
beard—barba, f
beautiful—bello, -a; hermoso, -a
because—porque
because of—a causa de; por
bed—cama, f
bedroll—mochila, f
bedroom—recámara, f
beef—res, f
beefsteak—bistec, m
beer—cerveza,f
beet—betabel, m
before (front of)—delante de
before (time)—antes de
beprgar—mendigo, m
behind—detrás (de), atrás (de)
bell—campana, f
belly—panza, f
below—debajo (de), abajo (de)

belt—cinto, m; cinturón, m; faja, f
belt maker—talabartero, m
bench—banco, m; banca, f
beneath—debajo (de)
beside—al lado (de) ; cerca (de)
besides—además (de)
best—mejor
better—mejor
between—entre
B-girl—fichera, f (slang)
big—grande
bigamist—bigamo, m
bigamy—bigamia
big belly—panzón, -a
bilí—billete, m; cuenta, f
billiard room—billar, m
billfold—billetera, f; cartera, f
binoculars—gemelos, m; lentes de larga distancia, m
biology—biología, f
bird—pájaro, m; ave, f (el)
birth—nacimiento, m
birth certifícate—certificado de nacimiento, m; acta de nacimiento, f (el)
birthday—cumpleaños, m
birthmark—estigma, f; marca de nacimiento, f
biscuit—bollo, m; bizcocho, m
black—negro, -a
blackboard—pizarra, f; pizarrón, m
blacksmith—herrero, m; forjador, m
blame—culpa, f; falta, f
blanket—cobija, f; frazada, f
blind—ciego, -a
block (city)—cuadra, f; manzana, f
blond—rubio, -a; huero, -a
blood—sangre, f
blouse—blusa, f
blue—azul
boat—bote, m; barco, m; lancha, f
body—cuerpo, m
bond—fianza, f
bone—hueso, m
bookkeeper—tenedor de libros, m
boot—bota, f
border—frontera, f; orilla, f

Border Patrol—Patrulla de la Frontera, f; migra, f (slang)
boss—patrón, m; jefe, m
both—ambos, los (las) dos
bottle—botella, f
bottom—fondo, m
bow-legged—patizambo, -a
box—caja, f; cajón, m
boxear—furgón, m
boy—muchacho, m; chamaco, m (slang) chavalo, m (slang), niño
bracelet—pulsera, f; braceleta, f
brake—freno, m
branch—ramo, m; rama, f
brave—valiente, bravo, -a
brawl—barulla, f; disputa, f
bread—pan, m
breakfast—desayuno, m; almuerzo, m
breast—pecho, m
brewery—cervecería, f
brick—ladrillo, m
brickmason (layer)—albañil, m
bridge—puente, m
bridle—freno, m broad—ancho, -a
broken—roto, -a; quebrado, -a
brood—cría, f
broom—escoba, f
broomcorn—millo de escoba, m
brother—hermano, m
brother-in-law—cuñado, m
brown—café
brunette—moreno, -a; trigueño, -a
brush—chaparral, m; monte, m; matorral, m
bucket—cubeta, f; balde, m; bote, m
building—edificio, m
bull—toro, m
bullet—bala, f; balazo, m
bulletin—boletín, m
bundle—bulto, m; chiva, f (slang)
burn—quemada, f
burn scar—quemada, f
bus—autobús, m; camión, m; ómnibus, m
bus boy—mozo, m
business—negocio, m
busy—ocupado, -a
but—pero, sino, mas
butcher—carnicero, m

butter—mantequilla, f
button—botón, m
by—por, para
by (near)—cerca
by day—de día
by means of—por medio de
by night—de noche

C

cabbage—repollo, m
cafe—café, m
cake—bollo, m; pastel, m
calendar—calendario, m; cromo, m
calí—becerro, -a
camp—campo, m
can—bote, m; lata, f
candy—dulce, m
canoe—canoa, f; chalupa, f
cap—cachucha, f; gorra, f
capital—capital, f
car—carro, m; auto, m; coche, m
card—tarjeta, f
care—cuidado
careful—cuidado; cuidadoso, -a
carefully—cuidadosamente
carpenter—carpintero, m
carpenter shop—carpintería, f
carrot—zanahoria, f
cash—al contado
cashier—cajero, m; contador, m
cat—gato, -a
cattle—ganado, m
cattleguard—guardavacas, m
cattleman—ganadero, m
cause—causa, f
cave—cueva, f
ceiling—cielo, m
cemetery—cementerio, in; panteón, m
cent—centavo, m
century—siglo, m
certain—seguro, -a; cierto, -a
certainly—ciertamente; ¿cómo no?
certifícate—certificado, m
chair—silla, f
chalk—tiza, f
chance—oportunidad, f
change—cambio, m

charming—simpático, -a
chauffer—chofer, m
cheap—barato, -a
check (commercial)—cheque, m
cheek—mejilla, f
cheese—queso, m
cherry—cereza, f
chest—pecho, m; baúl, m
chicken—pollo, m; gallina, f
chief—jefe, m; patrón, m
child—niño, -a
child's nurse—nana, f
chin—barba, f
Christian ñame—nombre de pila; m; primer nombre, m
Christmas—Navidad, f
Christmas Eve—Nochebuena, f
church—iglesia, f
cigar—puro, m; cigarro, m
cigarette—cigarrillo, m; cigarro, m
citizen—ciudadano, -a
citizenship—ciudadanía, f
city—ciudad, f
civil—civil
class—clase, f
clay—barro, m.
clean—limpio, -a
clear—claro, -a
clearly—claramente
clerk—dependiente, m-f
clock—reloj, m
clóse—cerca (de)
clothes—ropa, f
clothing—ropa, f
cloud—nube, f
coach—coche, m
coat—saco, m; abrigo, m
cobbler—zapatero, m
cock—gallo, m
coffee—café, m
cold—frío, -a; frío, m
collar—cuello, m
colusión—choque, m
colony—colonia, f
color—color, m
commission merchant—comisionista, m-
communist—comunista, m-f
companion—compañero, -a

company—compañía, f
compartment—compartimiento, m
complaint—queja, f
complete—completo, -a
complexión—tez, f
concerning—acerca de, tocante a, de
constable—alguacil, m
cónsul—cónsul, m
consulate—consulado, m
content(ed)—contento, -a
contents—contenidos, m
contract laborer—bracero, m
contractor—contratista, m
convict—convicto, m
cook—cocinero, -a
cool—fresco, -a
cop—chota, f (slang)
copper—cobre, m
cord—cordón, m; cuerda, f
corn (dry)—maíz, m
corn (fresh)—elote, m
córner—esquina, f; rincón, m
cornfield—milpa, f
corral—corral, m
correct—correcto, -a
cotton—algodón, m
cotton picking—pizca, f
cottonwoodT—álamo, m
counsel,—consejo, m; aviso, m
country—país, m; campo, m
country house—villa, f
countryman—campesino, m
countryman (fellow)—paisano, m
county—condado, m
court—corte, f
courthouse—casacorte, f
cousin—primo, -a
cow—vaca, f
cowboy—vaquero, m
coyote—coyote, m
crate box—cajón, m
crazy—loco, -a
cream—crema, f
credit (on)—al fiado; crédito, m
creek—arroyo, m; riachuelo, m
crew (ship)—tripulación, f
crewman—tripulante, m
crime—crimen, m; delito, m
criminal—criminal, m; reo, m
cripple—rengo, -a; cojo, -a

cross—cruz, f
crude—crudo, -a
crutch—muleta, f
cry—grito, m
crybaby—llorón, -a
cucumber—pepino, m
cup—taza, f
curve—curva, f
custom—costumbre, f; moda, f
customs—aduana, f
customs officer—aduanero, m
cut—cortada, f
cute—bonito, -a; lindo, -a
cut scar—cortada, f

D

dad—papá, m
daily—diario, -a
daily newspaper—diario, m
dairy—lechería, f
damage—daño, m
dance—baile, m
dancer—bailarín, -a
danger—peligro, m
dangerous—peligroso, -a
dark—o(b)scuro, -a
date—fecha, f; cita, f
daughter—hija, f
daughter-in-law—nuera, f
day—día, m
day after tomorrovv—pasado mañana
day before yesterday—anteayer
day laborer—jornalero, m
day off—día de descanso, m
dead—muerto, -a
deaf—sordo, -a
dear (affection)—querido, -a
dear (costly)—caro
death—muerte, f
debt—deuda, f
December—diciembre
deed—hecho, m; acto, m
deep—hondo, -a
deer—venado, -a
defect—defecto, m
delicious—delicioso, -a
dentist—dentista, m-f
departure—salida, f
dependent—dependiente, m-f

deportation—deportación, f
description—descripción, f
desert—desierto, m
destination—destinación, f
detail—detalle, m
detective—detective, m; detective, m
detention camp—corralón, m (slang)
devil—diablo, m
difference—diferencia, f
different—diferente
difficult—difícil, duro, -a (slang)
difficulty—dificultad, f
dinner—cena, f; comida, f
direction—dirección, f; rumbo, m
director—director, m
dirt—polvo, m; tierra, f
dirty—sucio, -a; mugroso, -a (slang)
dispute—disgusto, m; mitote, m
distance—distancia, f
distant—distante
district—distrito, m
ditch—zanja, f; acequia, f; canal, m
divisional—divisorio, -a
divorce—divorcio, m
doctor—doctor, -a; médico, m
document—documento, m
dog—perro, -a
doll—muñeca, f
dollar—dólar, m
domestic—doméstico, -a
domicile—domicilio, m
donkey—burro, -a
door—puerta, f
double—doble
doubt—duda, f
dough—masa, f
dove—paloma, f
dovvn—abajo
dozen—docena, f
drag—rastra, f
drag trail—sendero rastreado, m
drawer—cajón, m
dress—vestido, m; traje, m
dressmaker—costurera, f; modista, f
driver—chofer, m
drug—droga, f
druggist—droguero, m; boticario, m
drug store—botica, f; farmacia, f; droguería, f
drunk—borracho, ebrio, tomado
drunkard—borrachón, m

drunkenness—borracher(í)a, f; borrachez, f
dry—seco, -a
duck—pato, -a
during—durante
dusk—anochecer, m
dust—polvo, m
duty—obligación, f; deber, m
duties (customs)— derechos; impuestos, m

E

each—cada
eagle—águila, f (el)
ear (inner)—oído, m
ear (outer)—oreja, f
early—temprano
earring—arete, m
earth—tierra, f
easily—fácilmente
east—este, m; oriente, m
eastern—oriental
easy—fácil
ebony—ébano, m
echo—eco, m
education—educación, f
egg—huevo, m; blanquillo, m
eight—ocho
eighth—octavo, -a
either—o
elbow—codo, m
election—elección, f
electric—elétrico, -a
electricity—electricidad, f
elegant—elegante
embassy—embajada, f
emigrant—emigrante, m
employee—empleado, -a; trabajador, -a
employment—empleo, m; trabajo, m; chamba, f (slang)
empty—vacío, -a
enemy—enemigo, -a
engine—locomotora, f; máquina, f
engineer—ingeniero, m; maquinista, m
English—inglés, -a
English (language)—inglés, m
enough—bastante, suficiente, basta
entire—entero, -a
entrance—entrada, f
entrance gate—garita, f (slang)
entry—entrada, f

envelope—sobre, m
equal—igual
eraser—borrador, m
errand—mandado, m; recado, m
error—error, m; falta, f
especial—especial
even—llano, -a; liso, -a
evening—tarde, f; noche, f
ever—alguna vez
every—cada; todos los------; todas las ____
everybody—todos, todo el mundo
everywhere—por todas partes, por donde-quiera
evidence—evidencia, f
ewe—oveja, f
exact—exacto, -a; mero, -a (slang)
exactly—exactamente, mero (slang)
examination—examen, m
example—ejemplo, m
excellent—excelente
except—menos
exclusión—exclusión, f
excuse—excusa, f
exercise—ejercicio, m
expenses—gastos, m
expensive—caro, -a
express—expreso, m; exprés, m
extensión—extensión, f
extra—extra
eye—ojo, m
eyebrow—ceja, f
eyeglasses—anteojos, m; lentes, m
eyelash—pestaña,
eyelid—párpado, m

F

face—cara, f
fací—hecho, m
factory—fábrica, f
fair—claro, -a
faith—fe, f
fall—otoño, m
false—falso, -a
falsehood—falsedad, f; mentira, f
family—familia, f
far—lejos
fare—pasaje, m
farm—rancho, m; hacienda, f

farmer—hacendado, m; ranchero, m; campesino, m
farm laborer—labrador, m; cultivador, m; sembrador, m
father—más lejos
fashion—moda, f; manera, f
fast—rápido, -a
fat—gordo, -a
father—padre, m; papá, m
father-in-law—suegro, m
fault—culpa, f
February—febrero
federal—federal
fee—derecho, m
fellow countryman—paisano, m
female—hembra, f
fence—cerca, f; cerco, m
fence jumper—alambrista, m-f (slang)
few—pocos, -as; unos, -as
fewer—menos
field—campo, m; labor, f
fifteen—quince
fifth—quinto, -a
fifty—cincuenta
fight—pelea, f; pleito, m
file—archivo, m; lima, f
film—película, f
final—final, último, -a
finally—al fin, por fin
fine—multa, f
finger—dedo, m
fingernail—uña, f
fingerprints—huellas digitales, f; huellas de los dedos, f
fire—lumbre, f; fuego, m
fireman—bombero, m; fogonero, m
firewood—leña, f
first—primer(o), -a
fish—pez, m; pescado, m
fisherman—pescador, -a
fishing—pesca, f
five—cinco
five hundred—quinientos, -as
flag—bandera, f
flame—llama, f
flashlight—luz de mano, f (slang); foco de mano, m
flat (tire)—llanta pinchada, f
flat-nosed—chato, -a
flight—vuelo, m

flood—inundación, f; diluvio, m
floor—piso, m; suelo, m
flour—harina, f
flower—flor, f
fly—mosca, f
following—siguiente
food—alimento, m; comida, f
fool—tonto, -a
foot—pie, m
foot bridge—puente de a pie, m
footpath—senda, f; sendero, m; vereda, f
for—por, para
forearm—canilla, f
forehead—frente, f
foreign—extranjero, -a
foreman—mayordomo, -a
forest—selva, f; bosque, m
forgery—falsificación, f
fork—tenedor, m; horca, f
form—forma, f
former—anterior
formerly—anteriormente, antes
for that reason—por eso, así que
fortnight—quincena, f
forty—cuarenta
forward—adelante
four—cuatro
fourteen—catorce
fourth—cuarto, -a
fowl—ave, f (el)
fox—zorro, -a
frank—franco, -a
frankness—franqueza, f
free—libre
freedom—libertad, f
freight—carga, f
freight train—trend de carga, m
French—francés, -a
frequently—frecuentemente, a menudo
fresh—fresco, -a
friar—fraile, m
Friday—viernes, m
friend—amigo, -a
f rom—de, desde
from time to time—de vez en cuando
front of—delante de
front seat—asiento de enfrente, m
fruit—fruta, f
fryer (chicken)—pollo, m
frying pan—sartén, f

full—lleno, -a
furniture—muebles, m
furniture store—mueblería, f
future—futuro, m; porvenir, m

G

gain—ganancia, f
gambler—tahúr, m
garage—garage, m
garlic—ajo, m
generally—generalmente
gentleman—caballero, m
Germán—alemán, -a
gift—regalo, m
girdle—faja, f; cinto, m
girl—muchacha, f; niña, f
glance—mirada, f; ojeada, f
glass—vidrio, m
glass (drinking)—vaso, m
glove—guante, m
goat—cabra, f; chivo, -a
goathered—pastor, m; chivero, m; borreguero, m; cabrero, m
God—Dios
goddaughter,—ahijada, f
godfather—padrino, m
God grant—ojalá
godmother—madrina, f
godson—ahijado, m
gold—oro, m
good—bueno, -a
goodbye—adiós
governess—nana, f
government—gobierno, m
grain combine—segadora de combinación, f
grandchild—nieto, -a
grandfather—abuelo, m
grandmother—abuela, f
grape—uva, f
grapefruit—toronja, f
grass—sacate, m; yerba, f
graveyard—panteón, m; cementerio, m
gray—gris; (hair) pelo canoso, m
great—grande, famoso, -a
green—verde
grocer—abacero, m
groceries—abarrotes, m
ground—suelo, m; tierra, f
group—grupo, m

guarantee—garantía, f
guard—guardia, m-f
guest—huésped, -a
guide—guía, m-f
guilt—culpa, f
guilty—culpable
gulf—golfo, m
gun—fusil, m; (shotgun—escopeta, f)
gunshot—tiro, m; disparo, m; balazo, m

H

hair—pelo, m; cabello, m
hairy—peludo, -a; velludo, -a
half—medio, -a; mitad, f
half-brother—medio hermano, m
half-sister—media hermana, f
hand—mano, f
handcuffs—esposas, f; manillas, f
handkerchief—pañuelo, m
handsome—guapo, -a
hangover—crudo, -a
happy—feliz, alegre, contento,- a
harbor—puerto, m
hard—duro, -a; difícil
harm—daño, m
harvest—cosecha, f
harvester—cosechero, m; segadora, f
harvest season—pizca, f
hat—sombrero, m
hate—odio, m
hawk—gavilán, m
hay—heno, m; sacate, m
head—cabeza, f
health—salud, f
hearing—audiencia, f
heart—corazón, m
heat—calor, m
heater—calorífero, m
heavy—pesado, -a
heel—talón, m
helicopter—helicóptero, m
hell—infierno, m
helio—hola, bueno
help—ayuda, f
hen—gallina, f
herb—hierba, f; yerba, f
herd—ganado, m; rebaño, m
here—aquí, acá
hide—piel, f

hidden---rescondido, -a
high—alto, -a
high priced—caro, -a; costoso, -a
highway—carretera, f; calzada, f
hill—loma, f; cerro, m
hip—cadera, f
history—historia, f
hoe—azadón, m
hog—marrano, -a; puerco, -a
hole—agujero, m; pozo, m; hoyo, m
holiday—día de fiesta, m
holster—funda, f
horae—casa, f; hogar, m; domicilio, m
honre (at)—en casa
homeland—patria, f; tierra, f
homework—tarea, f
honest—honesto, -a
hope—esperanza, f
horse—caballo, m
horn (auto)—bocina, f; pito, m
horn (animal)—cuerno, m
horseshoe—herradura, f ..
horse stable—.caballeriza, f
hose—media, f
hose (garden)—manguera, f
hospital—hospital, m
host—huésped, m
hostess—huéspeda, f; fichera (B-girl), f (slang)
hot—caliente
hotel—hotel, m
hour—hora, f
house—casa, f
household goods—muebles, m; menaje de casa, m
housekeeper—ama de llaves, f; doméstica, f
housemaid—sirvienta, f; criada, f
house trailer—casa de remolque, f
housewife—ama de casa, f (el)
how—como
however—sin embargo
how long—cuanto tiempo
how many—cuantos, -as
how much—cuanto, -a
hundred—cien (to)
hunger—hambre, f (el)
hungover—crudo, -a (slang)
hurricane—huracán, m
hurry!—¡ándale!; ¡apresúrese!
husband—esposo, m; marido, m

I

ice—hielo, m
ice cream—helado, m; nieve, f
idea—idea, f
identical—idéntico, -a
identifica tion—identificación, f
idiot—idiota, m-f
if—si
if (that is) so—si es así
ill—enfermo, -a; malo, -a
illegal—ilegal
illegally—ilegalmente
ilegítimate child—hijo, -a natural; hijo, -a ilegítimo, -a illiterate—analfabeto, -a
illness—enfermedad, f
immediately—en seguida, inmediatamente
immigrant—inmigrante, m
immigrant inspector—inspector de inmigración, m
immigrafion—inmigración, f
immoral—inmoral
importance—importancia, f
important—importante
impossible—imposible
impression—impresión, f
in—en
inch—pulgada, f
incident—incidente, m
independence—independencia, f
independent—independiente
Indian—indio, -a
indolence—desidia, f; indolencia, f
industry—industria, f
in front—en frente, delante
inhabitant—habitante, m
ink—tinta, f
innocent—inocente
in order (to)—para
in order that—de manera que, para que
insane—loco, -a
insecticide—insecticida, f
inside—dentro (de)
inspector—inspector, m
in spite of—a pesar de
instead of—en vez de
intelligent—inteligente
intention—-intención, f
interest—interés, m
interior—interior, m
international—internacional
intestine—tripa, f; intestino, m
intímate—intimo, -a
investigation—investgación, f
iron—hierro, m; fierro, m
iron (clothes)—plancha, f
irrigation ditch—acequia, f
island—isla, f
is there?—¿hay?
Italian—italiano, -a
Italy—Italia

J

jack (auto)—gato, m; yaque, m (slang)
jacket—chaqueta, f
jack rabbit—liebre, f
jail—cárcel, f
janitor—portero, m; conserje, m
January—enero
jaw—quijada, f; mandíbula, f
jewel—joya, f
jeweler—joyero, m
jewelry—alhajas, f; joyas, f
jewelery shop—joyería, f
Job—trabajo, m; chamba, f (slang)
journey—viaje, m
judge—juez, m
juice—jugo, m
July—julio
June—junio
jury—jurado, m
just—no más, nada más, justo, -a
justice—justicia, f
justice of peace—juez de paz, m

K

key—llave, f
khaki—kaki, caqui
kid—cabrito, m; chavalo, -a (slang); chamaco, -a (slang)
kidnaper—secuestrador, m
kidnaping—secuestro, m
kidney—riñon, m
kilogram—kilogramo, m
kilometer—kilómetro, m
kind—clase, f; bondadoso, -a
kiss—beso, m
kitchen—cocina, f

kitchen utensils—trastos de cocina, m
kite—papalote, m
knapsack—mochila, f
knee—rodilla, f
knife—navaja, f; cuchillo, m
knife (large)—machete, m
knowledge—sabiduría, f; conocimiento, m

L

labor—labor, f; trabajo, m
laborer—trabajador, m; jornalero, m
lack—falta, f
lad—mozo, m; joven, m
lady—señora, f; señorita, f
lake—lago, m; laguna, f
lamb—borrego, -a; cordero
lame—rengo, -a; cojo, -a
land—tierra, f; terreno, m
landing (airplane)—aterrizaje
landlord—patrón, m
language—idioma, m; lengua, f
lard—manteca, f
large—grande
large-bellied—panzón, -a
lariat—lazo, m
lasso—lazo, m
last—último, -a
last month—el mes pasado
last ñame—apellido, m
last night—anoche
last week;—la semana pasada
last year—el año pasado
late—tarde
lately—últimamente
later—después, más tarde
launch—lancha, f; chalupa, f
laundress—lavandera, f
laundry—lavandería, f
law—ley, f
lawyer—abogado, -a; licenciado, -a
laziness—desidia, f; pereza, f
lazy—perezoso, -a; flojo, -a (slang)
lead—plomo, m
leader—líder, m; jefe, m
leaf—hoja, f
lean—delgado, -a; flaco, -a
least (at)—a lo menos, por lo menos
leather—cuero, m; baqueta, f
leatherworker—talabartero, m

left—izquierdo, -a
leg—pierna, f
legal—legal
legally—legalmente
lemon—limón, m
length—longitud, m;
largo-less—menos
lesson—lección, f
let's see—vamos a ver
letter—carta, f; letra, f
level ground—llano, m; plano, m
liberty—libertad, f
license—licencia, f
license píate—placa, f
lie—mentira, f
life—vida, f
light—luz, f
light (weight)—ligero, -a
light (color)—claro
light, (electric)—luz eléctrica, f
light (bulb)—foco, m
lighter (cigarette)—encendedor, m
like—como
like—semejante
like that—así
like this—así
likewise—también
lime—lima, f
limit—límite, m
line—línea, f
lip—labio, m
list—lista, f
little—poco, -a (quantity); pequeño, -a (size)
livestock—ganado, m
living—vida, f; subsistencia, f
living room—sala, f
load—carga, f
lobster—langosta, f
local—local
location—lugar, m; sitio, m
long—largo, -a
look out!—¡cuidado!
loose—flojo, -a; suelto, -a
love—amor, m
low—bajo, -a
luck—suerte, f
lunch—merienda, f; lonche, m (slang)
lunch counter—lonchería, f (slang)
lung—pulmón, m

M

machine—máquina, f
machinery—maquinaria, f
machinist—maquinista, m-f
mad—loco, -a; enojado, -a
magazine—revista, f
maid—criada, f
mail—correo, m
mailman—cartero, m
maimed—mocho, -a
main boss—mero gallo, m (slang)
maize—maíz, m
maize field—milpa, f
mamma—mamá, f
man—hombre, m; señor, m
manager—gerente, m; director, m
mandate—orden, m-f
manrier—manera, f; modo, m
many—muchos, -as
map—mapa, m
March—marzo
mare—yegua, f
margin—margen, m; orilla, f
marijuana—marijuana, f
mark—marca, f; seña, f; signo, m
market—mercado, m
market place—mercado, m
marriage—casamiento, m; matrimonio, m
marriage certifícate—certificado de matrimonio, m
married—casado, -a
masón—albañil, m
mass—misa, f (church); conjunto, m (people)
matches—cerillos, m; fósforos, m
matter—asunto, m
May—mayo
maybe—quizá, quizás, tal vez
mayor—presidente municipal, m; alcalde, m
meal—comida, f
mean—malo, -a
meanwhile—mientras tanto, entre tanto
meat—carne, f
meat market—carnicería, f
mechanic—mecánico, m
medallion—medalla, f
medicine—medicina, f
meeting—junta, f
member—miembro, -a
menú—carta, f; lista, f; menú, m
merchant—comerciante, m
metal—metal, m
method—método, m; modo, m
Mexican—mexicano, -a
Mexican dollar—peso, m
mid-day—mediodía, m
middle—medio
midnight—medianoche, f
midwife—partera, f
mile—milla, f
milk—leche, f
milkman—lechero, m
mili—molino, m
miller—molinero, m
mine—mina, f
miner—minero, m
mineral—mineral, m
minor—menor (de edad)
minus—menos
minute—minuto, m
miracle—milagro, m
Miss—señorita, f
mistake—falta, f; error, m
mistress—mujer de pie, f; querida, f
mode—modo, -a; manera, f
mold—moho, m
mole—lunar, m
Mom—mamá, f
moment—momento, m
Monday—lunes, m
money—dinero, m; moneda, f
month—mes, m
moon—luna, f
more—más
morning—mañana, f
mosquito—zancudo, m; mosquito, m
moss—moho, m
mother—madre, f; mamá, f
mother-in-law—suegra, f; madre política, f
motive—motivo, m
motor—motor, m
mountain—montaña, f; monte, m
mouse—ratón, m
mouth—boca, f
movie (theatre)—cine, m
Mr.—señor, m
Mrs.—señora, f
much—mucho, -a
mud—lodo, m
mulé—muía, f

municipality—municipio, m
murder—asesinato, m; homicidio, m
murderer—asesino, -a
music—música, f
musician—músico, m
mustache—bigote, m
mustard—mostaza, f
mutilated—mocho, -a

N

name—nombre, m
namesake—tocayo, -a
narcotic—narcótica, m
narrow—angosto, -a; estrecho, -a
nation—nación, f
national—nacional
nationality—nacionalidad, f
native—nativo, -a
native country—tierra, f; patria, f
naturalization—naturalización, f
near—cerca (de)
nearly—casi
necessary—necesario, -a
neck—cuello, m; pescuezo, m
neighbor—vecino, -a
neighborhood—barrio, m; vecindad, f
neither—ni, tampoco
neither . . . ñor—ni ... ni
nephew—sobrino, m
nervous—nervioso, -a
never—nunca, jamás
nevertheless—sin embargo
new—nuevo, -a
news—noticia(s), f
newspaper—periódico, m; diario, m
New Year—año nuevo, m
next—después, siguiente, luego, próximo, -a
next month—el mes que viene, el mes que entra
next week—la semana que viene, la semana que entra
next year—el año que viene, el año que entra
nickname—sobrenombre, m; apodo, m
niece—sobrina, f
night—noche, f
night before last—anteanoche
nightfall—anochecer, m
nine—nueve
ninth—noveno, -a

no—no
nobody—nadie
noise—ruido, m
no longer—ya no
no more—ya no
none—ninguno, -a
nook—rincón, m
noon—mediodía, m
no one—nadie
nor—ni
north—norte, m
nose—nariz, f
not—no
not any—ningún (o), -a
not anymore—ya no
nothing—nada
not yet—todavía no
November—noviembre
novice—novicio, -a
now—ahora
nowadays—hoy día
number—número, m
nurse—enfermera, f
nurse (for children)—niñera, f
nut—nuez, f

O

oak—roble, m
oath—juramento, m
oats—avena, f
occupation—ocupación, f
occupied—ocupado, -a
October—octubre
of—de
of course—claro, por supuesto, seguro que sí
off duty—franco, -a
offense—ofensa, f
offer--oferta, f
office—oficina, f
officer—oficial, m
official—oficial, m
offspring—cría, f
often—a menudo
oil—aciete, m
okay—está bien
oíd—viejo, -a; anciano, -a
older—mayor
oldest—mayor
on—en, sobre

once—una vez (at)
once—en seguida
one—un(o), -a
one-eyed—tuerto, -a
one hundred—cien (to)
on foot—a pie
onion—cebolla, f
only—nada más, no más, sino, so único, -a
on the outside—por fuera
on time —a tiempo
open—abierto, -a
opium—opio, m
opportunity—oportunidad, f
opposite—opuesto, -a
or—o, u
orange—naranja, f
orange tree—naranjo, m
order—orden, f
orphan—huérfano, -a
organization—organización, f
orient—oriente, m; este, m
oriental—oriental
origin—origen, m
original—original
other—otro, -a
otherwise—de otra manera, de ot modo
our—nuestro, -a, etc.
ours—el nuestro, etc.
out—afuera, fuera
outside—afuera, fuera
over—sobre, encima
overalls—pantalón de pechera
overcoat—abrigo, m; sobretodo, m
over there—allá
owner—dueño, -a; amo, -a (el)
oyster—ostión, m

P

package—paquete, m
packing shed—bodega, f
page—página, f
pain—dolor, m
painter—pintor, -a
pair—par, m
pants—pantalones, m
paper—papel, m
papa—papá, m
pardon—perdón, m
parents—padres, m

park—parque, m
part—parte, f
party—fiesta, f
pass—paso, m
passage—pasaje, m
passenger—pasajero, -a
past—pasado, -a; último, -a
pasture—potrero, m ; pasto, m
path—vereda, f; senda, f; sendero, m
patrol—patrulla, f; tnigra, f (slang)
patrol inspector—patrullero, m
paved—pavimentado, -a
paw—pata, f
pay day—día de pago, m
peach—durazno, m
peace officer—alguacil, m
pear—pera, f
pen (writing)pluma, f
pen (stock)—corral, m
pencil—lápiz, m
penitentiary—penitenciaría, f; casa de corrección, f
penknife—navaja, f
penny—centavo, m
pepper—chile, m; pimiento, m; pimienta, f
people—gente, f
perhaps—quizá, quizás, tal vez
perjury—perjurio, m
permanent—permanente
permission—permiso, m
permit—permiso, m
person—persona, f
pharmacy—farmacia, f; botica, f
photograph—fotografía, f; foto, f
pick(axe)—pico, m
picker—pizcador, -a
picking season^pizca, f
picture—retrato, m; foto, f
picture show—cine, m; vistas, f (slang)
picture film—película, f
piece—pedazo, m; pieza, f
pig—marrano, -a; puerco, -a
pillow—almohada, f
pillow case—funda de almohada, f
pilot—piloto, m; aviador, m
pimp—alcahuete, m
pin—alfiler, m; broche, m
pineapple—pina, f
pistol—pistola, f
pity—lástima

place—lugar, m; sitio, m
plant—planta, f
planter—plantador, m; sembrador,
píate—plato, m; placa, f
plaza—plaza, f
please—por favor
plow—arado, m
plumber—plomero, m
pocket—bolsa, f; bolsillo, ai
pocket-book—bolsa, f: portamoneda, m
pocketknife—navaja, f
poison—veneno, m
point—punto; m; punta, f
pole—palo, m; vara, f
pólice force—policía, f
policeman—policía, m
pool—charco, m; billares, m
pool hall—billar, m; salón de billares, m
poor—pobre
Pope—Papa, m
poplar—álamo, m
pork—puerco, m
port—puerto, m
porter—portero, m
port of entry—puerto de entrada, m; garita, f (slang)
portrait—retrato, m
possible—posible
post—poste, m; palo, m
postman—cartero, m
postmaster—administrador de correos, m
post office—correo, m; estafeta, f
potato—papa, f; (sweet) camote, m tio- und—libra, f
power—poder, m; fuerza, f
prayer—oraclón, f
preceding—anterior
precise—preciso, -a
presence—presencia, f
present—presente, regalo, m
president—presidente, m
pretty—bonito, -a; lindo, -a
price—precio, m
priest—cura, m; sacerdote, m; padre, m
print—huella, f; impresión, f
prison—prisión, f; cárcel, f
prisoner—prisionero, -a; preso, -a
problem—problema, m
proceedings—procedimientos, m; actás, f
process—proceso, m

product—producto, m
professor—professor, -a
promise—promesa, f
prometer—promotor, m; empresario, m
proof—prueba, f
property—propiedad, f
prostituta—prostituta, f
prostitution—prostitución, f
provided (that)—con tal que, siempre que
puddle—charco, m
pug-nosed—chato, -a
pulse—pulso, m
pump—bomba, f
punctual—puntual
pupil—alumno, -a; pupila, f (eye)
pure—puro, -a
purpose—propósito, m
purse—bolsa, f; bolsillo, m

Q

quail—codorniz, f
quarrel—disgusto, m; riña, f
quart—cuarto, m
quarter—peseta, f (coin); cuarto, m (measure)
question—pregunta, f
quick—pronto, -a
quickly—pronto quota—cuota, f

R

rabbit—conejo, -a
race—raza, f
radish—rábano, m
radio—radio, m-f (instrument, m;
transmission, f)
raf t—balsa, f
rag—trapo, m
railroad—ferrocarril, m
railroad track—traque de------, m; vía, f
rain—lluvia, f
rake—rastrillo, m
ram—carnero, m
ranch—rancho, m
rancher—ranchero, m
ranch foreman—caporal, m
rape—rapto, m; estupro, m
rapid—rápido, -a
rare—raro, -a

rarely—muy raro (coll); casi nunca (coll)
rascal—picaro, m
rat—rata, f
rattle snake—víbora de cascabel, f
ravine—arroyo, m; cañada, f
raw—crudo, -a
ready—listo, -a
real—real, mero, -a (slang)
really—de veras
reason—razón, f; causa, f
receipt—recibo, m
recent—reciente
recently—recientemente
record—récord, m; transcripición, f; disco, m (phono)
red—rojo, -a; colorado, -a
relative—pariente, -a
rendezvous—cita, f
rent—renta, f
report—reporte, m
republic—república, f
requirement—requisito, m
residence—residencia, f; domicilio, m
resources—bienes, m; riquezas, f
restaurant—restaurante, m
rest room—servicio, m; cuarto de baño, m; excusado, m
retall—al por menor
reunión—reunión, f
review—repaso, m
revolver—revólver, m
rib—costilla, f
rice—arroz, m
rich—rico, -a
rifle—rifle, m; fusil, m
right?—¿verdad?
right—derecho, -a; derecho, m
right away—pronto, prontito, en seguida, inmediatamente
right now—ahorita, ahora mismo
ring—anillo, m
river—río, m
road—camino, m
robber—ladrón, m; ratero, m
robbery—robo, m
rock—piedra, f; roca, f; peñasco, m
rod—vara, f
rogue—picaro, m
roof—techo, m
room--cuarto, m

rooster—gallo, m
rope --soga, f; reata, f
rose—rosa, f
rough—áspero, -a
round—redondo, -a
round trip fare—pasaje de ida y vuelta, m; pasaje redondo, m
route—rumbo, m; vía, f; ruta, f
row boat—bote de remos, m
rubber—hule, m; goma, f
rule—regla, f
ruler—regla, f (measure); gobernador, m (person)
ruralman—campesino, m
rust—moho, m

S

sabotage—sabotaje, m
sack—costal, m (cloth); bolsa, f (paper)
sad—triste safe—seguro, -a
sailor—marinero, m
saint—santo, -a; san
salary—sueldo, m; salario, m
sale—venta, f
saloon—cantina, f; salón, m
salt—sal, f
same—igual, mismo, -a
sample—muestra, f
sand—arena, f
sandal—sandalia, f; hurache, m
sandwich—sandwich, m (slang) ; emparedado, m
Saturday—sábado, m
sausage—chorizo, m; salchicha, f
scale—balanza, f; báscula, f; escala, f
scar—cicatriz, f
scarcely—apenas
school—escuela, f
sea—mar, m
season—estación, f
seat—asiento, m
second—segundo, m; segundo, -a
secretary—secretario, -a
seed—semilla, f
sentence—sentencia, f; oración, f
sentry box—garita, f
September—septiembre
servant—sirviente, -ta

service—servicio, m
seven—siete
seventeen—diez y siete
seventh—séptimo, -a
several—varios, -as
sex—sexo, m
shame—vergüenza, f; lástima, f
sharecropper—mediero, m
sharp—filoso, -a; en punto (time)
sheep—borrego, m; carnero, m ;
oveja, f sheriff—jerif e, m; sherif e, m (slang)
shin—canilla, f
ship—barco, m; buque, m; vapor, m
shirt—camisa, f shoe—zapato, m shoe
shop—zapatería, f shop—taller, m
shore—costa, f; playa, f; orilla, f (bank oí a stream)
short—bajo, -a; corto, -a; chaparro, -a; chapo (slang)
shorts—calzoncillos, m
short time—rato
shot—tiro, m; disparo, m; balazo, m
shot gun—escopeta, f
shoulder—hombro, m
shovel—pala, f
shrimp—camarón, m
sick—enfermo, -a; malo, -a
side—lado, m
sidewalk—banqueta, f; acera, f
sight—vista, f
sign—seña, f; marca, f; signo, m; rótulo, m; letrero, m
signature—firma, f
silk—seda, f
silver—plata, f
since—desde
single—soltero, -a
sir—señor, m
sister—hermana, f
sister-in-law—cuñada, f
site—sitio, m; lugar, m
six—seis
sixteen—diez y seis; dieciséis
sixth—sexto, -a
sixty—sesenta
size—tamaño, m
skin—cutis, m; piel, f
skinny—flaco, -a
skirt—falda, f

skunk—zorillo, -a
sky—cielo, m
sl-ender—delgado, -a; flaco, -a
sling—honda, f
slip—fondo, m
slipper—chancla, f; sandalia, f
slow—despacio; lento
slowly—despacio, lentamente
small—pequeño, -a; chico, -a
smoke—humo, m
smooth—suave, liso, -a; llano, -a
smuggled goods—contrabando, m
smuggler—contrabandista, m-f
snake—víbora, f; culebra, f
snow—nieve, f
so—así que, conque, tan, por eso
soap—jabón, m
social security card—tarjeta de seguro social, f
sock—calcetín, m
soft—suave, blando, -a
soil—tierra, f; suelo, m
soldier—soldado, m
so many—tantos, -as
some—algún(o), -a; unos, -as
somebody—alguien; alguna persona
someone—alguien, alguna persona
some place—algún lugar
something—alguna cosa, algo
sometimes—a veces
so much—tanto, -a
son—hijo, m
son-in-law—yerno, m
soon—pronto
sort—clase, f; modo, m
soul—alma, f (el)
soup—caldo, m; sopa, f
south—sur, m
Spain—España
Spaniard—español, -a
Spanish—español (language), m; español, -a
special—especial
spectacles—anteojos, m; lentes, m
speed—velocidad, f
spider—araña, f
spinach—espinaca, f
spoon—cuchara, f
spoon (tea)—cucharilla, f
sport—deporte, m
sporting:—deportivo, -a

spring—primavera, f; ojo de agua, m
spy—espía, m-f
squall—chubasco
square—plaza, f; cuadrado, -a
squash—calabaza, f
stair—escalón, m
stall—puesto, m
stamp—timbre, m; estampilla, f; sello, m
stand—puesto, m
star—estrella, f
state—estado, m
statement—declaración, f
station—estación (de), f
stationwagon—camioneta, f
status—estado, m
steam—vapor, m
steer—novillo, m; rez, f
step—paso, m; escalón (stairs), m
stepchild—hijastro, -a
stepfather—padrastro, m
stepmother—madrastra, f
stick—palo, m; vara, f
still—todavía, aún
stocking—media, f; calcetín, m
stomach—estómago, m
stone—piedra, f
stop—alto, basta, parada, f
store—tienda, f
storeroom—bodega, f; almacén, m
storm—tormenta, f; chubasco, m
story—cuento, m; historia, f
story (floor)—piso
stove—estufa, f
stowaway—polizón, m
straight—derecho, -a; recto, -a
stranger—extranjero, -a; desconocido, -a
statue—estatua, f
straw—paja, f
street—calle, f
streetcar—tranvía, m
strength—fuerza, f; poder, m
strike—huelga, f (work stoppage)
string—cordón, m; hila, m; cuerda, f
striped—listado, -a
strong—fuerte; poderoso, -a
stub (ticket)—talón, m
student—estudiante, m-f; alumno, -a
study—estudio, m
subject—sujeto, m
suburb—barrio, m

such—tal
suddenly—de repente
sufficient—suñciente
sugar—azúcar, m
suit—traje, m
suit (law)—queja, f; pleito, m
suitcase—maleta, f; veliz, m
sum—suma, f
summer—verano, m
sun—sol, m
Sunday—domingo, m
supper—cena, f
sure—seguro que sí, seguro, -a
súmame—apellido, m
suspicion—sospecha, f
suspicious—sospechoso, -a
swarthy—trigueño, -a; moreno, -a
sweater—suéter, m; chamarra, f
sweet—dulce
sweetheart—novio, -a
swimsuit—traje de baño, m

T

table—mesa, f
tail—cola, f; rabo, m
tailor—sastre, m
tailor shop—sastrería, f
tall—alto, -a
tangerine—mandarina, f; tangerina, f
tank—tanque, m
target—blanco, m
task—tarea, f
tatoo—tatuaje, m; tatú, m
taxi—taxi, m; carro de sitio, m
tea—té, m
teacher—maestro, -a
teeth—dientes, m
telegram—telegrama, m
telephone—teléfono, m
television—television, f
television set—televisor, m
ten—diez
tenth—décimo, -a
tequila—tequila, m
terrible—terrible
territory—territorio, m; terreno, m
test—prueba, f; examen, m
testimony—testimonio, m
Texas—Texas (Tejas)

than—que
thanks—gracias, f
that—ese, -a; aquel, -Ha; eso, que
that's why—por eso, así que
that which—lo que
the—el, la, los, las
theater—cine, m; teatro, m
then—entonces, luego, después
there—allí, allá, ahí
there are—hay
therefore—por eso, así que
there is—hay
there was—había
there were—había
these—estos, -as
thick—grueso, -a; espeso, -a; denso, -a
thief—ladrón, m; ratero, m
thin—delgado, -a; flaco, -a
thing—cosa, f
third—tercero, -a
thirteen—trece
thirty—treinta
this—este, esta, esto
those—esos, -as; aquellos, -as
though—aunque
thousand—mil
thread—hilo, m
threat—amenaza, f
three—tres
through—por
thumb—pulgar, m
Thursday—jueves, m
thus—así
ticket—boleto, m; billete, m
tie—corbata, f
time—tiempo, m; vez, f; hora, f
tin—lata, f; hojalata, f; estaño, m
tire—llanta, f
tired—cansado, -a
title—título, m
to—a, para
tobáceo—tabaco, m
today—hoy
toe--dedo (del pie), m
toenail—uña, f
together—junto(s), -a(s)
toilet—servicio, m; excusado, m
tomate—tomate, m
tomorrow—mañana
tongue—lengua, f

tonight—esta noche, a la noche
too—también
tools—herramienta (s), f
too many—muchos, -as; demasiados, -as
too much—mucho, -a; demasiado, -a
tooth—diente, m
top—cima, f; cumbre, f
tourist—turista, m-f
toward—hacia
town—pueblo, m
tracks—huellas, f
track (railroad)—vía, f; riel, m; traque, (slang)
tractor—tractor, m
tractor driver—tractorista, m-f
trail—pisada, f; huellas, f; vereda, f; sendero, m
train—tren, m
trainee—novicio, m
traitor—traidor, -a
travejer—viajero, -a
tree—árbol, m
trial—juicio, m
trip—viaje, m
trousers—pantalones, m
truck—camión, m; troque, m (slang); troca, f (slang)
truck driver—troquero, m (slang)
true—verdad, cierto
trunk—baúl, m; petaca, f
trunk (car)—cajuela, f
truth—verdad, f
Tuesday—martes, m
turkey—guajalote, m; cócono, m (coll)
twelve—doce
twenty—veinte
twig—vara, f
twin—gemelo, m; cuate, m
two—dos

U

ugly—'feo, -a
únele—tío, m
under—debajo (de), bajo, abajo
under oath—bajo juramento
undershirt—camiseta, f
underwear—ropa interior, f
uniform—uniforme, m
United States—Estados Unidos, m
university—universidad, f

unjust—injusto, -a
unknown—desconocido, -a
unless—a menos que
until—hasta, hasta que
up—arriba
upon—sobre, al
upright—justo, -a
upstairs—arriba
up to—hasta
useful—útil
usually—generalmente, usualmente

V

vacation—vacación (es), f
vaccination—vacuna, f
valid—válido, -a
valise—veliz, m
valley—valle, m
value—valor, m; precio, m
various—varios, -as
vegetable—legumbre, f; verdura, f
verb—verbo, m
very—muy
vest—chaleco, m
view—vista, f
village—aldea, f; villa, f; población, f
vinegar—vinagre, m
violation—violación, f
violence—violencia, f
visa—visa, f
visible—visible
visit—visita, f
visitor—visitante, m
voice—voz, f
voluntarily—voluntariamente
voluntary—voluntario, -a
volunteer—voluntario, -a
vote—voto, m

W

wages—sueldo, m
wagon—vagón, m
waist—cintura, f
waiter—mesero, -a
waiting room—sala de espera, f
walking cañe—bastón, m
wall—pared, f

war—guerra, f
warehouse—bodega, f; almacén, m
warm—tibio, -a; caliente
warning—aviso, m
warrant of arrest)—orden de arresto, m-f, fallo de arresto, m
wart—verruga, f
was there?—¿había?
watch—reloj, m
watchmaker—relojero, m
watch out!—¡cuidado!
water—agua, f (el)
waterhole—tanque, m; charco, m
wave—ola, f; onda, f
wax—cera, f
way—rumbo, m; camino, f; vía, f
weak—débil
weapon—arma, f (el)
weather—tiempo, m
wedding—boda, f; casamiento, m
Wednesday—miércoles, m
weed—hierba, f; yerba, f
week—semana, f
weight—peso, m
well—noria, f; pozo, m; pues, bien
were there?—¿había?
west—oeste, m; poniente, m; occidente, m
wet—mojado, -a
wetback—mojado, -a (slang)
what—lo que
what?—¿qué?
what color—de que color
whatever—cualquier (a)
what for—para que
wheat—trigo, m
wheel—rueda, f
when—cuando
where—donde
whether—si
which—cual, que
while—mientras -.
white—blanco, -a
who? — ¿quién?; ¿quiénes?
who—quien, -es; que
whole—entero, -a
wholesale—al por mayor
wholesale house—almacén, m
whom—quien, -es
whose—de quien, -es, cuyo
why—por que

wide—ancho, -a
widow—viuda, f
widower—viudo, m
width—anchura, f; ancho, m
wiener—salchicha, f
wife—esposa, f
wig—peluca, f
wild—salvaje, silvestre
willing—dispuesto, -a
wind—viento, m
windmill—papalote, m; molino de viento, m
windshield—parabrisa, m
window—ventana, f
wine—vino, m
winter—invierno, m
wire—alambre, m
wise—sabio, -a; erudito, -a
with—con
within—dentro (de)
without—sin
witness—testigo, -a
wolf—lobo, -a
woman—mujer, f; señora, f
wood—madera, f
wood (fire)—leña, f
wood chopper—leñador, m
woods—monte, m; bosque, m
wool—lana, f

word—palabra, f
work—trabajo, m; empleo, m; labor, f; chamba, f (slang)
worker—trabajador, -a; obrero, -a
workshop—taller, m
world—mundo, m
world war—guerra mundial, f
worse—peor
wreck—choque, m
wrinkle—arruga, f
wrist—pulso, m; muñeca, f

Y

yard—yarda
year—año, m
yellow—amarillo, -a
yes—sí
yesterday—ayer
yet—todavía, aún
yonder—allá
young—joven, m-f
young lady—señorita, f
young lád—mozo, m
young goat—cabrito, m
youngster—chamaco,-a (coll); chavalo, -a (slang)

SPANISH-ENGLISH VOCABULARY

A

a—to, at
abajo—under, below, down
abierto, -a—open
abogado, m—lawyer
abrigo, m—coat, overcoat
abril—April
abuela, f—grandmother
abuelo, m—grandfather
acá—here
acento, m—accent
acequia, f—(irrigation) ditch

acera, f—sidewalk
acerca de—about, concerning
acre, m—acre
acta de nacimiento, f (el)—birth certifícate
acumulador, m—battery (storage)
además (de)—besides
adicto, -a—addict
adiós—good-bye
admisión, f—admission
aduana, f—customs
aduanero, m—customs agent
aeropuerto, m—airport

afuera—outside, out
agosto—August
agua, f (el)—water
agujero, m—hole
ahijado, -a—godchild
ahora—now
ahora mismo—right now
ahorita—right now aire, m—air
a la caída de la tarde—at sun down
a la caída del sol—at sun down
a la madrugada—at dawn
al amanecer—at dawn
alambre, m—wire
alambrista, m-f—fence jumper (slang)
álamo, m—cottonwood, poplar
a la noche—tonight
al anochecer—at dusk
albañil, m—bricklayer, masón
alcahuete, m—pimp
aldea, f—village
alemán, -a—Germán
al fin—finally, at last
al fin de—at the end of
algo—something, anything
algodón, m—cotton
alguacil, m—constable, peace officer
alguien—someone, somebody, anyone, anybody
alguna cosa—something, anything alguna vez—ever
algún lugar—anywhere, some place, any place, somewhere
algún(o), -a—some, any
alhajas, f—jewelry
alimento, m—food
al lado (de)—beside
alma, f (el)—soul
almacén, m—wholesale house, ware- house
almohada, f—pillow
al principio—at first, at the begin-ning
alrededor—around
alto—stop
alto, -a—tall, high
alumno, -a—pupil, student
allá—over there, yonder, there
allí—there
ama de casa, f (el)—housewife
amanecer, m—dawn, daybreak
amarillo, -a—yellow

amenaza, f—threat
a menos (de)—unless
americano, -a—American
amigo, -a—friend
amo, m—owner
analfabeto, -a—illiterate
anciano, -a—oíd
anillo, m—ring
anoche—last night
anochecer, m—nightfall, dusk
anteanoche—night before last
anteayer—day before yesterday
anteojos, m—eyeglasses
anterior—preceding, former
anteriormente—formerly
antes (de)—before, formerly
anuncio, m—announcement
año, m—year
año nuevo, m—new year
apellido, m—last ñame, súmame
apenas—scarcely, barely
a pesar de—in spite of
a pie—on foot
aquel—that (at a distance)
aquella—that (at a distance)
aquellos, -as—those (at a distance)
aquí—here
arado, m—plow
araña, f—spider
árbol, m—tree
archivo, m—file, archive
arena, f—sand
arete, m—earring
arma, f (el)—weapon (arm)
arreglo, m—arrangement
arriba—above, up
arroz, m—rice
artista, m-f—artist
asesinato, m—murder
asesino, m—murderer
así—thus, like this, like that
asiento, m—seat
asiento de atrás, m—back seat
asiento de enfrente, m—front seat
así que—therefore, for that reason, so
asunto, m—matter
a tiempo—on time
atrás (de)—behind, back
audiencia, f—hearing

aun—yet, still
aunque—although, though
auto, m—auto, car
autobús, m—bus
automóvil, m—automobile
autoridad, f—authority
ave, f (el)—fowl, bird
a veces—at times, sometimes
avenida, f—avenue
aviador, m—pilot
avión, m—airplane
aviso, m—warning, advice
ayer—yesterday
ayer por la mañana—yesterday morning
ayuda, f—help
azteca—Aztec azúcar, m—sugar
azul—blue

B

bailarín, -a—dancer
baile, m—dance
bajo—low, short, under
bajo juramento—under oath
balsa, f—raft
banco, m—bank
banco, -a—bench
bandera, f—flag, banner
bandido, m—bandit
banquero, m—banker
banqueta, f—sidewalk
baño, m—bath
baqueta, f—leather
barato, -a—cheap
barba, f—chin, beard
barbacoa, f—barbecue
barbería, f—barber shop
barbero, m—barber
barco, m—boat, barge, ship
barraca, f—barrack
barril, m—barrel
barrio, m—neighborhood, suburb
barro, m—clay
base, f—base
basta—enough, stop
bastante—enough
bastardo, -a—bastard, born out of wedlock
bastón, m—walking cañe
batería, f—battery
baúl, m—trunk, chest

becerro, -a—calí
bello, -a—beautiful
beso, m—kiss
betabel, m—beet
bien—vvell
bigote, m—mustache
billar, nv—billiard room, pool hall
billete, m—bilí
billetera, f—billfold
biología, f—biology
bistec, m—beefsteak
bizcocho, m—biscuit
blanco, m—target
blanco, -a—vvhite
blusa, f—blouse
boca, f—mouth
boda, f—wedding
bodega, f—storeroom, warehouse
bola, f—ball
boletín, m—bulletin
boleto, m—ticket
bolsa, f—purse, pocket, bag, sack
bolsillo, m—purse, pocket
bollo, m—biscuit (small), cake
bomba, f—pump
bonito, -a—pretty, cute
borrador, m—eraser
borrego, -a—lamb
bota, f—boot
bote, m—boat, can, jail (slang)
bote de remos, m—rowboat
botella, f—bottle
botón, m—button
braceleta, f—bracelet
bracero, m—contract laborer, manual laborer
brazo, m—arm
bueno—helio, all right
bueno, -a—good
bulto, m—bundle
burro, m—donkey
buque, m—ship

C

caballeriza, f—stable
caballero, m—gentleman
caballo, m—horse
cabello, m—hair
cabeza, f—head
cabra, f—goat

cabrito, m—young goat, kid
cachucha, f—cap
cada—each, every
cadera, f—ship
café, m—coffee, brown
caja, f—box
cajón, m—crate box, drawer
cajuela, f—car trunk
calcetín, m—sock
calendario, m—calendar
caliente—warm, hot
calvo, -a—bald
calzón, m—vvhite pants
calzoncillos, m—shorts
calle, f—street
callejón, m—alley
cama, f—bed
cambio, m—change
camino, m—road, way
camión, m—truck, bus
camioneta, f—stationwagon
camisa, f—shirt
camiseta, f—undershirt
campana, f—bell
campesino, m—ruralman, farmer
campo, m—field, camp, country
canilla, f—forearm, shin
canoa, f—canoe
cantina, f—bar
cantinera, f—barmaid
cantinero, m—bartender
cansado, -a—tired
caporal, m—ranch foreman
cara, f—face
cárcel, f—jail
carga, f—load, freight, cargo
carne, f—meat
carnero, m—-sheep, ram
carnicero, m—butcher
caro, -a—expensive
carpintero, m—carpenter
carretera, f—highway
carro, m—car, automobile
carta, f—letter
cartera, f—billfold
cartero, m—mailman, postman
casa, f—house, home
casacorte, f—courthouse
casa de remolque, f—house trailer
casado, -a—married

casi—almost, nearly
casi nunca (coll)—rarely
causa, f—cause
ceja, f—eyebrow
cena, f—dinner, supper
centavo, m—cent
cerca, f—fence
cerca (de)—near, cióse, about, beside
certificado, m—certifícate
certificado de nacimiento, m—birth certifícate
cerveza, f—beer
cicatriz, f—scar
ciego, -a—blind
cielo, m—sky, ceiling
cien(to)—one hundred
cierto, -a—certain, true
cigarrillo, m—cigarette
cigarro, m—cigar, cigarette
cinco—five
cine, m—theater, movie
cinto, m—belt, girdle
cintura, f—waist
cinturón, m—belt
cita, f—date, rendezvous, appointment
ciudad, f—city
ciudadanía, f—citizenship
ciudadano, -a—citizen
claramente—clearly
claro, -a—clear
claro—of course
clase, f—class, kind, type
cobija, f—blanket
cocinero, -a—cook
cócono, m—turkey
coche, m—car, coach
codo, m—elbow, stingy (slang)
codorniz, f—quail
cojo, -a—cripple, lame
color, m—color
colorado, -a—red
comadre, f—cióse friend
comerciante, m—merchant
comida, f—dinner, food
comisionista, m-f—commission merchant
como—as, like, about, how
compadre, m—cióse friend
compañero, -a—companion
compañía, f—company
compartimiento, m—compartment
completo, -a—complete

con—with
condado, m—county
conejo, -a—rabbit
conmigo—with me
conocido, -a—acquaintance
conocimiento, m—knowledge
conque—so
consigo—with you
cónsul, m—cónsul
consulado, m—consulate
con tal que—provided
contento, -a—content(ed)
contestación, f—answer
contigo—with you (familiar)
contra—against
contrabandista, m-f—smuggler
contrabando, m—smuggled goods
contraseña, f—baggage check
corazón, m—heart
corbata, f—tie
cordón, m—cord, string
corral, m—corral
corralón, m (slang)—detention camp
correcto, -a—correct
correo, m—post office, mail
cortada, f—cut, cut scar
corte, f—court
corto, -a—short
cosa, f—thing
cosecha, f—harvest
costal, m—sack
costilla, f—rib
costumbre, f—custom
coyote, m—coyote
crema, f—cream
cría, f—brood, offspring, suckling
criada, f—maid
crimen, m—crime
cromo, m—calendar
crudo, -a—raw, crude, hungover
cruz, f—cross
cuadra, f—block
cual—which
cualquier, -a—any, anyone, anybody
cualquier lugar—anywhere, anyplace
cuando—when
cuanto, -a—how mucli
cuantos, -as—how many
cuanto tiempo—how long
cuarenta—forty

cuarto, m—room
cuarto, -a—fourth
cuatro—four
cuchillo, m—knife
cuello, m—neck, collar
cuenta, f—bilí
cuero, m—leather
cuerpo, m—body
cueva, f—cave
cuidado, m—care, careful, watch out, look out
cuidadosamente—carefully
cuidadoso, -a—careful, cautious
culpa, f—guilt, fault, blame
culpable—guilty
cumpleaños, m—birthday
cuñada, f—sister-in-law
cuñado, m—brother-in-law
cuota, f—quota
cura, m—priest
curva, f—curve

CH

chaleco, m—vest
chalupa, f—launch, snfiall vessel, boat, canoe
chamaco (slang)—youngster, boy, kid
chamarra, f—sweater
chamba, f (slang)—work, Job
chancla, f—oíd shoe, slipper
chaparral, m—low brush
chaparro, -a—short
chapo (slang)—short
chaqueta, f—jacket
charco, m—pool, puddle, waterhole
chato, -a—flat-nosed, pug-nosed
chavalo (slang)—youngster, boy, kid
chico, -a—small
chiva, f (slang)—bundle, personal ítem
chivo, -a—goat
chofer, m—chauffeur, driver
choque, m—wreck
chorizo, m—sausage
chubasco, m—squall, storm

D

de—of, from, about, as
debajo (de)—under, beneath, below
décimo, -a—tenth
declaración, f—statement
de cualquier modo—any way
de día—by day
dedo, m—finger
delante (de)—in front, before, ahead
delgado, -a—thin, slender, lean
delito, m—crime, offense
de manera que—ia order that
demasiado, -a—too much
demasiados, -as—too many
de noche—by night, at night
dentista, m-f—dentist
dentro (de)—within, inside
de nuevo—again
de otra manera—otherwise, (in) another way
de otro modo—otherwise, (in) another way
dependiente, m-f—clerk
deporte, m—sport
deportivo—sporting
de que color—what color
de quien, -es—whose
derecho, -a—right, straight
desconocido, -a—stranger, unknown
descripción, f—description
desde—since, from
desierto, m—desert
despacio—slow, slowly
después (de)—after, later, next, then
detalle, m—detail
de todo modos—anyhow, anyway
detrás (de)—behind, after, back ¡
de veras!—really!
de vez en cuando—from time to time
día, m—day
diablo, m—devil día
de descanso, m—day off, day of rest
día de fiesta, m—holiday
diario, m—daily newspaper
diario, -a—daily
diciembre—December
diente, m—tooth
diez—ten
difícil—difficult, hard
dificultad—difficulty, trouble
dinero, m—money
dirección, f—direction, address
disgusto, m—argument, disagree-ment
dispuesto, -a—willing
distrito, m—district
doble—double
doctor, -a—doctor
documento, m—document
dólar, m—dollar
dolor, m—pain, ache
doméstico, -a—domestic
domicilio, m—doinicile, abode, home
domingo, m—Sunday
donde—where
droga, f—drug
dueño, -a—owner
dulce, m—candy, sweet
durante—during
duro, -a—hard, difficult (slang)

E

ébano, m—ebony
eco, m—echo
edad, f—age
edificio, m—building
educación, f—education
ejemplo, m—example
ejercicio, m—exercise
ejército, m—army
el—the
el año pasado—last year
el año que viene—next year
elección, f—election
el mes pasado—last month
el mes que viene—next month
elote, m—corn (fresh)
embajada, f—embassy
empleado, -a—employee
empleo, m—employment, work
en—in, on, at
en contra de—against
en cuanto—as far as
enemigo, -a—enemy
enero—January
enfermera, f—nurse
enfermo, -a—sick, ¡ll
en frente—in front
enojado, -a—angry, mad
en punto—sharp (on the dot)
en seguida—immediately

entero, -a—whole
entonces—then
entrada, f—entry, entrance
entre—between, among
en vez de—instead of
equipaje, m—baggage
esa—that
escopeta, f—shotgun
escuela, f—school
ese—that eso—that (neuter)
esos, -as—those
espalda, f—back (of body)
español, m—Spanish (language)
español, -a—Spanish, Spaniard
esperanza, f—hope
espía, m-f—spy
espinaca, f—spinach
esposa, f—wife
esposo, m—husband
esquina, f—córner
esta—this
está bien—okay, all right
estación, f—season
estación de, f—. . . . station
estado, m—state, status
Estados. Unidos, m—United States
estafeta, f—post office
esta noche—tonight
este—this
este, m—east, orient
estómago, m—stomach
esto—this (neuter)
estos, -as—these
estudiante, m—student
evidencia, f—evidence
examen, m—test, examination
excitado, -a—excited
excusado, m—restroom, toilet
extranjero, -a—stranger, alien, foreigner

F

fábrica, f—factory
fácil—easy
fácilmente—easily
faja, f—belt, girdle
falda, f—skirt
falso, -a—false
familia, f—family
farmacia, f—pharmacy

fe, f—faith
febrero—February
fecha, f—date
fe de bautismo, f—baptismal certifícate
federal, m—federal
feliz—happy
feo, -a—ugly
ferrocarril, m—railroad
fianza, f—bail, bond
fichera, f—B-girl, hostess (slang)
fiesta, f—fiesta, party
filoso, -a—sharp
flaco, -a—skinny, thin, lean, slender
flojo, -a—loóse, lazy (slang)
fondo, m—bottom, slip
forma, f—form
francés, -a—French
franco, -a—frank, off duty
frazada, f—blanket
freno, m—brake, bridle
frente, f—forehead
frijol, m—bean
frío, m—cold
frío, -a—cold
frontera, f—border
fuego, m—fire
fuera—out, outside
funda, f—holster, pillow case
furgón, m—boxear
fusil, m—rifle

G

gallina, f—hen, chicken
gallo, m—rooster, cock
ganado, m—cattle, herd, livestock
ganancia, f—gain, earning
garage, m—garage
garita, f—sentry box, entrance
gate, port of entry (slang)
garantía, f—guarantee
gastos, m—expenses
gato, -a—cat
gavilán, m—hawk
generalmente—generally, usually
gente, f—people
gobierno, m—government
gorra, f—cap
grande—large, big
granero, m—granary

gris—gray
grupo, m—group
guajalote, m—turkey
guante, m—glove
guapo, -a—handsome
guardavacas, m—cattleguard
guerra, f—war
guerra mundial, f—world war

H

había—there was, there were
¿había?—was there?, were there?
hace—ago
hacendado, m—farmer
hacia—toward
hacienda, f—farm
hacha, f (el)—axe
hambre, f (el)—hunger
hasta—until, as far as, up to, to
hay—there is, there are
¿hay?—is there?, are there?
hermana, f—sister
hermano, m—brother
hermoso, -a—beautiful
herradura, f—horseshoe
herramienta(s), f—tools
herrero, m—blacksmith
hierba, f—weed, herb
hija, f—daughter
hijastro, -a—stepchild
hijo, m—son
hijo -a ilegítimo -a—illegitimate child
hijo -a natural—illegitimate child
hilo, m—thread, string
hogar, m—home
hola—helio
hombre, m—man
hombro, m—shoulder
honda, f—sling, wave
hondo, -a—deep
honesto, -a—honest
hora, f—hour, time
hotel, m—hotel
hoy—today
hoy día—nowadays
hoyo, m—hole
huarache, m—sandal
huelga, f—strike

huella, f—track, print, impression
huellas de los dedos, f—fingerprints
huellas digitales, f—fingerprints
huero, -a—blonde
hueso, m—bone
huésped, m—guest, host
huéspeda, f—guest, hostess
huevo, m—egg
hule, m—rubber
huracán, m—hurricane

I

idéntico, -a—identical
identificación, f—identification
iglesia, f—church
¡gual—same
ilegal—illegal
ilegalmente—illegally
importante—important
imposible—impossible
impresión, f—impression
incidente, m—incident
inglés, m—English, Englishman
inglés, -a—English
injusto, -a—unjust
inmigración, f—immigration
inocente—innocent
inspector, m—inspector
inteligente—intelligent
internacional—international
intestino, m—intestina
íntimo, -a—intímate
investigación, f—investigation
invierno, m—winter
izquierdo, -a—left

J

jamás—never
jamón, m—ham
jefe, m—chief, boss, leader
jornalero, m—day-laborer, manual laborer
joven, m-f—young person
joven—young
joyas, f—jewels, jewelry
joyería, f—jewelry shop
joyero, m—jeweler
jueves, m—Thursday

juez, m—judge
juicio, m—trial
julio—July junio—June
junta, f—meeting
junto(s), -a(s)—together
jurado, m—jury
juramento, m—oath
justicia, f—justice
justo, -a—just, upright

L

la, -s—the
labio, m—lip
labor, f—field, work
lado, m—side
ladrillo, m—brick
ladrón, m—thief, robber
lana, f—wool
lancha, f—launch, boat, barge
lápiz, m—pencil
largo, -a—long
la semana pasada—last week
la semana que viene—next week
lástima—shame, pity
lavandera, f—laundress, washer-woman
lazo, m—lasso, lariat
leche, f—milk
lechería, f—dairy, dairy farm
lechero, m—milkman
legal—legal
legalmente—legally
legumbre, f—vegetable
lejos—far lengua, f—tongue
lentes, m—eyeglasses
leña, f—firewood
ley, f—law
libertad, f—freedom, liberty
libra, f—pound
libre—free
licencia, f—license
líder, m—leader
liebre, f—jackrabbit
lima, f—lime, file
límite, m—limit
limón, m—lemon
limpio, -a—clean
lindo, -a—pretty, cute
línea, f—líne
listo, -a—ready

local—local
loco, -a—mad, crazy
lodo, m—mud
loma, f—hill
lo más pronto posible—as soon as possible
lo que—that which, what
luego—then, next
luego que—as soon as
lugar, m—place, location
lumbre, f—fire
luna, f—moon
lunar, m—mole
lunes, m—Monday
luz, f—light
luz de mano, f—flashlight

LL

llama, f—flame
llano, m—level ground
llanta, f—tire
llave, f—key
llegada, f—arrival
lleno, -a—full
llorón, -a—crybaby
lluvia, f—rain

M

madrastra, f—stepmother
madre, f—mother
madrina, f—godmother
madrugada, f—dawn, wee hours of the morning, early morning
maestro, -a—teacher
maíz, m—corn (dry), maize
mal—badly
maleta, f—suitcase
malo, -a—bad, sick, ill, mean
mamá, f—mamma, mom, mother
manera, f—manner, fashion, way
mano, f—hand
mantequilla, f—butter
manzana, f—apple, block (city)
mañana—tomorrow
mañana, f—morning
mapa, m—map
máquina, f—machine
maquinaria, f—machinery
maquinista, m-f—machinist

mar, m—sea
marca, f—mark, sign
margen, m—margin
marido, m—husband
marijuana, f—marijuana
marinero, m—sailor
marrano, -a—hog, pig
martes, m—Tuesday
marzo—March
más—more
mas—but
masa, f—dough
más tarde—later
mayo—May
mayor, m—older, oldest
mayordomo, m—foreman
mecánico, m—mechanic
medalla, f—medal, medallion
media, f—hose, stocking
medianoche, f—midnight
módico, m—doctor
medio, -a—half
mediodía, m—noon, midday
mejilla, f—cheek
mejor—better, best
mendigo, m—beggar
menos—less, minus, except
mentira, f—lie
mercado, m—market, market place
mero, -a (slang)—real
mes, m—month
mesa, f—table
metal, m—metal
método, m—method
mexicano, -a—Mexican
miembro, -a—member
mientras—while
miércoles, m—Wednesday
migra (slang), f—Border Patrol
milagro, m—miracle
milpa, f—cornfield, maize field
milla, f—mile
mina, f—mine
minero, m—miner
minuto, m—minute
mirada, f—glance
misa, f—mass (church)
mismo, -a—same
mochila, f—knapsack, bedroll
mocho, -a—maimed, mutilated

moda, f—fashion, mode, custom
modo, m—method, manner
moho, m—rust, moss, mold
mojado, -a—wet, wetback (slang)
molino de viento, m—windmill
moneda, f—money
montaña, f—mountain
monte, m—high brush, mountain
moreno, -a—brunette, swarthy, dark
mosca, f—fly
mosquito, m—mosquito
mostaza, f—mustard
motivo, m—motive
motor, m—motor
mozo, m—bus boy, young chap, lad
muchacha, f—girl
muchacho, m—boy
mucho, -a—much, a great deal of, a lot of, too much
muchos, -as—many, too many
muebles, m—furniture
muerte, f—death
muerto, -a—dead
muestra, f—sample
mujer, f—woman
mujer de pie, f—mistress
muía, f—mulé
muleta, f—crutch
munición (es), f—ammunition
municipio, m—municipality
mundo, m—world
muñeca, f—wrist, dolí
música, f—music
músico, m—musician
muy—very

N

nacimiento, m—birth
nación, f—nation
nacional—national
nacionalidad, f—nationality
nada—nothing, anything
nada más—just, only
nadie—nobody, no one, anyone, anybody
nana, f—governess, child's nurse
naranja, f—orange
naranjo, m—orange tree
narcótico, m—narcotic

nariz, f—nose
nativo, -a—native
navaja, f—knife, penknife, pocket-knife
Navidad, f—Christmas
necesario, -a—necessary
negocio, m—business
negro, -a—black
nervioso, -a—nervous
ni—neither, nor
nieto, -a—grandchild
nieve, f—snow
ningún(o)-a—none, not any
niño, -a—child
no—no, not
noche, f—night
Nochebuena, f—Christmas Eve
no más—just, only
nombre, m—name
nombre de pila, m—Christian name
noria, f—well
norte, m—north
noticia(s), f—news, notice
noveno, -a—m'nth
novicio, -a—novice, trainee
noviembre—November
novio, -a—sweetheart
nuera, f—daughter-in-law
nueve—nine
nuevo, -a—new
número, m—number
nunca—never, not ever

O

obrero, m—worker
o(b)scuro, -a—dark
octavo, -a—eighth
octubre—October
ocupación, f—occupation
ocupado, -a—occupied, busy
ocho—eight
odio, m—hate
oeste, m—west
ofensa, f—offense
oferta, f—offer
oficial, m—officer, official
oficina, f—office
oído, m—(inner) ear
ojalá—God grant
ojo, m—eye

ola, f—wave
ómnibus, m—bus
opio, m—opium
oportunidad, f—opportunity
opuesto, -a—opposite, opposed
oración, f—sentence, prayer
orden, f—order, mándate
oreja, f—(outer) ear
organización, f—organization
oriental—oriental, eastern
oriente, m—orient, east
origen, m—origin
original—original
orilla, f—border, margin, shore, bank
oro, m—gold
oso, -a—bear
otoño, m—autumn, fall
otra vez—again
otro, -a—another, other
oveja, f—sheep, ewe

P

padrastro, m—stepfather
padre, m—father, priest
padrino, m—godfather
página, f—page
país, m—country
paisano, m—fellow countryman
paja, f—straw
pájaro, m—bird
palabra, f—word
paloma, f—dove
pan, m—bread
panadería, f—bakery
panadero, m—baker
pantalones, m—trousers, pants
panza, f—belly
panzón, -a—large bellied, big belly
pañuelo, m—handkerchief
Papa, m—Pope
papá, m—dad, father
papa, f—potato
papalote, m—windmill, kite
papel, m—paper
paquete, m—package
para—in order (to), for, by, to
para que—what for
pared, f—wall
pariente, -ta—relative

párpado, m—eyelid
parque, m—ammunition, park
partera, f—midwife
pasado mañana—day after tomorrow
pasaje, m—passage, fare
pasaje de ida y vuelta, m—round trip fare
pasaje redondo, m—round trip fare
pasaporte, m—passport
paso, m—step, pass
pastel, m—cake
patituerto, -a—deformed (leg)
patizambo, -a—bow-legged
pato, -a—duck
patria, f—homeland
patrón, -a—boss, chief
patrullero, m—patrol inspector
pecho, m—chest
pelea, f—fight
película, f—film (movie)
peligro, m—danger
peligroso, -a—dangerous
pelo, m—hair
pelota, f—ball
peluca, f—wig
peluquería, f—barber shop
peluquero, m—barber
peor—worse
pequeño, -a—small, little
pera, f—pear
perezoso, -a—lazy
periódico, m—newspaper
permanente—permanent
permiso, m—permit, permission
pero—but
perro, -a—dog
persona, f—person
pesado, -a—heavy
pesca, f—fishing
pescado, m—fish
pescador, m—fisherman
pescuezo, m—neck
peseta, f—quarter (coin)
peso, m—Mexican dollar
pestaña, f—eyelash
petaca, f—trunk
pez, m—fish
picaro, -a—rascal, rogue
pie, m—foot piel, f—skin, hide
pierna, f—leg

pila, f—battery, holy-water basin
piloto, m—pilot
pintor, -a—painter
piso, m—floor
pista, f—trail
pistola, f—pistol,
pizarra, f—blackboard
pizarrón, m—blackboard
pizca, f—harvest season, picking season
pizcador, m—picker
placa, f—badge, license píate
planta, f—plant
plata, f—silver
plato, m—píate
plaza, f—plaza, square
pleito, m—fist fight
plomero, m—plumber
plomo, m—lead
pluma, f—pen
pobre—poor
poco, -a—little (amount)
pocos, -as—few
policía, m—policeman
policía, f—pólice forcé
pollo, m—fryer (chicken)
poniente, m—west
por—for, through, by
por dondequieira—everywhére
por eso—for that, reason, thereforé, that's why, so
por favor—please
por fin—finally, at last
por fuera—on the outside
porque—because
por que—why
por supuesto—of course
portamoneda, f—billfold
portero, m—porter
por todas partes—everywhere
posible—possible
potrero, m—pasture, meadow
pozo, m—hole, well
precio, m—price
preciso, -a—precise, necessary
pregunta, f—question
presa, f—dam
presencia, f—presence
presente—present
preso, -a—prisoner
primavera, f—spring

primer nombre, m—first name, given name
primer(o), -a—first
primo, -a—cousin
prisión, f—prison
prisionero, -a—prisoner
problema, m—problem
proceso, m—procesa
producto, m—product
profesor, -a—professor
promesa, f—promise
prontito—quickly, right away
pronto—quick, soon, right away
propiedad, f—property
propósito, m—purpose
prostitución, f—prostitution
prostituta, f—prostitute
próximo, -a—next
prueba, f—proof, test
pueblo, m—town
puente, m—bridge
puerco, m—pork, pig
puerta, f—door
puerto, m—port, harbor
puerto de entrada, m—port of entry (sea)
pues—well
puesto, m—stand, stall
pulgada, f—inch
pulgar, m—thumb
pulmón, m—lung
pulsera, f—bracelet
pulso, m—pulse, wrist
puntual—punctual
puro, -a—puré
puro, m—cigar

Q

que—that, who, than
¿qué?—what?
queja, f—complaint
quemada, f—burn, burn scar
queso, m—cheese
querida, f—mistress
quien, -es—who, whom
quijada, f—jaw
quincena, f—fortnight
quinto, -a—fifth
quizá(s)—maybe, perhaps

R

rábano, m—radish
radio, m-f—radio
ranchero, m—ranchar, farmer
rancho, m—farm, ranch
rápido, -a—rapid, fast
raro, -a—rare
rata, f—rat
ratero, -a—thief, robber
ratito, m—very short time (slang)
rato, m—short time
ratón, m—mouse
raza, f—race
razón, f—reason
real—real
reata, f—rope, riata, lariat
recámara, f—bedroom
recibo, m—receipt
record, m—record
regalo, m—present, gift
reloj, m—dock, watch
relojero, m—watchmaker
remo, m—oar
rengo, -a—cripple, lame
renta, f—rent
repaso, m—review
repollo, m—cabbage
reporte, m—report
res, f—beef, steer
respeto, m—respect
respuesta, f—ánswer, response
restaurante, m—restaurant
retrato, m—picture
reunión, f—reunión
revista, f—magazine
revólver, m—revolver
rico, -a—rich
rifle, m—rifle
río, m—river
rincón, m—córner, nook
riñon, m—kidney
rodilla, f—knee
rojo, -a—red
ropa, f—clothes, clothing
ropa interior, f—underwear
rosa, f—rose
rótulo, m—sign
rubio, -a—blonde
ruido, m—noise
rumbo, m—way, direction, route

S

sábado, m—Saturday
sabiduría, f—knowledge
sabotaje, m—sabotage
sacerdote, m—priest
saco, m—coat
sal, f—salt
sala, f—living room
sala de espera, f—waiting room
salario, m—salary
salchicha, f—wiener, sausage
salida, f—departure, exit
salud, f—health
salvaje—wild
san, m—saint
sandalia, f—slipper, sandal
santo, -a—saint
sartén, f—frying pan
sastre, m—tailor
seco, -a—dry
secretario, -a—secretary
seda, f—silk
según—according to
segundo, -a—second
seguro, -a—sure, certain, safe
seguro que sí—sure, of course
seis—six
semana, f—week
senda, f—path, footpath
sendero, m—path, trail
sentencia, f—sentence
seña, f—sign, mark
señor, m—Mr., sir, man
señora, f—Mrs., woman, lady
señorita, f—Miss, lady (unmarried)
septiembre—September
séptimo, -a—seventh
servicio, m—service, restroom, toilet
sexto, -a—sixth
sí—yes
si—if
siem pre—always
siempre que—provided (that)
si es así—if so, if that is so
siete—seven
siglo, m—century
signo, m—sign, mark
siguiente—following, next

silvestre—wild
silla, f—chair
sin—without
sin embargo—nevertheless
sino—but, only
sirvienta, f—servant, housemaid
sitio, m—place, location, site
sobre, m—envelope
sobre—on, upon
sobrenombre, m—nickname, alias
sobretodo, m—overcoat
sobrina, f—niece
sobrino, m—nephew
soga, f—rope, riata, lariat
sol, m—sun
soldado, m—soldier
solo—alone
sólo—only
soltero, -a—single
sombrero, m—hat
sordo, -a—deaf
sospechoso, -a—suspicious
suave—soft
sucio, -a—dirty
suegra, f—mother-in-law
suegro, m—father-in-law
sujeto, m—subject
sueldo, m—salary, wages
suelo, m—floor, ground
suerte, f—luck
suéter, m—sweater
suficiente—sufficient, enough
sur, m—south

T

tabaco, m—tobáceo
tahúr, m—gambler
tal—such
talabartero, m—leather worker, beltmaker
talón, m—stub, heel
tal vez—perhaps
taller, m—shop
tamaño, m—size
también—also, too, likewise, as well
tampoco—either, neither
tan—as, so
tan pronto como—as soon as
tanque, m—tank, waterhole
tanto, -a—as much, so much

tantos, -as—as many, so much
tarde, f—afternoon, evening
tarde—late
tarea, f—homework, task
tarjeta, f—card
taxi, m—taxi
taza, f—cup
té, m—tea
teatro, m—theater
techo, m—roof
teléfono, m—telephone
televisión, f—television
televisor, m—televisión set
temprano—early
tenedor de libros, m—bookkeeper
tequila, m—tequila
tercer(o), -a—third
territorio, m—territory
terreno, m—territory, land
terrible—terrible
testigo, -a—witness
testimonio, m—testimony
tez, f—complexion
tía, f—aunt tibio, -a—warm
tiempo, m—time, vveather
tienda, f—store
tierra, f—earth, native country, land, soil
tinta, f—ink
tío, m—unele
tiro, m—shot
titulo, m—title
tiza, f—chalk
tobillo, m—ankle
tocante a—about, concerning
tocayo, -a—namesake
tocino, m—bacon
todavía—still, yet
todavía no—not yet
todo, -a—all, everything
todo el mundo—everybody
todos, -as—everybody, all
tomate, m—tomato
tormenta, f—storm
toro, m—bull
trabajador, -a—worker, employee
trabajo, m—work, employment, Job
tractor, m—tractor
tractorista, m—tractor driver
traidor, -a—traitor
traje, m—suit

traje de baño, m—swimsuit
tranvía, m—street car, trolley
tren, m—train
tren de carga, m—freight train
tres—three
trigo, m—wheat
trigueño, -a—swarthy, dark
tripa, f—gut, intestine
trique, m (slang)—personal belong-ing, personal item
triste—sad
troca, f (slang)—truck
troque, m (slang)—truck
troquero, m (slang)—truck driver
tuerto, -a—one-eyed
turista, m-f—tourist

U

últimamente—lately
último, -a—last
un, -a—a, an, one
único, -a—only
uniforme, m—uniform
universidad, f—university
unos, -as—few, some
unos, -as cuantos, -as—a few
unos, -as pocos, -as—a few
uña, f—fingernail, toenail
útil—useful
uva, f—grape

V

vaca, f—cow
vacaciones, f—vacation
vagón, m—wagon
válido, -a—valid
valiente—brave
vamos a ver—let's see
vapor, m—ship, steam
vaquero, m—cowboy
vara, f—twig, pole, rod
varios, -as—several, various
vaso, m—(drinking) glass, tumbler
vecindad, f—neighborhood
vecino, -a—neighbor
veliz, m—valise, suitcase
venado, m—deer
ventana, f—window

verano, m—summer
verdad, f—truth, true
¿ verdad ?—right ?
verde—green
verdura, f—vegetable
vereda, f—trail, path
vestido, m—dress
vez, f—time
vía, f—way, route, railroad track
viaje, m—trip, journey
vida, f—life
vidrio, m—glass
viejo, -a—old
viento, m—wind
viernes, m—Friday
villa, f—village, country house
vino, m—wine
violencia, f—violence
visa, f—visa
visible—visible
visita, f—visit
vista, f—sight, view
viuda, f—widow
viudo, m—widower

voluntariamente—voluntarily
voluntario, -a—volunteer, voluntary

Y

y—and
ya—already
ya mero—almost
ya no—no more, not anymore, no longer
yarda, f—yard
yegua, f—mare
yerba, f—weed, herb
yerno, m—son-in-law

Z

zancudo, m—mosquito
zapatería, f—shoe shop
zapatero, m—cobbler
zapato, m—shoe
zorillo, -a—skunk
zorro, -a—fox

SUPPLEMENTAL VOCABULARY, LEGAL AND CRIMINAL

accessory—cómplice
accomplice—cómplice
accountability—responsabilidad
accuse—acusar
acquired rights—derechos adquiridos
acquittal—absolución, descargo
act—acto, hecho
addict—ad icto
adjourn—levantar o aplazar la sesión
advócate (v.)—abogar, apoyar
affidavit—declaración jurada
aforementioned—ya mencionado, susodicho
alcoholic—alcohólico
alias—sobrenombre, alias
alter—alterar
anarchist—anarquista
anarchy—anarquía
annul—anular, cancelar
appeal (v.)—apelar
appellate court—tribunal de apelaciones

application—petición, aplicación
arraignment—emplazo, emplazamiento
arson—incendio malicioso
attorney—licenciado, abogado
Attorney General—Procurador General
bearer—portador
Board of Immigration Appeals— Tribunal de Inmigración de Apelación
change of venue—traslado de jurisdicción
charge—cargo, (v.) acusar
charity—caridad
Commissioner of Immigration—Comisionado de Inmigración
commit (v.)—cometer
complain—quejarse
complaint—queja
conceal—esconder
condone—perdonar
congress—congreso
congressman—diputado, congresista

contagious—contagioso
convict—convicto, reo
counsel—consejero, abogado
crime (major)—crimen
crime (lesser)—delito
crime involving moral turpitude— crimen u ofensa de depravación moral
crowd—gentío
custody—custodia, guardia
customs duties—derechos de aduana
decree—decreto
defendant—demandado, acusado
defendant—defensor
delinquent—delincuente
detention facility—campo de detención, corralón (slang)
deputy—delegado, comisario, diputado
disorderly conduct—conducta contra la moral pública, desorden público
district attorney—fiscal
embassy—embajada
embezzle—hurtar, apropiar
embezzler—estafador
enabling act—ley de autorización
encarcerate—encarcelar
enforce—hacer cumplir,
ejecutar engage—ocupar,
emplear enroll—matricular, inscribir
equity—equidad
evidence—evidencia
execution—ejecución
exile—destierro
exile (person)—desterrado ,
exi'le (v.)—desterrar
expire—expirar, cumplirse el plazo, vencer
feeble-minded—falto de inteligencia
felony—felonía
forge (v.)—falsificar, forjar
fraud—fraude, engaño
fraudulent—fraudulento
free under bond—libre bajo fianza
gang—pandilla
grace period—período de espera
Grand Jury—Gran Jurado
guarantee—garantía
guilt—culpa
guilty—culpable
harbor (v.)—abrigar, resguardar,
defender hearing—audiencia
indict (v.)—acusar por el Gran Jurado

ineligible—no tener las calificaccio-nes, ineligible
information—información
immoral—inmoral
immunity—inmunidad
imprison—encarcelar
inadmissible—no admisible, inadmisible
invalid—inválido
investigator—investigador, indagador
killer—aesino
knowledge—ciencia, conocimiento
leader—líder, jefe
legislatura—legislatura
liable—sujeto, expuesto
loathsome—aborrecible
malice—malicia
mándate—mandato
mania—manía, locura
mercy—clemencia, perdón
misdemeanor—crimen de menor cuantía, delito, crimen
menor mistreat—maltratar
moral turpitu'de—depravación moral
murder—asesinato, (v) asesinar
murderer—asesino
natural born citizen—ciudadano por nacimiento
naturalization certifícate—certificado de ciudadanía o naturalización
naturalized citizen—ciudadano naturalizado
notary public—escribano o notario público
off en se—ofensa
officer in charge—jefe, oficial encargado
order to show cause—orden para mostrar (enseñar) causa
overdue—sobrevencido, demoroso
overthrow—vencer, derrotar
parole—perdón condicional
pardon—absolución
pauper—pobre, indigente
penalty—pena, castigo
petition—petición
plaintiff—demandante
plea—súplica
political—político
polygamy—poligamia
post bond—poner fianza
prosecute—enjuiciar
psychopathic—personalidad psicopática
public charge—carga pública

public welfare—bienestar público
publish—publicar
reasonable doubt—duda razonable
refugee—refugiado
reprieve—suspensión temporal
respondent—respondedor
revolution—revolución
right of appeal—derecho de recurso
rule to show cause—orden de presentar motivos justificantes
search—(person) esculcar; (vehicle) registrar
search and seizure—registro e incautación
search warrant—orden de registro
sentence—condena, sentencia
sexual—sexual
shoplifting—ratería de tiendas
Special Inquiry Officer—Juez de la Inmigración, Oficial de Interrogaciones Especiales
stillbirth certifícate—certificado de natimuerto
subject—sujeto
subpoena—(v.) citar, comprendo
suit—pleito, acción judicial
summons—citación
supporting documents—documentos justificativos
surrender (v.)—ceder, entregar
suspect (v.)—sospechar, suponer
suspect—persona sospechada

suspensión—suspensión
suspicion—sospecha, desconfianza
súmame—apellido
term—plazo, término
threat—amenaza
trial—juicio
trial attorney—abogado de la inmigración
U.S. Attorney—Fiscal Federal
U.S. Marshal—Mariscal Federal
venue—jurisdicción
verba tim—al pie de la letra
verdict—veredicto, fallo
verification—verificación
verify—verificar, averiguar, comprobar
versus—contra
vest—dar posesión
viólate—violar, infringir
void—nulo, inválido
waiting list—causas en espera
warning—advertencia, aviso
warrant—comprobante, autorización
wedlock—matrimonio
whom it may concern—a quien pueda interesar
wilful—premeditado, intencional
witness (mat.)—testigo material
written notice—aviso escrito